THE EXPRESS ON SUNDAY

COMPLETE GUIDE
TO
CRYPTIC
CROSSWORDS

J.A.COLEMAN

Brockhampton Press

© James Coleman 1994

This edition published 1994

Published by Eric Dobby Publishing Ltd,
12 Warnford Road, Orpington, Kent BR6 6LW

This edition Published 1998 by Brockhampton Press,
A member of Hodder Headline PLC Group

ISBN 1 86019 3021

British Library Cataloguing in Publication Data
Coleman, James
    The complete guide to cryptic crosswords
    1. Cryptic crossword puzzles. Encyclopedias.
    I. Title
    793.73'2

ISBN 185882 024 3

Printed and bound in Great Britain by
Creative Print and Design Wales, Ebbw Vale

INTRODUCTION

Many people who regularly do crosswords for pleasure shy away from cryptic crosswords, thinking that they are too difficult. If they made the effort, they might well discover that not only are they not as difficult as they had thought but they can give even greater pleasure to the solver than non-cryptic versions.

Crosswords are not difficult because they are labelled 'cryptic', nor simple because they are labelled 'easy', 'quick' or 'concise'; the degree of difficulty largely depends on the vocabulary of the solver in relation to that used by the compiler. Where solutions are within the solver's vocabulary, it is often the case that cryptic crosswords are easier than concise crosswords. In the concise version, a very specific clue, 'King of beasts (4)', obviously permits only one solution, LION, and needs no further clues. A somewhat less specific clue, 'Large animal (4)', could be BEAR, KUDU, LION, etc., and help in the form of a letter from another intersecting solution might be required before the correct solution can be entered. An even less specific clue, 'Animal (4)', could have many possible solutions and, even when the first letter of the solution is known to be L, it could still be LAMB, LION or LYNX. The cryptic version of the same clue, '*Animal* with broken loin (4)', has the same direct clue ('*animal*') - always in italics in these notes - but the indirect clue 'broken loin' immediately suggests LION (an anagram of 'loin') rather than LAMB or LYNX. Similarly, 'Floor covering (8)' could be LINOLEUM or OILCLOTH but, if the clue is '*Floorcovering* is too chill (8)', the anagram of 'too chill' confirms OILCLOTH as correct. If both direct and indirect clues give the same answer, this can usually be entered as the correct solution with some degree of confidence (but *see* Double-Checking, Part 2:29).

Where the solution lies outside the solver's vocabulary, cryptic clues will often point to a solution which would not have been possible with the single direct clue that appears in the concise type of puzzle. Faced with the straight clue, 'American bird (5)', one might be at a loss even if the stage _ _ER_ has been reached. The cryptic version of the same clue, 'Turn away from the wind with unknown American bird (5)', allows the solution to be built up from 'Turn away from the wind' (VEER) and 'unknown' (Y), and the solution VEERY can be entered even before the dictionary confirms that this is the name of a North American thrush. In some crosswords many of the solutions can be words not previously

3

encountered, but the puzzle can nevertheless be solved successfully from the indirect clues.

Since most cryptic clues provide at least two routes to the solution, there is some merit in the claim that this type of crossword is easier to solve than the concise type, although, because the compiler to some extent offsets the additional assistance given by the indirect clues by using less well-known synonyms for words in the clue, early attempts may prove frustrating. Always check the published solutions to see how the answers you failed to get were arrived at; in this way, you will gradually come to recognise some of the devices which compilers use and which seem endless in their variety! In the example quoted above, you may not have recognised 'unknown' as Y (an algebraic symbol for an unknown quantity), but you will almost certainly recognise it the next time you come across it.

Consider this. In a concise crossword, you might find the three separate clues 'Youngster (5)', 'Preserves (4)' and 'Islanders (9)', and you would probably have little difficulty in arriving at the correct solutions MINOR, CANS and MINORCANS. In the cryptic version you would be given the single clue 'Youngster preserves *islanders* (9)'. If you treat each part of the indirect clue as a separate clue, you will arrive at the solution in the same way as with the concise version. Since many of the clues in cryptic crosswords contain 'mini-crosswords' of this sort, you are getting at least two crosswords for the price of one and, hence, at least twice as much pleasure.

A final point. You will be reading the examples given in these notes as isolated examples and you may think, in some cases, that you could never have found the solution without the explanation. But remember that you are rarely asked to solve a clue in isolation; in most cases you will have some letters from previously solved clues to help you. As a result of this help, you may sometimes spot a solution without fully understanding how it was derived from the clue. If this happens, go back to the clue and work out how the solution was derived from it (*see* Double-Checking, Part 2:29 and Making a Start, Part 2:30).

CONTENTS

PART 2: GENERAL HINTS

APPENDICES

PART 1: TYPE OF CLUE

1

DEFINITIONS AND CLASSIFICATION

Anagram: a word or phrase the letters of which can be rearranged into another word or phrase

Homonym: same spelling, different meaning and sometimes different sound, e.g. fast =speedy; fast =abstain from food

Homophone: same sound, different spelling, different meaning, e.g. throne and thrown

Palindrome: a word that is spelled the same in each direction, e.g. repaper

Synonym: same meaning, different spelling, different sound, e.g. fast and speedy

In these notes the following definitions and symbols are used:

Direct clue: the clue (or part) that will alone give the solution

Indirect clue: that part of the clue from which words are deduced to form part of the solution

Given word: a word printed in the clue which will form part of the solution

Derived word: a word derived from an indirect clue which will form part of the solution

Pointer: a word or phrase in the clue which indicates which words or letters in the clue, or which operation, will be used to arrive at the solution

In the clues, numbers in round brackets indicate the number of letters in the solution

· (7)

Solutions are in full capitals
Direct clues are in italics

· EXAMPLE
· *Shoe cleaner, a downtrodden type* (7)=DOORMAT

Given words used in the solution are shown in small capitals in square brackets

· Gives me [ME] grim [GRIM] *pain* (6)=MEGRIM

7

Derived words are shown in the same way, whether in the solution or not

• Villain [ROTTER] gets mother [DAM] a *large port* (9)=ROTTERDAM

Letters selected for retention are underlined

• Leaders of t̲he o̲ld m̲en e̲ntered in *book* (4)=TOME

and where they form only part of the solution are also shown in small capitals in square brackets

• *African* mother [MA] with s̲ome [S] A̲merican-I̲ndian [A, I] origins (5)=MASAI

Letters selected for elimination or substitution are in round brackets

• *Don't sit* on shore [ST(R)AND] right [R] out (5)=STAND

Hidden words are shown between slash strokes (solidi)

• *Producing sound* in uni/son? I c/onduct (5)=SONIC

Letters to be used to form an anagram are underlined

• D̲octor c̲an change *pact* (9)=CONCORDAT

A dash within a word in square brackets indicates that other letters will be written in that space in the solution

• See [SE–E] about uncle [SAM] getting *a plant* (6)=SESAME

The sign =, when used inside square brackets in the clue, indicates a given or derived word which has been changed by reversal, homophone or anagram, etc.

• Rat [RAT] returns [=TAR] to achieve [GET] *object* (6)=TARGET

The length of a clue is no guide to the length of the solution: the single letter O can generate a solution with fourteen letters, e.g. CIRCULAR LETTER; whereas a clue with many words can yield a very short solution, e.g. *Record* a soccer error [OG] by a learner [L]=LOG.

Most clues indicate the number of letters in the solution by figures in round brackets, such as (6) for single words, (4,2) for two words, (3,2,5) for three words, (4-2) or (4-3-5) for hyphenated words, and so on, but in some crosswords only the total number of letters required is given in the brackets, even if the solution comprises several words. In some specialised types of crossword no numbers are given at all.

Some clues will contain one direct clue, others will have two or more direct clues, but most will have a combination of direct and indirect clues. You can be almost certain, in the last case, that the direct clue will be at the beginning or end of the clue; it is rarely in the middle, and where this occurs in the examples in these notes attention is drawn to this somewhat unusual construction.

It follows from this that the middle part of a multi-part clue is very likely to be an indirect clue, the answer to which will be in the middle of the solution (if an inclusion is involved) or at the beginning or end of the solution in most other cases. It is worthwhile, if you happen to spot the answer to this part of a clue, to pencil it in, in the hope that it may assist with the complete solution or with the solution of intersecting clues.

In most cases, the indirect clues, when combined by addition, subtraction, etc., will give the same result as the direct clue

- Business [CO] paid for [MET] by *space traveller* (5)=COMET

Occasionally, if the solution is not difficult, only one indirect clue may be given to the solution. This may be a **given word**

- *Dolly* has her art [ART] (6)=PARTON

- *Punched* out [OUT] in the centre (7)=CLOUTED

- *Consider* rather more than ink [INK] (5)=THINK

or a **derived word**

- *Poetry* supporter [LEG] in the middle (5)=ELEGY

- *Works on the farm* though sick [ILL] at heart (6)=TILLER

- *Took over the plane* with sailor [JACK] aboard (8)=HIJACKED

Sometimes a clue will serve the double function of direct and indirect clue

- Southeastern [SE] French *town* [VILLE] (7)=SEVILLE
(The direct clue 'town' =SEVILLE, but 'French town' [VILLE] acts as an indirect clue)

- *Sort of roll* A-E, etc. (9)=ELECTORAL
(The direct clue 'sort of roll' =ELECTORAL, but 'sort of' acts as a pointer to an anagram, and 'roll' itself forms part of that anagram)

• *Bay* [B-AY] with some p/isca/torial content (6)=BISCAY
(The direct clue 'bay' functions as an indirect clue to the word to be written outside 'isca')

The sort of oddity that ignores usual rules is shown in the adjoining example. Here there is no direct clue in the first clue because it is linked to the second and the solution in both cases is some form of miscreant.

• <u>Counsel</u> perplexed [SCOUN-EL] about medical man [DR] ... (9) = SCOUNDREL

• ...a *miscreant* in li/fe lon/g detention (5) =LIFER

In some cases it is difficult to determine which is the direct clue

• Programme finding gold in part of Central America (8)
(The solution might be another word for 'programme' or it might be the name of part of Central America, such as Panama. In this case, the fact that 'gold' is said to be 'in' part of Central America makes it easy to arrive at 'gold [OR] in part of Central America [PAN-AMA]' to give PANORAMA, the TV programme)

• Old silver coin is a mark showing precision of detail (7)
(Is the solution an 'old silver coin', made up from other words meaning 'mark' and 'precision of detail', or is it a word meaning 'precision of detail', made up from words meaning 'old silver coin' and 'mark'? Since 'mark' is the central part of the clue, it is not likely to be the direct clue and is therefore most likely to be the first or last part of the solution. 'Mark' is often abbreviated to M which, combined with the given word 'is' [IS], gives -ISM, a probable word

ending. This indicates 'old silver coin' [REAL] as the beginning, to give the solution as REALISM =precision of detail)

Occasionally one direct clue serves for two entries

- Stand [DAIS] over unknown [Y] ... (5) =DAISY (down clue)

- ...flower – many [LOT] useless [US] (5) =LOTUS

As is evident from the foregoing examples, the direct clue is usually a straightforward synonym and the 'cryptic' part of the clue is in the indirect clues. Sometimes, all parts are cryptic.

- *Rigger, say,* using rope [STRING], in French style [EN], extremely cleverly [CY] (10)=STRINGENCY (The direct clue, *Rigger, say,* is a homophone of 'rigour', a synonym for the solution STRINGENCY)

There are so many ways of phrasing a clue that it is virtually impossible to classify them all, and any attempt to do so will inevitably result in some overlapping. Some of the more usual types are given in Part 1 as a general guide to the thinking that lies behind them. It is not, of course, necessary for the solver to analyse each clue to determine which type it is before attempting a solution; the various categories are given merely as a convenient way of covering the many and varied options. When reading these notes the classification can be ignored since, in practice, the pointer, and in other cases the absence of a pointer, will indicate how to proceed to find a solution.

Compilers of crosswords take a very broad view of what constitutes a word. They will use straightforward English words, foreign words, obsolete words, dialect words, prefixes that do not normally stand on their own as words, abbreviations, parts of words, letters from other words, and even numbers written as letters.

The raw materials for the solution, the words and letters, must, of course, come from the clue (except in the case of direct quotations), and they can be in the form of given words or letters, derived words or letters, abbreviations, selected letters, hidden words, homophones, or a combination of any of these. What you then do with this material depends on the operation indicated by the pointer. It may require you to add words together or form letters into an anagram or to combine two or more such operations.

The operations that may be required are addition, subtraction, reversal, inclusion, substitution, and the construction of an anagram.

11

Because anagrams are such a regular feature of crosswords, they have been treated separately in these notes as a class in their own right.

Most clues contain a pointer. Pointers for the use of words and letters are given in each of the following sections, but some of those most frequently used for the various operations are listed below:

Addition:
  across: and, after, before, beside, given, joining, meeting, next to, receiving, with
  down: over, supporting, under
Subtraction: disbarred, dropping, leaving, losing, moving, no, removing, without
Reversal:
  across: back, backing, backwards, coming back, overthrow, rejected, retrograde, returning, reverse, revolutionary, travelling west, turning
  down: above, below, carries, climbing, going up, mounting, over, subscribed, under, upset
Inclusion:
  inside: among, carrying, catching, covered by, disconnected, holding, imprisoned by, in, including, interrupting, introducing, keeping, retained by, swallowed by

  outside: about, around, capturing, embracing, out, outside, round, surrounding, without
Substitution: change, difference, end-to-end, head-to-tail, replaces

Occasionally you will find a clue in which one word functions both as a clue and as a pointer

• *Upset* many mouthpieces (5)= SPILL (down clue) ('Many' [L] plus 'mouthpieces' [LIPS] together and reversed = SPILL. 'Upset' is a direct clue to 'spill' and also acts as a pointer to the reversal)

The guidelines given in these notes are no more than that; they are not rules that cover every case. Given the clue 'On Avon clumsy boat takes in water (7)', you would quite properly expect to find that 'clumsy' was intended as a pointer to an anagram and that 'takes in' is a pointer to an inclusion of some word meaning 'water', the result being a town, perhaps, on the River Avon. In fact, the solution is 'on Avon' (BATH) plus 'clumsy boat' (TUB), giving BATHTUB, which 'takes in water'.

The following sections in Part 1 deal with the various types of clue. Any explanation of a solution that is not immediately explicit should become clear after you have read the general hints in Part 2.

2

SYNONYMS

Solutions dealt with under the overall title of synonyms fall into four separate categories: straight synonyms, oblique descriptions, opposites and negatives, and one of a class. These are dealt with in the sections which follow.

It is usually not too difficult to find a solution for a clue, provided that it is clear what the clue means. The English language is notorious not only for words that have many meanings as one part of speech but for words that double as nouns, verbs or adjectives and have different meanings in each role. It is usually clear from the context which role any particular word is playing but, in the style adopted for crosswords, it is not always so evident.

In solutions we are looking for words which have the same meaning as the clue but which are spelt differently (synonyms), but the clue may be a word that has more than one meaning and, unless we are clear as to which meaning is intended, we may look for the wrong synonym. For example, given the word 'stable' one might look for a synonym based on the assumption that the compiler intended it to mean 'horsebox' when, in fact, he really intended it as an adjective meaning 'steady'.

The different meanings may arise either from general usage or from the fact that the words come from different roots but, whatever the reason, you must be clear as to what a clue really means. A few examples will make the point:

grave:	tomb (noun) serious (adj.)	sanction:	embargo (noun) allow (verb)
kind:	class (noun) caring (adj.)	seal:	sea animal (noun) fasten (verb)
relation:	kinsman (noun) telling (noun)	worst:	opposite to best (adj.) overcome (verb)

Typical examples

- *Staff* employed by the Royal Household (7) =SCEPTRE
  (The use of 'employed' leads one to think of 'staff' as employees instead of 'rod')

- *Fairly good sum for orderly?* (4) =TIDY
  ('Orderly' could be a hospital attendant getting good wages, but here it means TIDY, as in 'a tidy sum')

The above are words which are spelt the same and have the same pronunciation but which have different meanings.

Another problem arises with words which are spelt the same but which have different meanings according to how they are pronounced. Because the clues are printed and not spoken, differences in stress are not apparent and can mislead. The following pairs of words illustrate the point:

ab'stract = theoretical (adj.)
abstract' = draw away (verb)

en'trance = gateway (noun)
entrance' = delight (verb)

con'tent = capacity (noun)
content' = satisfied (adj.)

wound' = injury (noun)
wound' = twisted (verb)

Typical examples

- *Tarry rope* (4) =STAY
  ('Tarry' can mean 'covered in tar', as a ship's rope might be, or 'linger', both meaning STAY)

- *Meeting to overhaul military tower* (3-2-3) =TUG-OF-WAR
  ('Tower' is used to mean 'one who tows', not a building)

Even when you are dealing with clues that give only direct clues to straightforward synonyms, it is not always easy to spot the connection. Some words are exact synonyms for each other but most are near-synonyms. For example, if you look up 'furze' in a dictionary you will find it defined as 'gorse or whin'; 'gorse' is defined as 'furze or whin'; and 'whin' is defined as 'furze or gorse'. All three words are exact synonyms for each other.

You would not expect to find exact synonyms used as direct clues since the solution could be easily found by reference to the dictionary.

If you look up 'shore' you will find that it can mean 'land', 'sewer', 'prop' or 'warn' (among other things), but if you look up each of the four words, none will be defined as 'shore'. The result is that you can have four direct clues meaning 'shore' and not be able to find the required synonym in an ordinary dictionary; if you could, the solution would be too simple.

Dictionaries of synonyms are available and may be of some use to the solver, but often the solution to such clues depends on recognising a near-synonym of one of the direct clues and then checking with a standard dictionary to see if that word satisfies the rest of the clue.

Compilers use language to suit their own convenience and have developed their own vocabulary in which flowers become bloomers or rivers, rivers are bankers or flowers, kings and queens are cards, cattle are neat, and so on. Some of the more common uses are given in A Compiler's Vocabulary, Appendix 4.

You can be quite sure that, where a word has several meanings, the compiler will select the least well known for the clue and will also attempt to phrase his clue in such a way as to lead you towards one interpretation when he intends another. In the clue 'Measure in cabaret (3)', the pointer 'in' presupposes a hidden word and there are several three-letter words to be found in 'cabaret' — CAB, ABA, BAR, ARE and RET. Of these, you might well opt for ARE as a metric measurement of area; the compiler intends the solution to be CAB, an ancient Hebrew measure.

Moral: before considering solutions, be clear what the clue means; not only will you be wise to rephrase the wording of the clue (*see* Phrasing, Part 2:25) but you should also read the individual words with varying stresses so that you can distinguish between, for example, en'trance and entrance'.

2.1 STRAIGHT SYNONYMS

The clue usually consists of two or more direct clues and you are required to find a synonym which satisfies each part, or it will contain indirect clues, the answer to which will give you the same solution as the direct clue.

Pointers: makes, getting, giving, producing, etc.

In some simple cases, only one indirect clue is given and letters are added arbitrarily for the solution

• Up [UP] in *price!* (5) = RUPEE

• *Burner* of buns [BUNS] and more (6) = BUNSEN

15

• *Childish* enough to annoy [RILE] in the end (7) =PUERILE

The more usual case requires a synonym for two or more direct clues
Note that many words, particularly short ones, have many meanings (*see* third example)

• *Synonyms for first and last half in football* (5) =DANCE
(Both 'foot' and 'ball' =DANCE)

• *Watch* for *cheat's mannerism* (5) =TRICK

• *Able to preserve tin chimneypot* in *prison* (3) =CAN

Synonyms may be formed by **addition**

of **derived** words

• Very little [WEE] for [PER] *hired mourner* (6) =WEEPER

• Thrash [WHIP] bad [POOR] playwright [WILL] for getting the *bird* (12) =WHIPPOORWILL

• Two aspects of goal [BAR, NET] give *Yorkist win* (6) =BARNET

of **given** and **derived** words

• Turns [WINDS] or [OR] makes *chair* (7) =WINDSOR

• *Tragic woman* gives me [ME] means of death [ROPE] (6) =MEROPE

• *That reminds* me [ME] to [TO] get the chaps [MEN] in (7) =MEMENTO

or of **parts** of words

• Fed [FED] some oranges [ORA(NGES)] in *play* (6) =FEDORA

• *Candles* are quite tall [TAL(L)] with a bit of glow [(G)LOW] (6) =TALLOW

• *Caper* of worker [ANT] with some ice [IC(E)] (5) =ANTIC

Note that some additions are not in the same order in the solution as in the clue

- Own [HAVE] first live [BE] *bear* (6)=BEHAVE
- Cheat [CON] one [I] over the *picture* (4)=ICON (down clue)
- Contemptible fellow [TWERP] subscribing to an article [AN] *in Belgium* (7)=ANTWERP (down clue)

and some are phrased as if they were subtractions

- Without Queen [ER] *this bid* would not be on [OFF] (5)=OFFER
- Without beds [COTS] the *expenses* would be a shilling [S] (5)=COSTS (Note two examples of the direct clue in the centre)
- *Verse* would be an essay [TRY] without the writer [POE] (6)=POETRY

You might expect a clue containing the word 'behind' to indicate an addition with one word placed behind another; this is not always the case

- There's a medical man [DR] behind [AFT] the *plan* (5)=DRAFT
- Place bet [BACK] on the team [SIDE] *behind* (8)=BACKSIDE
- Way [ST] behind [RUMP] and French [ET] *prostitute* (8)=STRUMPET

A special case of addition of synonyms, which might be called 'cognate addition', has an indirect clue acting also as the direct clue

- With mouth [TRAP] quiet [P], one [I] *holy person* [ST] (8)=TRAPPIST

In some cases you are required to deduce a derived word from an indirect clue in a roundabout fashion

- *Writer* after his title (4)=NIBS ('Nibs' is associated with 'his' in the phrase 'his nibs' — a person of importance)

There are many devices for the subtraction of letters or parts of words (*see* Selected Letters, Part 1:4) but so far as the **subtraction** of complete words is concerned, the usual cases are as follows:

derived words minus **derived**

- Minute organism [PLANK(TON)] losing weight [TON] in *wood* (5) =PLANK

- *For example,* a bird [MINA] leaving name [NO(MINA)TE] (4) =NOTE

- Wheatless (CORNless) tropic [CAPRI(CORN)] *island* (5) =CAPRI

derived words minus **given**

- *Oriental* shacks [SHAN(TIES)] without ties [TIES] (4) =SHAN

- Unpreferred girl's [BRU(NET)TE] net [NET] loss — *he's no gentleman* (5) =BRUTE

- Every character [ALPHA(BET)] lost bet [BET] for a *start* (5) =ALPHA

given words minus **given**

- *The time* to whiten [WH(IT)EN] without it [IT] (4) =WHEN

- Another [(AN)OTHER] without an [AN] *alternative* (5) =OTHER

- *Punished* as a result of having gathered [GAT(HER)ED] without her [HER] (5) =GATED

given words minus **derived**

- *Attempt* to remove witches [COVEN] from Coventry [(COVEN)TRY] (3) =TRY

- *Pass* a long way [LEAGUE] from a colleague [COL(LEAGUE)] (3) =COL

- French one [UN] debarred from funeral [F(UN)ERAL] is *wild* (5) =FERAL

In some cases, the clue requires the inference of a derived word from which a

- *Disagreement* plain in court (4) =TIFF (Infer 'plaintiff')

part is subtracted for the solution

- Takes delight in being *sweet* (7)=TURKISH
  (Infer 'Turkish delight')

- *Ship* on show in show (4)=BOAT
  (Infer 'Showboat')

and some subtractions are phrased as if they were additions

- When it gets hot [H], *this river* can be fierce [TIGRIS(H)] (6)=TIGRIS
  (Note the direct clue in the centre)

- Buccaneers [(P)IRATE(S)] given no extra thought [PS] are *angry* (5)=IRATE

In some cases, some words are added, others are subtracted

- *Exhalation* from Hermia's [(HER)MIAS] mother [MA]? Not her [HER] (6)=MIASMA

- Going by rail [R(A)I(L)], Al [AL] left car [MINI] in *Italian town* (6)=RIMINI

- *Payments* for writers [PENS] of reduced editions [(EDIT)ION(S)] (7)=PENSION

Reversal of the answer given by the indirect clue may be required to give the solution to the direct clue

- Orgy [REVEL] back in *bar* (5)=LEVER

- *PM's mate* sinned [SINNED] in revolutionary style (6)=DENNIS

- Sort of water [EVIAN] turned *green* (5)=NAIVE

Some reversals affect more than one word

- *Nasty type* returns best [TOP] woollens [KNITS] (8)=STINKPOT

- *One who causes damage* and recurrent regret [RUE] to [TO] scholars [BA'S] (8)=SABOTEUR

- Fixes responsibility for [PINS] crime [RAP] back at the *root* (7)=PARSNIP

but in other cases only one word is reversed

- *To do this,* get all [ALL] to [TO] reverse [=OT] (5)=ALLOT

- *Parapet* built by party [LAB] backing [=BAL] American [US] commerce [TRADE] (10) =BALUSTRADE

- Gun [LUGER] brought back [=REGUL] on a [A] mount [TOR] for the *governor* (9) =REGULATOR

In the case of down clues, the principles are the same but the pointers are different

- *Prosperity* rising time [ERA] passed quickly [FLEW] (7) =WELFARE

- *Praise* double [DUAL] upturn [=LAUD] in mine [P-IT] (7) =PLAUDIT

- Fixes [PINS] up [=SNIP] the favourite [PET] in a *scrap* (7) =SNIPPET

The act of reversal may be incorporated as part of the solution

- Pets down [=STEP UP] *get promotion* (4-2) =STEP-UP (down clue)

- *Ascending* down, draw back [=UPWARD] (6) =UPWARD (down clue)

- *Thrash* low-down climber [=WOL UP], they say (6) =WALLOP (down clue)

Inclusions are words written one inside another. If word A is written inside word B, it follows that B is written outside A and this difference of approach is reflected in the pointer to the solution. Note that in this context 'without' means 'outside' (*see* The Use of 'Without' and 'Within', Part 2:13)

Derived words may be written inside other **derived words**

- Solitary [LONE] in the cove [BA-Y]? *Rubbish!* (7) =BALONEY

- *Explosive substance* making horse [GE-E] swallow tongue [LATIN] (8) =GELATINE

- *Wandering* desert fighter [RAT] is captured by Red Norseman [ER-IC] (7)=ERRATIC

or outside
- Solitary [LONE] horse [B-AY] on the outside? *Rubbish!* (7)=BALONEY

- A month [OC-T] without a note [TE] from the *players* (5)=OCTET

- Lady's possessive [H-ER] about bird [OWL], a *mistake* (6)=HOWLER

Derived words may be written inside **given words**
- Monkey [APE] in part [PAR-T] of *coping* (7)=PARAPET

- *Brought on* by cad [CA-D] being out of employment [USE] (6)=CAUSED

- Tailless bird [GOOS(E)] in care [CAR-E] of another *bird* (8)=CARGOOSE

or outside
- Everybody [A-LL] is about to [TO] read *'Coral Island'* (5)=ATOLL

- Were [WERE] surrounded by fish [CO-D] and *showed* fear (7)=COWERED

- *Show* me [ME] into a box [KIS-T] (6)=KISMET

Derived words may be written backwards inside or outside other **derived words**
- People [MEN] turn up [=NEM] in secret service [CI-A] *pictures here* (6)=CINEMA (down clue)

- Members [PARTS] contrarily [=S-TRAP] have to go round as well as [AND] into *bunker* (8)=SANDTRAP

- *Fixed purpose* to be always [EVER] up [=RE-VE] about sun [SOL] (7)=RESOLVE (down clue)

or outside **given words**
- Raced [RAN] eight furlongs [I MILE]

back [=ELIM, I, NA-R] about to [TO] complete the *race* (10)=ELIMINATOR

The reversal may be indicated by 'rising' in down clues

• *Pierce* mammals [BATS] rising (5) =STAB

but this word can also refer to a physical feature

• Make a mistake [ERR] in rising [T-OR] *panic* (6) =TERROR

Given words may be written backwards inside **derived words**

• *He* puts back the car [CAR=RAC] tool [HO-E] outside (6)=HORACE

• It's [ITS] turned [=STI] and locked in part of ladder [RU-NG] and *corroding* (7)=RUSTING

• *The underside* or reverse if [IF=FI] in piano [SOF-T] (6)=SOFFIT

or outside

• *Cruel* king [R] secure [BAR] I [I] found in returning cab [CAB=BA-C] (8)=BARBARIC

• *He retracts* approval [OK] in Rover's [ROVER] return [=REV-OR] (7)=REVOKOR

• Everybody [ALL] in step [STEP] back [=P-ETS] to *platform* (7)=PALLETS

Given or **derived words** written one inside the other may both then be reversed

• *Shellfish* add [S-UM] less [LESS] in, by return (7)=MUSSELS

• *Curse* always [E-VER] about one pound [LI] return (6)=REVILE

• It's [ITS] locked in at all times [EV-ER], withdrawn and *uneasy* (7)=RESTIVE

Occasionally you will find double inclusions — one word inside another with both inside a third

• People [M-EN] outside trudge [PLOD] into it [I-T] with a *deflated sound* (9)=IMPLODENT

In some cases the solution is the result of what would

• *Impulse* a boy [S-ON] must swallow to become a man of the theatre

happen if an inclusion were made in a **derived word**

[S-URGE-ON] (4)=URGE

- *Wine* would be poison [H-EML-OCK] with wood [ELM] crushed [=EML] inside (4)=HOCK

- *Exhibition* would be superficial [SH-ALL-OW] if it had everything [ALL] in it (4)=SHOW

or a **given word**

- *Being* included in card [CAR-D] would get you treated affectionately [CAR-ESSE-D] (4)=ESSE

- You'd have to rebuild [RE-EDIFY] if [IF] limited by this *like some native huts* (5)=REEDY

- *Girl* in bed [B-ED] would be prohibited [B-ANN-ED] (3)=ANN

A frequent pointer to an inclusion is 'covered by'; note that it may be used to refer to physical objects rather than words

- *Transport system* covered by foreign capital (5)=METRO

Other pointers used for inclusion are 'round' and 'around' but they can be misleading; they may indicate reversal

- Bear [POOH] round [=HOOP] Los Angeles [LA] is *fair game* (4-2)=HOOP-LA

- Jack [AB] has little brothers [BROS] around [=SORB] *entrance* (6)=ABSORB

and 'round' can mean O

- Whip-round [CAT, O] for *Roman statesman* (4)=CATO

Another favourite is 'interrupts'

- I [I] interrupted male [MA-N] *chief* (4) =MAIN

which can be doubled up

- *Faithful* soldier [GI] returns [=I-G] and twice interrupts general [L-E-E] (5) =LIEGE

'Admitted' often indicates an inclusion

- He [H-E] admitted the queen [ER] *at this very spot* (4) =HERE

23

but can have other uses

(*see also* Letter Groups, Part 2,28)

Substitution of words may involve replacing given or derived words by others

• Doctor [DR] admitting [OWNING] *murder, perhaps* (8)
=DROWNING

• Replacing Jack [JACK] in amphibian [NATTER(JACK)], Edward [ED] *grumbled* (8)=NATTERED

• Bill [POSTER] supplants six [VI] in previous [PRE(VI)OUS] setting? *Ridiculous!* (12)=PREPOSTEROUS

• *Near* where Jack's detailed [JAC(K)] to replace girl [HER] hidden by supporter [AD(HER)ENT] (8)=ADJACENT

or the switching of words from one position to another

• *House-porter partly re-arranged* [=PORTERHOUSE] neat [BEEF] version of Keats (9)=BEEFSTEAK

• *Reverse mail chain* [=CHAIN MAIL] for king [R] in love [A-MOUR] (6)=ARMOUR

• *Turn over centre garden* [=GARDEN CENTRE] and attend to [NURSE] edges of rockery [R,Y] (7)=NURSERY

or switching the order of parts of given words

• *She's* riding the first half [RID] last (6)=INGRID

For the substitution of letters

see Selected Letters, Part 1:4.

2.2 OBLIQUE DESCRIPTIONS

The clue describes the solution in rather elaborate phraseology — Churchill's description of a lie as a 'terminological inexactitude' is a typical example — or by a punning allusion. In most cases, the whole clue is a direct clue and, since there is no need to distinguish between direct and indirect clues, no part of the clue is in italics in the examples quoted.

Pointers: use of ? and !
elaborate phraseology

The usual form of clue has no indirect clue	• A distressing blow for the Italians (7)=SIROCCO
	• High-rise accommodation for the workers? (7)=ANTHILL
	• Does it fix a tile to a shingle? (3-3)=HAT-PIN
	• It's a great fiddle! (5)=CELLO
	• National power supply in the Caribbean? (7,4)=SPANISH MAIN
	• The long arm of the paw! (6,3)=POLICE DOG
	• Race starter? (4)=ADAM
	• Subject to 'income' tax (8)=DUTIABLE

2.3 OPPOSITES/NEGATIVES

The solution is the opposite or negative of the word(s) derived from the indirect clue(s) or the meaning of the clue is reversed to arrive at the solution.

Pointers: forms of negative
apparently, contrary, opposite, presumably, scarcely, reverse

Typical examples	• Is *she* OK for looks? The reverse, apparently (7)=STUNNER (Reverse=looks for KO)
	• Obviously not a tax-free *country* (8)=SCOTLAND (Scot=tax)
	• *Information* not about high country (7)=LOWDOWN
In some cases, 'opposite' is used in the sense that, once the answers to the indirect	• *Changed into* insect [BE-E] in the river [CAM]? Quite the reverse! (6)=BECAME

25

clues have been found, they are written in the reverse order for the solution

(CAM into BE—E, not BEE into CAM)

Note that these clues are similar to some referred to in Straight Synonyms, Part 1:2.1, but the phrasing is somewhat different

- Makes me [ME] crazy [MAD] about tool [HOE]? Just the opposite, that's *plain* (4-4) =HOME-MADE (HO-E about ME-MAD, not ME MAD about HOE)

- *Club* to beat [LICK] a writer [NIB]? On the contrary (7)=NIBLICK

There are exceptions, as usual: the solution may require a word that means 'opposite' and not one that is the opposite of the clue

- Evil [VICE] kind of poet [VERSER], apparently [=VERSA]. *Exactly the opposite* (4,5)=VICE VERSA

- Mark [ANTONY] going to Malta [M]? *Just the opposite* (7)=ANTONYM

- Chat? *Quite the opposite* (8) =CONVERSE

- Opposed to making whisky? *It's contrary to nature* (7,3,5)=AGAINST THE GRAIN

or 'opposite' may indicate reversal

- *To bribe* leader of <u>n</u>ation [N] is not quite healthy [ROBUS(T)] — the opposite (6)=SUBORN

- *Image* is fine [OK] in Northern Ireland [N-I]? Just the opposite (4)=IKON

- One [I] wet place [BOG]? Just the opposite, *a dry place* (4)=GOBI

2.4 ONE OF A CLASS

The solution is a word defining a general class, of which a particular example is given in the clue, or defining a particular example from the general class mentioned in the clue.

Pointers: use of ?
  for example or e.g., for instance, maybe, perhaps, possibly, sometimes, sort of

Typical cases where the particular example is given	• *India*, perhaps, affected by the moon (5) =OCEAN
	• *Mosquito*, maybe, with fixed wings (9) =AEROPLANE
	• *Private*, perhaps, but nevertheless in company (7) =SOLDIER
Typical cases where the general class is given	• *Cat*, perhaps, of small weight (5) =OUNCE
	• *Dog* that may go the rounds (5) =BOXER
	• *An example of Flora*, bursting into tears (5) =ASTER
This type of clue may be combined with other **derived words**	
by **addition**	• Persian, maybe [CAT], related to [KIN] *amentum* (6) =CATKIN
	• Siamese [CAT, EG] love [O] to move up [RISE] in *class* (10) =CATEGORISE (Note the pointer EG included)
	• Maxim, for example [GUN], a *pointer*, perhaps [DOG] (3-3) =GUN-DOG (Note two examples in one clue)
or by **inclusion** in a given or derived word	• Boxer, for example [DO-G], involved in [IN] *management* (5) =DOING
	• Put in [IN] furniture of a sort [SOFA] right [R] *to that end* (7) =INSOFAR
	• A [A] receiver [F-ENCE] taking in Asian, for example [FLU], gets *abundant money* (9) =AFFLUENCE
A variation on these themes uses towns, people, etc., to represent a particular	• *Fair maid of Perth*? (6) =SHEILA (Perth in Australia, where a girl is a 'sheila')

country or area. The clue 'street in Paris' means RUE (French for 'street', in Paris or elsewhere in France)

—Arm's Park fervour =high feeling in Wales =HWYL
—De Gaulle's change of policy =French VOLTE FACE
—Dublin lad =boy in Ireland =SEAN
—is in Bonn ='is' in German =IST
—man from Glasgow =any Scot =MON (or IAN or MAC)
—Oxford Street =street in Oxford =BROAD or HIGH
—Roman unmoved =Latin IN SITU
—St Andrew's club =iron in Scotland =AIRN
—wild dog in Melbourne =anywhere in Australia =DINGO

A particular town or county may be given as representing a general area of the country

Cornwall/Devon =SW
Durham =NE
Home Counties/Kent =SE
Humberside =NE

Sometimes the country in general is used as the clue to a particular town, city, etc.

• *Oil-refining product* of Scottish Isle [BUTE] and Aberdeen area [NE] (6) =BUTENE
(Aberdeen is in the Northeast)

• Ambassador [HE] to Havana [CUBA] *tragic figure* (6) =HECUBA

• *Plant* nothing [O] in Cornwall [S-W] (3) =SOW

• *Appear* to measure [EM] beyond Home Counties [SE] (4) =SEEM

• *Kidnap* in China (8) =SHANGHAI

• Unable [CANT] to get ahead [ON] *in China* (6) =CANTON

• The French [LA] desert the courtesan [DELI(LA)H] ruined *in India* (5) =DELHI

In the general class of letters, 'Greek character' may be PLATO but is more likely to be a letter of the ancient Greek alphabet such as CHI, PI, PHI, etc.
(Note that another adjective, such as Sophoclean or Attic, may be used instead of 'Greek')

- *Fashion* [TON] *seen on Greek* character [CHI] (6) = CHITON
  (Note the direct clue used also as an indirect clue)

- In American city [LA], one's bound [BD] to find a [A] *Greek character* (5) = LABDA

- Letter from Greek [MU] student [L] is [IS] hard [H] and *awkward* (6) = MULISH

and 'Hebrew character' may be MOSES but is more likely to be a letter of the Hebrew alphabet such as ALEPH, RESH, etc.

- *Censured* second-class [B] Hebrew character [LAMED] (6) = BLAMED

- The Hebrew character [YOD] and the Spanish [EL] *sing* (5) = YODEL

- *Change* Hebrew letter [RESH] and copy [APE] (7) = RESHAPE

Note that characters from alphabets other than English are often referred to as 'exotic letters', 'classical characters', 'foreign letters', or just 'letters'

- *Bring to a successful conclusion* an [A] exotic letter [CHI] to a lady [EVE] (7) = ACHIEVE

- Graduates [ALUM-NI] including one [I] retired classical character [MU = UM] discover *element* (9) = ALUMINIUM

- *One corresponding to you,* say [= U], among foreign letters (7) = UPSILON
  (Upsilon = U)

- Put on order [OM] a long time [AGE] back [= EGA] by *letter* (5) = OMEGA

Sometimes you may find combinations of characters and people, both representing one of a class

- One slip ruined a *character in Homer* (7) = EPSILON
  (Epsilon = E in Homer)

For classes such as Harpies, etc.

see Numbers, Part 2:23.

3

ABBREVIATIONS

Abbreviations (including initial letters and symbols) are extensively used in crosswords and it is essential to become familiar with those most frequently used by compilers. In the majority of cases, abbreviations form only part of a solution but, occasionally, they may form the whole.

A good dictionary, with a comprehensive list of abbreviations, is an essential tool for the solver. Such a list gives the accepted or authorised versions of the abbreviations, but as the compiler is apt to use his own versions, be prepared to use initial letters (usually capitalised) of words that may not have an accepted abbreviation.

The compiler may use abbreviations such as

DG =Director-General
SI =South Island
NP =North Pole

while the accepted versions are

DG =Dei Gratia (by the Grace of God)
SI =Système Internationale
NP =New Providence
      Notary Public
Np =Neptunium
np =new paragraph
     no place

The same abbreviations can have different meanings according to the style of typeface used in printing (*see* NP, etc., above). The dictionary gives B =Baron, British, Bachelor, boron, bel, black, Belgium; *B*=magnetic flux density; b =born, book, bowled; *b*=breadth. Since solutions are entered in capitals, the compiler makes no distinction between upper and lower case, italic and roman, etc., and, for his purpose, B can stand for all the words listed above.

A full list of abbreviations will be found in a dictionary. Some abbreviations, together with others peculiar to crossword compilers, are given in A Compiler's Vocabulary, Appendix 4.

Abbreviations are usually taken from **given words**

- *Native* of Northern Australia [NA] with story [TAL(E)] cut short (5) = NATAL

- *Quiet* Southern Irish [SI] fast [LENT] (6) = SILENT

- *Mad* card game [LOO] at New Year [NY] (5) = LOONY

but occasionally need to be taken from **derived words**

- BBC boss [DIRECTOR-GENERAL = D-G] taking artist [RA] in to *draw* (4) = DRAG

- One [I] First Lord of the Treasury [PRIME MINISTER = PM] without a thick slice [CH-UNK] of *American squirrel* (8) = CHIPMUNK

Remember that the plural of noun abbreviations doubles the letter (pages = PP, etc.), even — in crosswords — in unusual cases,

- I [ONE] love [O] fellows [FF] — that's *not to be repeated* (3-3) = ONE-OFF

- Graduate [BA] students' [LL] *dance* (4) = BALL

but doubling the letter of an adjective abbreviation acts as an intensifier (very black = BB; very quiet = PP, etc.)

- *Unique* unit [ONE] — nothing [O] very loud [FF] (3-3) = ONE-OFF

Pointers: briefly, contracted (Thomas, the contractor = THOS), initially, shortly, small.
Where no pointers are given, the abbreviation may often be deduced from the clue itself.

The following are frequently used examples and are worth noting for future reference:

bridge
(the card game) denotes players as North, South, East and West, so 'bridge players' are N, S, E and W; 'bridge partners' are NS or EW; 'bridge opponents' are NE,

- Rock python's [KA-AS] catching partners [NS] in *this state* (6) = KANSAS

- *Latest* bridge opponents [NE] and partners [WE] sit [S(I)T] when I [I] leave (6) = NEWEST

NW, SE and SW; (*see also* 'point', 'quarter' below)

- Attractive [MAGNETIC] partner [POLE] *can give direction*
  (8,4) = MAGNETIC POLE
  (Note POLE instead of N or S)

This notation can be used to refer to partnerships in general

- *Fools* presenting no problem [SIMPLE] to [TO] partnership [NS]
  (10) = SIMPLETONS

The cards used by the players (hearts, clubs, diamonds and spades) can be abbreviated to H, C, D and S

- Some suspicion [BREA-TH] about diamond's [D] *size*
  (7) = BREADTH

- Clubs [C] about [ON] in [IN] the east [E] carrying *poison* (6) = CONINE

- Hearts [H] one [ONE] leads to suit [S] the [T] Yankee [Y]. *Truth!*
  (7) = HONESTY

chess
pieces are represented by abbreviations:
  pawn = P
  knight = N
  bishop = B
  rook/castle = R
  queen = Q
  king = K

- *Swindler's* impressive [NOB-LE] capture of bishop [B] with rook [R]
  (7) = NOBBLER

- *Expert* use of knight [N], a [A] rook [R] and king [K] (4) = NARK

- *Check* with bishop [B] and a [A] rook [R] (3) = BAR

although 'queen' in most cases is ER

- *Tradesman* in vehicle [CAR] shut up [PENT] queen [ER]
  (9) = CARPENTER

countries
are often represented by the International Vehicle Registration (IVR) letters

- *What oppressors seek* in Poland's [PL] subjection [UNDER]
  (7) = PLUNDER

- *Tree* given in Libya's [LAR] honour [CH] (5) = LARCH

- *Measure* through [PER] Switzerland [CH] (5) = PERCH
  (Note CH for Companion of Honour and for Switzerland)

but can also appear under their full names

- *Yoke to vehicle* in [IN] country [SPA(I)N] I [I] left (6) =INSPAN

- *Privilege* which belongs to him [HIS] in the country [FRAN-CE] (9) =FRANCHISE

- *Heated* iron [FE] in an African Republic [CHA-D] (6) =CHAFED

element
may sometimes refer to one of the four elements of the ancient world (air, earth, fire, water) but almost always to one of the symbols for one of the hundred plus elements known to modern physics, including those known as 'rare earths'
(*see* A Compiler's Vocabulary, Appendix 4)

- *Sharpness* of the last word [A-MEN] about copper [CU] (6) =ACUMEN

- *Sherry* can turn gold [OR] poured in one [S-OLO] [=OLOROS] with nothing [O] added (7) =OLOROSO

- *Was violent* silver [AG] in colour [R-ED] (5) =RAGED

- *Element* found by listener [EAR] in rather unusual [=RARE-TH] circumstances (4,5) =RARE EARTH

gas
will probably indicate the symbol for one of the elements that are gases in their natural state (e.g. oxygen) or one of the compounds (e.g. carbon monoxide) (*see* A Compiler's Vocabulary, Appendix 4)

- *Prince* sticks head [P-ATE] outside oxygen [O] tent [TENT] (9) =POTENTATE

- There is chlorine [CL], yes [AY], in the *earth* (4) =CLAY

- *Gas* identified initially by chemical [C] osmosis [O] (6,8) =CO =CARBON MONOXIDE (Note that CO has many other meanings: cobalt, commanding officer, conscientious objector, etc.)

but sometimes the full name may be called for

- Missiles [AMMUNITION] appearing briefly [=AMMO] in a riot [=NIA]? No, *gas* (7) =AMMONIA

IC

is often used as a homophone for 'I see' (*see* Homophones, Part 1:6)

• *Drink* is in fashion [TON], I see [IC] (5)=TONIC

but can mean 'in charge'

• A [A] northern [N] chief [ARCH] in charge [IC] is *disorderly* (8)=ANARCHIC

or 'integrated circuit'

• *Gummy acid's* used a lot [MUC(H)], but not wholly on integrated circuit [IC] (5)=MUCIC

or 'one hundred'

see Numbers, Part 2:23

lines

usually refers to railway lines and is frequently abbreviated to BR (British Rail) or RY (railway)

• *Wide* lines [BR] with no [O] publicity [AD] (5)=BROAD

• *True* victory [VE] lines [RY] (4)=VERY

and BR is sometimes used as an abbreviation for 'transport'

• Transport [BR] everyone [EACH] to *The Gap* (6)=BREACH

point

may sometimes refer to a literal point (spike, punctuation mark, etc.)

• There may be some point in *serving meat in this way* (5)=KEBAB

• Woman [ADA] and man [MAN] on point [TINE] of being *inflexible* (10)=ADAMANTINE

• *Accept* a small point [PT] after a fuss [ADO] (5)=ADOPT

but frequently means 'course', 'direction' or 'way' in the sense of a point of the compass, using the abbreviations N, S, E and W (*see also* 'bridge' above, 'quarter' below)

• *Inert* animal [STAG] takes point [N] with an insect [ANT] (8)=STAGNANT

• *Admiral* set [JELL] one [I] firm [CO] course [E] (8)=JELLICOE

• *Diamond*, for instance, to [TO] go in three directions [S-NE] (5)=STONE

Note that courses or directions such as ESE may be referred to as 'directions' or 'direction'

and 'move' and 'direction' together may imply switching the position of N, S, E or W

or their elimination

By analogy, 'pointed' can mean 'with a point'

although occasionally 'point' requires the compass bearing in full

A given bearing may operate as an adjective, not requiring abbreviation

and 'way' can frequently mean 'street' (ST), 'road' (RD) or 'mews' (*see also* 'ST' below) or, in a different sense, 'mode' (*see also* The Use of 'Out' and 'In', Part 2:12)

Since two of the major compass points (N and S) are the poles, a clue including 'pole' will often require N or S

although it can sometimes have a different sense

• Give father [PA] directions [SSE] — he's *faded* (5) =PASSE

• *Subtlety* of good [FINE] direction [SSE] (7) =FINESSE

• *Cut* when moving west [W] (4) =HEWN

• Ship moving south [S] for *fruit* (4) =HIPS

• Move west [W] from (W)ales for *drink* (4) =ALES

• *Girl* with a pointed [N] heel, possibly (5) =HELEN

• Homer's [PIGEON] lines [BR] point [EAST] to a *chest deformity* (6-6) =PIGEON-BREAST

• *Vessel* [C-AN] going round a [A] western river [TAMAR] (9) =CATAMARAN

• Find a way [ST] to tear [RIP] or *take off* (5) =STRIP

• A [A] very loud [FF] ring [O], the way [RD] to *give* (6) =AFFORD

• A [A] way [MEWS], it is said [=MUSE], to *make people laugh* (5) =AMUSE

• A way [MODE] to estimate value [RATE] *avoiding extremism* (8) =MODERATE

• Poles [SN] rode madly [=ORED] and *slept noisily* (6) =SNORED

• Talk [PATTER] to the Pole [N] by *design* (7) =PATTERN

• Pole [SPAR] Russian [RED] *boxed* (7) =SPARRED

- Pole [MAST], with some hesitation [ER], will *overcome* (6) =MASTER

and 'terminal' may require POLE in the solution

- *Runaway* king [ER] by the up-terminal [POLE=ELOP] (6) =ELOPER (down clue)

quarter
may be used to mean 'ghetto'

- *Fairly slow movement* by the French [LA] king [R] to give quarter [GHETTO] (9) =LARGHETTO

or to mean 'fraction' (*see also* Numbers, Part 2:23)

- A whole suit on ship? (7-4) =QUARTER-DECK

but usually means a course or compass bearing, either a point of the compass (N, S, E, W) or a quarter (NE, NW, SE, SW) (*see also* 'bridge', 'point' above)

- Course [NE] for a ship [SS] on *loch* (4) =NESS

- Call [TERM] it [IT] one quarter [E] of *an insect* (7) =TERMITE

- Quarter [S] size of old type [PICA] *spiral bandage* (5) =SPICA

These abbreviations (and others) may be used to refer to London (postal) districts

- *Place* it [IT] in the London area [S-E] (4) =SITE

- *Wandering* king [R] deserter [RAT] I [I] found in London district [E-C] (7) =ERRATIC

- Westminster [WI] Street [ST] — song [ARIA] for *climber* (8) =WISTARIA

with 'the city' often implying EC

- *Shut up* for a time [AGE] after being born [N] in the City [E-C] (6) =ENCAGE

You may also find clues that do not refer to 'points' or 'quarters' but still include compass points

- Auster [south wind=S WIND] operating [ON] *town in Wiltshire* (7) =SWINDON

A frequent use of one bearing (E) is found in the phrase 'in the East' or 'in the Orient' to give -INE as a word ending

- *Being obstinate* is a [A] crime [SIN] in [IN] the East [E] (7) =ASININE

- Emperor [CONSTANT(INE)] in [IN] the East [E] has left *without changing* (8) =CONSTANT

- *Fishy* prawn starter [P] is [IS] caught [C] in [IN] the Orient [E] (7) =PISCINE

- *Father confessor* venerable [AUGUST] in the Orient [INE] (9) =AUGUSTINE

side
in sport, means 'team' which can be XI (soccer) or XV (rugby)

- *Turn aside* group of eleven [SIDE] dogs [TRACKS] (4-6) =SIDE-TRACKS

- Eastern [E] loch [LEVEN] *side perhaps* (6) =ELEVEN

- Learner [L] in the team [SID-E] will *move furtively* (5) =SIDLE

and the parties in a dispute take sides

- *Subordinate event* for parties [SIDES] — in what way [HOW]? (8) =SIDESHOW

and 'side' can mean 'facet'

- Side [FACET] given financial acknowledgments [IOUS]? Must be *joking* (9) =FACETIOUS

but in most cases, 'side' means 'right' or 'left', sometimes used in full

- *Not qualified* for County [DOWN] side [RIGHT] (9) =DOWNRIGHT

- *Cut* club [C] side [LEFT] (5) =CLEFT

but, more often, abbreviated to R or RT and L

- Elizabeth's [BE-THS] right [R] in that there are *beds* (6) =BERTHS

- Right [R-T] about the priest [ELI] being *fired again* (5) =RELIT

- Left [L] a girl [UNA] with a [A] twitch [TIC] as *mad* (7) =LUNATIC

- *Afterwards* goddess [ATE] parts the sides [L-R] (5) =LATER

In cricket, 'right' is 'off' and 'left' is 'on' or 'leg', referring to parts of the field

- *Affront* right [OFF] to the last [END] (6) =OFFEND

- You have left off. Right on! (5) =SIDES

• *Inscription* on side [LEG] edge [END] (6) = LEGEND

but, when referring to the teams, 'off' means 'out' (off the field) and 'on' means 'in' (batting)

see The Use of 'Out' and 'In', Part 2:12

and 'left' can also mean 'departed', 'resigned', etc.

• A hundred [C] departed [LEFT] and *split* (5) = CLEFT

• *Resigned* from the *side* (4) = LEFT

and, at sea, means 'port'

• *Ally* left at sea [PORT] in glorious [SUP-ER] surroundings (9) = SUPPORTER

which can mean 'wine'

• Fresh [NEW] filling for pipes [PORT] *in the Isle of Wight* (7) = NEWPORT (Pipe = wine cask)

while 'right' also means 'correct' (indicated by a tick)

• *In a little time,* does it show one's not altogether right? (4,1,4) = HALF A TICK

which can be abbreviated to OK or OKE

• *Game* between prince [P] and King Edward [ER] right [OK] (5) = POKER

• '*Observer,* look [LO] right [OKE].' 'Right [R]!' (6) = LOOKER (Note two versions of 'right')

or, in the legal sense, a claim

• *Customer* right [LIEN] in Connecticut [C-T] (6) = CLIENT

or, at sea, it means 'starboard'

• *It is right* to get second [S] sailor [TAR] on panel [BOARD] (9) = STARBOARD

SS
sometimes refers to Hitler's bodyguard

• Father [PA] Time [AGE] captures German soldiers [SS] in *alley* (7) = PASSAGE

or, in some cases, to two seconds

• '*Always*' — coda [END] takes artist [LE-LY] about two seconds [SS] (9) = ENDLESSLY

but is more often the favoured abbreviation for 'steamship', described in the clue as 'ship', 'liner', 'vessel', 'craft', etc.

- *Vessel* or its centres [SS] when enlarged (9) =STEAMSHIP

- *She'll welcome* those wrecked [=HOSTE] on ship [SS] (7) =HOSTESS

- *Common trouble* getting vessel [SS] into well [HA-LE] (6) =HASSLE

although not all references to 'vessel' imply the use of SS

- *Space* for vessels [PANS] in the river [EX-E] (7) =EXPANSE

- *Vessel* badly [ILL] missed by weapons [ART(ILL)ERY] (6) =ARTERY

- Study [CON] article [A] in vessel's [T-IN] *hold* (7) =CONTAIN

- Vessel [URN], when hemmed in, tries to get through [DI-ALS] *logs* (8) =DIURNALS

- *Vessel* making a number [TEN] in America [U-S] almost sick [IL(L)] (7) =UTENSIL

Perhaps the most frequent use is for the inclusion of other words, so that anything 'aboard', 'on board' or 'in the ship' is written between S-S

- *Hauls* fish [LING] into the ship [S-S] (6) =SLINGS

- *Flowers* for Welshman [DAI] that is [IE] aboard [S-S] (7) =DAISIES

- Drink [PORT] put on board [S-S] for *games* (6) =SPORTS

- *Catch* [NAIL] the ship is carrying [S-S] *will please the French* (6) =SNAILS

although these phrases may be used as alternatives for each other

- A [A] poet [B-ARD] who wrote about love [O] *on a ship* (6) =ABOARD

Occasionally the phrasing of the clue will imply S-S written outside other words rather than words written inside S-S

- Vessel [S-S] going out of port [PORT] for *yachting etc.* (6) =SPORTS

Note that there are other meanings for the phrase 'on board' so it must not always be taken to imply S-S

- *One may be on board* to wash [BATH] a mass of hair [BUN] (7)=BATHBUN (Board=table)

- *Keep* man on board (6)=CASTLE (Chess board)

- *Top men in the baking business* (10)=BREADBOARD (Board of directors)

- Approval of foreigners [Fr. OUI, Ger. JA] necessary on *board* (5)=OUIJA (Ouija board)

- Th(e) meal men out East [E] cook *for the board* (9)=EMMENTHAL (Cheese board)

and 'aboard' sometimes implies SS rather than S-S

- *The skill* needed to tackle power failure [=PROWE] on board [SS] (7)=PROWESS

or may simply mean 'on'

- Getting aboard [ON] in time [H-OUR] is a *privilege* (6)=HONOUR

and 'in a ship' has other uses

- *Pest* in a ship (5)=APHIS

ST

is the usual abbreviation for 'street' and RD stands for 'road'; both are often referred to as 'way' so that 'in the street/road/way' involves splitting ST (*see also* 'point' above)

- *Garment* for the fireplace [INGLE] in a way [S-T] (7)=SINGLET

- *Ran* with one [ACE] in the road [R-D] (5)=RACED

- Otherwise [OR] come up [=RO] with a [A] way [ST] to *cook* (5)=ROAST (down clue)

In some cases 'way' means 'via'

- *He* found a [A] way [VIA] to [TO] rise initially [R] (7)=AVIATOR

or 'lane'

- *Italian food* makes you hang heavy [SAG] in a way [LA-NE] (7)=LASAGNE or 'motorway'

- *Undertaking* to show the way [MI] in plain speech [PRO-SE] (7)=PROMISE

or 'path'

- *Inefficient* in a [A] way [PATH] — call [CITE] back [=ETIC] later (9)=APATHETIC

or it can be used to mean 'method'

- Came across [MET] tool [HOD] in the *way* (6)=METHOD

ST is also a common abbreviation for 'saint', 'good man', 'holy man', etc.

- Saint [ST] Peter [SAFE] overturned the *most reliable* (6)=SAFEST

- Good man [ST] travelled on horseback [RODE] and *walked* (6)=STRODE

although, in some cases, S is used instead of ST and 'good man' may have other meanings

- Holy man [S] deceived [KIDDED] — *went out of control* (7)=SKIDDED

- *A good man* may perhaps mar a saint (9)=SAMARITAN

state
as a verb, may require a synonym (aver, allege, etc.)

- *Mean* to state [AVER] time [AGE] (7)=AVERAGE

- A [A] very incomplete [VER(Y)] *state* (4)=AVER

- *State* support [LEG] in beer [AL-E] division (6)=ALLEGE

or it may indicate a homophone

- Chair [THRONE], they state, is *flung through the air* (6)=THROWN

As a noun, it will sometimes refer to a nation-state

- *State* of some slipperiness, it's said [GREASE] (6)=GREECE

- *State* to call [DUB] sloth [AI] (5)=DUBAI

including those of Ancient Greece

- Most of the [TH(E)] people [RACE] in *ancient state* (6)=THRACE

but, more frequently, to one of the 50 states of the USA, each of which, except Hawaii, has its appropriate abbreviation (*see* A Compiler's Vocabulary, Appendix 4)

- *Pleading* from state [CAL] suffering reversal [=LAC] in depression [P-IT] (6)=PLACIT
- *Sheep* from Ireland [ERIN] found in Missouri [M-O] (6)=MERINO
- *Build* before [ERE] coming to Connecticut [CT] (5)=ERECT

Less frequently, the name of the state will be required in full

- Country [INDI-A] surrounding an [AN] *American state* (7)=INDIANA
- Fail to find [MISS] our [OUR] little island [I]-*state* (8)=MISSOURI

or 'states' will mean US

- 'Say Ar [=R]', house [HO]-doctor [MB] states [US] — 'here's a *lozenge*' (7)=RHOMBUS

and 'state' can also mean 'condition'

- Note [E] condition [STATE] of *property* (6)=ESTATE

T
is often used to stand for associated words such as T-square, etc.

- Sort of square [T] stretcher [RACK] for *dog* (5)=TRACK
- Sort of road junction [T] which has a fixed line [AXIS] for *vehicles* (5)=TAXIS
- Kind of shirt [T] on the line [ROPE]? *A figure of speech* (5)=TROPE

or as an abbreviation for 'tea' or 'tee'

- *Kind of paper* for children [ISSUE] after tea [T] (6)=TISSUE
- *Giant* I [I] beat [TAN] behind the tee [T] (5)=TITAN
- *Trevino's tee* [T]? (7)=INITIAL

Note that 'tea mixture', 'tea break' or 'blend of tea' can be rendered as ATE or EAT

- *Repayment* concerning [RE] black [B] tea mixture [=ATE] (6)=REBATE

- Car company's [BL] <u>tea</u> break [=EAT] *complaint* (5) =BLEAT

- *Distinctive character* of strong [F] blend of <u>tea</u> [=EAT] on the river [URE] (7) =FEATURE

T can also be used to mean 'half-dry'

see TT below

TT
may stand for 'teetotal' or 'dry'

- *A church cantata* may move <u>me to</u> [=MOTE] showing abstinence [TT] (6) =MOTETT

- Keeping dry [TT] in river [A-IRE] in this *garment* (6) =ATTIRE

or for the Tourist Trophy motorcycle race

- *Run along* or [OR] turn up [=RO] during the race [T-T] (4) =TROT (down clue)

or for 'teas' or 'tees' or 'tease'

- Teas [TT] in a row [TI-ER] are *a bit of a laugh* (6) =TITTER

- *Contend with* tees [TT] in a bundle [BA-LE] (6) =BATTLE

- Strip [BAND]-tease, say [=TT], held by two [I-I] criminals (8) =BANDITTI

or for 'doublet'

- *It was worn once* in the middle of hot<u>te</u>r [TT=double T] spell (7) =DOUBLET

Since TT can mean 'dry', T can mean 'half-dry'

- *Author,* half-dry [T], is on the wagon [WAIN] (5) =TWAIN

You may also find TT split as T-T to allow an inclusion

- Almost rush [RUS(H)] into race [T-T] for *responsibility* (5) =TRUST

union
sometimes means 'match', 'marriage', etc.

- *Most important man at the union?* (10) =BRIDEGROOM

but usually implies an abbreviation for the name of a trade union

- *Entertain* union members [NUJ] dancing [=NJU] in the centre [CO-RE] (7) =CONJURE

- No [NO] railwaymen [NUR] get up and *talk nonstop* (3,2) = RUN ON (down clue)
- *Spice* given by union [NUT] girl [MEG] (6) = NUTMEG

unknown

In algebra, unknown quantities are designated X and Y

- Unknown character [X] cutting tree [TREE] up [=E-ERT] for *use* (5) = EXERT
- *Weak* joke [PUN] unknown [Y] (4) = PUNY

X is also the symbol for a kiss

- *Hidden* meaning of a symbolic kiss [X] (7) = UNKNOWN

and a cross

- 'X' is *far from pleased* (5) = CROSS

In arithmetic, an unknown number is often designated 'n' (N)

- Unknown number [N] circle [O] crazy [MAD] *rover* (5) = NOMAD

Occasionally, 'unknown' will be something other than an abbreviation

- Warwick's Saladin? *Unknown* (4,5) = DARK HORSE

Colloquial abbreviations are used in crosswords, sometimes as given words to be incorporated into the solution, sometimes as indirect clues written in full from which the appropriate colloquialism must be derived.

Given abbreviations

- *Sage* who made 'em snore (7) = EMERSON
- *Correct!* 'Tis [TIS] in pursuit [CHAS-E] (8) = CHASTISE
- Late 'cos of *sugar* (7) = LACTOSE

and derived

- It's going to [IT WILL] introduce *fabric* (5) = TWILL
- *Graduate* unable [CANT] to turn graduate [BA=AB] (6) = CANTAB

- *Meagre* imitation <u>fur</u> [=FRU] on common girl [GAL] (6)=FRUGAL

- *Stake* and it [ANT] has a point [E] (4)=ANTE

- *Virtuous* tinker [S-LY] is not commonly [AINT] put inside (7)=SAINTLY

- Expert [AC-E] had them briefly ['AD 'EM] inside *university* (7)=ACADEME

I am

as an admission, claim, confession or declaration becomes I'M (IM)

- 'King Charles [CR]', I declare [IM], with energy [E], *'sin!'* (5)=CRIME

For the use of AM, IM, IAM at the beginning of words

see Letter Groups, Part 2:28

I have

Similarly, 'I have' is usually abbreviated to I'VE (IVE)

- In the king [G-R], I have [IVE] a *patron* (5)=GIVER

For the use of IVE at the end of words

see Letter Groups, Part 2:28

I would

becomes I'D (ID) or IDE, say
—he would=HED or HEED, say
—she would=SHED
—we would=WED or WEED, say,

- Figure [C] I would [ID] get the *police* (3)=CID

- *Skin* is hard [H], I would [ID] say [=IDE] (4)=HIDE

I shall or I will becomes I'LL (ILL)
—he will=HELL or HEEL, say
—she will=SHELL
—we will=WELL, or WEAL, say, or WHEEL, say

- Bridge [BR] I shall [ILL] go under to *fish* (5)=BRILL (down clue)

Crosswords are composed of letters, and Roman numerals, which are written as letters, can play an important part in some clues (*see* Numbers, Part 2:23).

3.1 ABBREVIATIONS USED ALONE

Some solutions are composed entirely of **abbreviations**

- Credit [CR] a [A] tax [VAT] on *neckwear* (6) =CRAVAT
- *Wind* from Continental [EUR] country [US] (5) =EURUS
- Roman people [PR] are [A] Irish [IR] that is [IE] *plain* (7) =PRAIRIE

some of abbreviations written backwards as **reversals**

- *Large case* for thousand [K] railwaymen's [NUR] tea [T] to return in (5) =TRUNK
- English [E] exhibition site [NEC] second [S] in return to *place of action* (5) =SCENE
- *Clarify,* say [EG], football [RU] power [P] revolution (5) =PURGE

and some of abbreviations written inside other abbreviations as **inclusions**

- *Attack with missiles* from two directions [N-E] engulfing this country [UK] (4) =NUKE
- *College* ring [O] that is [IE] politically neutral (=between R and L) (5) =ORIEL
- English [E] transactions [TR] in foreign city [N-Y] gets *registration* (5) =ENTRY

Sometimes the solution depends on finding the abbreviation in the clue and then expanding it to the full word

- Str/etc/hed the centre [ETC] to its full length *and so on* (2,6) =ET CETERA
- *Do* [DO] fully (5) =DITTO
- *Dry* so race [TT] is fully run (8) =TEETOTAL

3.2 ABBREVIATIONS/SYNONYMS

Combinations of **abbreviations** and **synonyms** may involve **addition**

to **given words**

- Grand [G] state [ALA] had [HAD] a *knight* (7) =GALAHAD

• Value of acid test [PH] — this [THIS] is [IS] for *lung disease* (8) =PHTHISIS

• *Turned* and ran [RAN] with detectives [CID] in pursuit (6) =RANCID

to derived words

• *Viciously attacked* poet [SAVAGE] who died [D] (7) =SAVAGED

• *The quaint* mongrel [CUR] I [I] love [O] (5) =CURIO

• Junior [BABE] student [L] in *The Tower* (5) =BABEL

which may be reversed

• *Old marriage* lines [BR] united with one [I] returning youth [LAD=DAL] (6) =BRIDAL

• Non-professional [LAIC] returns [=CIAL] to international organisation [UN] for *ancient script* (6) =UNCIAL

• Artist [RA] one [I] rejects scarlet [RED=DER] *invader* (6) =RAIDER

or subtraction

• *Admitting* complete [TH(OR)OUGH] loss of gold [OR] (6) =THOUGH

• Fish [SAL(M)ON] not male [M] in *Paris exhibition* (5) =SALON

• *Money* that departing expert [PRO] set forth [(PRO)POUND] (5) =POUND

or inclusion
inside other words

• *Peace* proposal for Ireland [EIRE] and Northern Ireland [NI] for study [CON] (9) =EIRENICON

• *Nimble* soldier [GI] in the drink [A-LE] (5) =AGILE

• *Mad* without jolly [RM] cove [BA-Y] (5) =BARMY

or vice versa

- *Longing* for facts [DA-TA] about East [E] Side [SIDE] River [R] (10) =DESIDERATA

- *Wide view* of girl [NORA] held by her parents [PA-MA] (8) =PANORAMA

- One [I] will be seized by nationalists [SN-P], *that's certain* (4) =SNIP

with the inclusion sometimes reversed

- *Clever* enough to win union [TU] backing [=UT] in one [AC-E] (5) =ACUTE

- *Misquote* lines [BR] back [=RB] in a storm [GA-LE] (6) =GARBLE

- Artist [RA] came back [=AR] into building [SH-ED] and *split up* (6) =SHARED

Some clues that involve **subtraction** are phrased as additions

- *Plant* but five hundred [D] to one [I] on it being heavenly [(DI)VINE] (4) =VINE

- Attached to ship [SS], the *sewer* would be unnecessary [NEEDLE(SS)] (6) =NEEDLE (Note the direct clue in the centre)

In some combinations, the abbreviations may appear in the clue requiring the full word in the solution

- *Poet* or [GOLD] mighty man [SMITH] (9) =GOLDSMITH

- *Familiar policemen* said 'See you [CU =COPPER] Sunday [S]' (7) =COPPERS

- *Breathing apparatus*-ring [O =OXYGEN] many [M] request [ASK] (6,4) =OXYGEN MASK

and, in others, both the abbreviation and the full word are required

- *Opsimath is a late one* [L] to be a money-winner [EARNER] (7) =LEARNER

See also Numbers, Part 2:23
See also A Compiler's Alphabet, Appendix 3, and A Compiler's Vocabulary, Appendix 4.

4

SELECTED LETTERS

There are many cases where the compiler needs a letter or two to add to or deduct from a word in the clue to make up the solution he is aiming for and there are almost as many ways of achieving this end, some of which are mentioned below.

By definition, if you select some letters from a word for retention, you are selecting the rest for elimination and, where the compiler chooses to use about half the letters in any given word, the distinction between selecting for retention and selecting for elimination becomes rather blurred. Such cases could be described (as they have been in Synonyms, Part 1:2, 1) as the use of part-words. How they are described is of no real importance — the pointer in the clue will usually provide sufficient guidance.

Pointers: *see* lists below

Letters may be **selected for retention**

by reference to the position of the letter(s) in a word using

first letters
—an opening =A
—beginning of time =T
—Big Top =B
—bullhead =B
—capital of Rome =R
—early stages of his life =HL
—empty-headed =starts with O
—first character in Hamlet =H

* *Conciliate* a particular locality [PL-ACE] including a [A] town initially [T] (7) =PLACATE

* Initially offensive [O] and beastly [B] episode [SCENE] — how *disgusting!* (7) =OBSCENE

* Reptile [ASP] is furious [IRATE] and *starts to hiss* [H] (8) =H =ASPIRATE

—first of <u>A</u>pril =A
—front of <u>h</u>ouse =H
—<u>Ge</u>nesis I and II =GE
—head of <u>d</u>epartment =D
—initiate the <u>s</u>cheme =S
—leader of <u>m</u>en =M
—leading <u>s</u>eaman =S
—onset of <u>w</u>inter =W
—opening <u>n</u>otes =N
—opening of <u>P</u>arliament =P
—origins of <u>t</u>he
  <u>U</u>niversity =TU
—<u>o</u>verhead =O
—<u>p</u>leasant at first =P
—source of <u>r</u>iver =R
—<u>t</u>he beginning =T
—<u>T</u>he <u>L</u>ion's Head =L
—<u>t</u>hey initially =T
—<u>T</u>imes leader =T
—<u>t</u>ip of <u>i</u>ceberg =I
—<u>t</u>iptop =T
—top of <u>l</u>adder =L
—<u>t</u>radesmen's entrance =T

Note the difference between
'the beginning of <u>t</u>he play' =T
and 'the beginning of
<u>p</u>lay' =P

second letters
—runnner-up in r<u>a</u>ce =A
—second character in p<u>l</u>ay =L
—second of A<u>u</u>gust =U
—second w<u>i</u>nd =I
—t<u>h</u>e centre =H

• Observing [NO-TING] second bit of
  s<u>h</u>erry [H] in *trifle* (7) =NOTHING

• *Listen to* runners-up in t<u>h</u>ree-
  legged [H,E] r<u>a</u>ce [A] by ri<u>v</u>er [R]
  (4) =HEAR

• Followers of leaders of a<u>r</u>moured
  regiment m<u>a</u>y t<u>r</u>ack *back*
  (4) =REAR

middle letters
—ap<u>p</u>le core =P
—at<u>om</u>ic nucleus =OM
—central hea<u>t</u>ing =T

• *Wrangled* and stormed [RAG-ED]
  about the centre of Wigan [G]
  (6) =RAGGED

50

−central Wales =L or ALE
−centre half =AL
−centre of Paris =R
−centre of Universe =VE
−contents of crate =RAT
−half-hearted =AL
−hard-hearted =AR
−health-centre =AL
−heart of gold =OL
−Heart of Midlothian =OT
−middle of the . . . =H
−Middle School =HO
−mid-off =F
−midstream =RE
−midsummer =MM
  (thousands)
−sweetheart =E
−town centre =OW
−you in the middle =O

last letters
−arrived finally =D
−at last =T
−back of beyond=D
−bottom of ladder=R
−different conclusion =T
−end of June=E
−final part of play=Y
−last characters in Aida=DA
−last laugh=H
−last of the Mohicans=S
−root of evil=L
−shirt-tail =T
−stern of dinghy=Y
−the bitter end =R
−the end =E
−the end of it=T
−the final straw=W
−the finish =E
−West End =T

Note the difference between
'end of the world' =E and
'end of world' =D

• *Raphael,* for instance, in fresh
  clothes [CHANGE] breaking
  Charles's heart [AR-L]
  (9) =ARCHANGEL

• *Grub* unfashionable [OUT] after
  the middle of March [R]
  (4) =ROUT

• Left [L] over [ACROSS] the end of
  the [E] *game* (8) =LACROSSE

• Goes for a spin [CYCL-ES] round
  Trinidad's two furthest [AD]
  islands (8) =CYCLADES

• *Soil* covering the roots of the [E]
  deciduous [S] elm [M] tree [B-IRCH]
  (8) =BESMIRCH

alternate letters

—alternate intervals of
   time =TM or IE
—even characters in play=LY
—every other part of
   Spain =SAN or PI
—odd bits of food =FO

• Even clear characters [L, A] in this
   state (9) =LA =LOUISIANA

• Books I and III [B, O] about [RE]
   drill (4) =BORE

• Parts 1 and 3 of story [S, O] king
   [R] Edward [TED] *arranged*
   (6) =SORTED

other single letters

• *Such feeling* for Beethoven's Third
   [E] movement [MOTION]
   (7) =EMOTION

• 4th July [Y] right [OK] for the
   Spanish [EL] *countryman*
   (5) =YOKEL

• Fifth of November [M] party [DO]
   upset [=OD] *teenager* (3) =MOD

first and last letters

—banana skin =BA
—boundaries of Surrey=SY
—fringes of society=SY
—heartless woman=WN
—limits of patience=PE
—logical extremes =LL
—outlying parts of
   Manchester=MR
—outwardly calm=CM
—sides of bacon=BN
—skirting
   Southampton=SOON
—social ends =SL
—termini of railway=RY
—terribly heartless =TY
—the heartless . . . =TE
—vile outsiders =VE

• *Relative position* upset the
   outsiders [T, E] in Ontario
   (11) =ORIENTATION

• *Abstained* from weed [=EWED] and
   the outsides of cheese [CH, SE]
   perhaps (8) =ESCHEWED

• *Asian ruler* extremely knavish
   [K, H] and authoritarian [A, N]
   (4) =KHAN

• *Employer* and unions [U, S]
   endeavour [E, R] to be extremely
   selective (4) =USER

by reference to the position
of the letter(s) in the alphabet
—a follower =B
—first character =A or
   ALPHA

• First character [A] to head an
   orchestra [LSO], *what's more*
   (4) =ALSO

—first nine characters (A to I) sent back =IOTA
—followers of ABC=DE
—followers of CND=DOE
—from A-K to M-Z=no L=NOEL
—JAYS have eyes (=I's) in front
—plenty of scope=A-Z
—successor to Brand X=BRANDY
—tee=AFTERS (after S)
—water=H-O (H to O =H_2O)

by reference to parts or fractions
—bit of fun=F
—centre half=CEN or TRE
—50% of people=PEO or PLE
—half a jiffy=SEC(ond)
—half of bitter=BIT or TER
—half-mile=MI or LE
—half-volume=BO(ok)
—halfway=STR(eet)
—most parts=ARTS
—not quite 50% =HAL(f)
—piece of bread=B
—piece of collar=S (from S-chain)
—portion of stodge=GE
—quarterdeck=D, E, C or K
—three-quarters of an hour=OUR
—troubadour's poor piece =BAD

by reference to compound words which themselves indicate the letter(s) to be selected for retention
—bandleader=B
—egghead=E
—double-header=D
—eye-opener=E

• Dee's predecessor [C], the love of France [L'AMOUR], makes a *din* (7)=CLAMOUR

• Extreme characters [A, Z] introducing a [A] meadow [LEA] *plant* (6)=AZALEA

• *Necessary* quarter-pint [T] in small bottle [VI-AL] (5)=VITAL

• Half the vicinity [VICI] bears witness to *his* winning third act (6)=CAESAR (Veni, vidi, vici; note the direct clue in the centre)

• Three-quarter quick [LIV(E)] to no purpose [IDLY] *in a bruised way* (7)=LIVIDLY

• Headmaster [M] requests [ASKS] *disguises* (5)=MASKS

• Minehead [M] painting [ART] *market* (4)=MART

—fat-headed =F
—Gateshead =G
—headmaster =M
—pithead =P
—redhead =R
—ringleader =R
—seafront =S
—squadron leader =S
—startle can start LEopard
—centre forward =W
—midnight =G
—bookend =K
—cocktail =K
—Gravesend =E
—tail end =L

• Sailor's [TAR] tin-opener [T] is *sharp* (4) =TART
• Win [GAIN] after midday [A] *once more* (5) =AGAIN
• *Remove* transport [BR] in [IN] Bridgend [G] (5) =BRING
• *Small drink* for rat-tail [T] donkey [ASS] (4) =TASS

by reference to vitamins A-E

• Stars [SUNS] had [HAD] vitamin [E] as *protection from rays* (8) =SUNSHADE

by reference to music
—notes/keys: ABCDEFG

• Energetically begin [PITCH IN] to note [G] *movement of vessel* (8) =PITCHING
• *Witty retort* about [RE] member [PART] with duplicate key [EE] (8) =REPARTEE
(Here RE is not a note but E is)

—notes/scale: DO, DOH, UT, RE, ME, MI, FA, FAH, SO, SOH, LA, LAH, TE, TI, SI

• Note [RE] on building resort [=TRORSE] is *turned down* (8) =RETRORSE
(Here RE is a note and 'resort', which is a favourite pointer to an anagram, is itself made into an anagram)
• *Dirty* opinion survey [POLL] — socially acceptable [U] to part of the scale [TE] (7) =POLLUTE

—violin strings: A, D, E, G

• *Put off* string [A] vest perhaps (5) =STAVE

—but the seed of the ash tree is known as a key,

• Key producer [ASH] with little time [MO] to spare [LEAN] in *museum* (9) =ASHMOLEAN

—a key can be a piano key

—and a note can be 'natural', 'sharp' or 'flat'

— or paper money

by reference to aspiration to include H

by reference to stuttering to double a letter

—sometimes in reversal

—but duplication of letters can have other implications

by reference to love to include O

or simply by arbitrary choice

• Plant [I-VY] round gold [OR] *key* (5) =IVORY

• *Policeman* takes note [FLAT] to part of Yard [FOOT] (8) =FLATFOOT

• *Outstanding feature* of earth [LAND], note [MARK] (8) =LANDMARK

• In girl [AVA] and boy [LANC-E] aspiration [H] leads to *downfall* (9) =AVALANCHE

• *Rigorous* aspirations [H-H] about Roman art [ARS] (5) =HARSH

• *Failure* of aspiration [H] after pile-up of <u>cars</u> [=CRAS] (5) =CRASH

• *Have recourse to* a [A] stuttering sound [P'PEAL] (6) =APPEAL

• *Join* a [A] stammering fellowship [C'COMPANY] (9) =ACCOMPANY

• *Shorten* a [A] lawyer's brief [B'BREVIATE] with spasmodic repetition (10) =ABBREVIATE

• *Seeing who starts* to [TO] c-chant [S, SING] (7) =TOSSING

• *Way-out* s-stuff [S-SERGE] sent back (6) =EGRESS

• *P-pipe* (5-7) =PENNY-WHISTLE

• *C-cor* (4,4) =CAPE HORN

see Numbers, Part 2:23

• Form of <u>code</u> [=DECO]-letter [R] in *scenery* (5) =DECOR

• *March* some <u>troops</u> [TR] into the team [S-IDE] (6) =STRIDE

• For example, mad <u>love</u> [=VO-EL] about *what this isn't* (5) =VOWEL (VO-EL outside W, a consonant)

- *Demand* [ASK] part of a [A] rifle [RI] for a *soldier* (6)=ASKARI

- *Rogue's* letters [SC] to a [A] politician [MP] (5)=SCAMP

- *Black* as parts of the night sky may be (4)=INKY

- *Bird* or river [PO] in part of Canada [CA-N] (5)=CAPON

- *Wants* letters [TS] to a customer [COVE] (6)=COVETS

Letters may be **selected for elimination**

by the use of words which themselves indicate elimination of

beginnings
—(d)ance not started=ANCE
—decapitated=omit first letter
—executed=omit first letter
—(g)rand deficiency=omit G
—(h)aircut=AIR
—he leaves t(he) . . .=T
—headless (f)lower=LOWER
—leaderless (w)omen=OMEN
—lead off=omit first letter
—nameless (di)ve=VE
—(o)ne loses nothing=NE
—topless dress=(g)OWN

- *Popular* beauty treatment [(F)ACIAL] won't start to give a lift [=LAICA] over fifty [L] (6)=LAICAL (down clue)

- *Wrong* house [VILLA], very small [(T)INY] with no opening (8)=VILLAINY

- *A man-eater,* she removes the leading pair [PR] in advance [(PR)OGRESS] (6)=OGRESS

middles
—disheartened b(o)y=BY
—half-hearted bel(l)ow =BELOW
—heartless be(a)st=BEST
—m(an)y won't have an . . . =MY
—n(o)t without love=NT

- *In Scotland, hideous* cut [GASH] locally [L(OCALL)Y] destroys infrastructure (6)=GASHLY

- Drink [ALE] preceded disturbance [R(IO)T] stifling cry of triumph [IO] — *warn people* (5)=ALERT

- Yogi [Y(OG)I] disheartened by clergyman [ELDER] — *he gives up* (7)=YIELDER

ends
—almost al(l) =AL
—curtailed tri(p) =TRI
—cut-price =COS(t)
—detailed =omit last letter
—incomplete =omit last letter
—limited are(a) =ARE
—most fruit =MELO(n)
—most of th(e) . . . =TH
—nearly al(l) =AL
—nearly all gon(e) =GON
—nearly all th(e) . . . =TH
—no end of th(e) . . . =TH
—not quite certain =SUR(e)
—penniless tram(p) =TRAM
—premature end =omit last
    letter
—short tim(e) =TIM
—tailless rabbi(t) =RABBI
—t(he) non-male =T
—th(is) is missing =TH
—unfinished job =TAS(k)

both ends
—avoid extremes
—no ends
—tops and tails
—unlimited

other single letters
—anonymous =omit N
—ba(i)t I omitted =BAT
—eyeless, say =omit I
—give nothing away =omit O
—losing his shirt =omit T
—lost time =omit T

• *Standing up* before [ERE] being cast [C(AS)T] as [AS] not wanted (5) =ERECT

• The French [LA] cut off the end [TH(E)] of *a strip of wood* (4) =LATH

• First rate [AI], excellent [RARE] and almost delicate [NIC(E)] climbing *plant* (9) =CINERARIA (down clue)

• After humbug [SHAM], Winnie [POO(H)] needs an hour [H] off to *wash* (7) =SHAMPOO

• Top and tail layout [(S)PEN(D)] for *writer* (3) =PEN

• Unlimited speech [(O)RATIO(N)] shows *scale of representation* (5) =RATIO

• *Fast day* for non-extreme representatives [(M)EMBER(S)] (5) =EMBER

• Headless monster's [(D)RAG(ON)] on/off [ON off] *horseplay* (3) =RAG

• Lovelessly turn few quail (o)ut — *wholly bad* (5,5) =QUITE AWFUL

• Rare [CURIO(U)S] non-U *bric-a-brac* (6) =CURIOS

—loveless =omit O
—nameless =omit N
—non-U =omit U
—not a co(a)t =COT
—nothing less =omit O
—no time =omit T
—not married =omit M
—not noisy =omit F
—not right =omit R
—penniless =omit P
—pointless =omit N, S, E or W
—right away =R
—som(e) reduction =SOM
—unnamed =omit N
—un-English =omit E
—without a penny =omit P
—without money =omit L

parts of words

—abandon attempt =omit TRY
—abandoned by the
  French =omit LE
—badly missed =omit ILL
—cut-price =CO(st)
—drop in =omit IN
—fatherless =omit PA
—faultless ser(vice) =SER
—half-time =TI or ME
—heartless I(an Botha)m =IM
—judge not
  finished =REFER(ee)
—motherless =omit MA
—nonunion (tu)tor =TOR
—often reduced =OF or TEN
—senseless =omit NOUS
—short course =PUD(ding)
—skip it =omit IT
—small bottle =BOT(tle)
—thankless (ta)sk =SK
—(use)less building =HO(use)
—weightless
  package =CAR(ton)
—without hesitation =omit ER
—without my fa(m)il(y) =FAIL

• *Stone* identified by only [ON(L)Y]
  ten [X], not fifty [L] (4) =ONYX

• *Silently* destroyed the la(s)t city
  left societyless (7) =TACITLY

• *Money* raised [UP] staggering
  [R-EE(LING)] around without fish
  [LING] (5) =RUPEE

• *Dock manager* is one complaining
  [WH-INGER] about a [A] return of
  freight [FR(EIGHT)=RF] with
  number [EIGHT] missing
  (10) =WHARFINGER

• A [A] river [R] valley [VAL(LEY)]
  with no arable land [LEY] *like*
  ploughed fields (5) =ARVAL

• Child [BRAT] seized by violent
  [VI-O(LENT)] but not fast [LENT]
  throbbing (7) =VIBRATO

• *Cut* and come again [REAP(PEAR)]
  fruitlessly (4) =REAP

by reference to Cockney speech	• Joint [(H)INGE] pronounced by Eliza and *Dean* (4) =INGE
	• Face [DIAL] Cockney's feverish [(H)ECTIC] *disputation by logic* (9) =DIALECTIC
	• *Circuitous journey* for Cockney pair [ME AND (H)ER] (7) =MEANDER
or to careless or common speech to eliminate H	• *Animal* carelessly said to be more heated [(H)OTTER] (5) =OTTER
	• Common refuge [(H)ARBOUR] in *old garden* (6) =ARBOUR
by reference to aspiration, to eliminate H	• *Claim unjustly* that Yorkshire town [(H)ARROGATE] is without aspiration (8) =ARROGATE
	• Has [(H)AS] no aspiration — sure [CERTAIN] *to find out* (9) =ASCERTAIN
	• Henry [(H)AL] loses his aspiration, I [I] meant [MEANT] to say [=MENT], for *food* (7) =ALIMENT
or by the use of the apostrophe of omission	• Headless lady's [(H)ER] 'eadgear [(H)AT] and ring [O] *is one of nine* (5) =ERATO (one of the nine Muses)
	• *A brawl*'s [(I)S] almost crime [CRIM(E)] and ruins <u>game</u> [=MAGE] (9) =SCRIMMAGE
	• *Fruit* growin' [RAISIN(G)] (6) =RAISIN
Blind mice had their tails cut off	• *Funny* business [CO] with blind rodents [MIC(E)] (5) =COMIC
and Manx cats and, by association, all things Manx are tailless	• A Manx cat [PUS(S)] having lost one of its nine lives? (7) =OCTOPUS

• Manx pawnbroker [UNCL(E)] gives publicity [AD] to *nude* (6)=UNCLAD

In some instances, letters selected might be termed 'cognate letters' (on the analogy of cognate anagrams)

• <u>T</u>urnberry's first [T] (3)=TEE

see Straight Anagrams, Part 1:8.1

Out and **without** are also used to eliminate letters

see The Use of 'Out' and 'In', Part 2:12 and The Use of 'Without' and 'Within', Part 2:13.

4.1 SELECTED LETTERS ALONE

Where **selected letters are retained** they may be used for the whole solution using

first letters

• *Joint* leaders from <u>A</u>lliance <u>n</u>aturally <u>k</u>nock <u>L</u>abour's <u>e</u>fforts (5)=ANKLE

second letters

• Runners-up in r<u>a</u>ce w<u>i</u>n o<u>r</u>dinary i<u>s</u>sue *songs* (4)=AIRS

third letters

• Third out of fo<u>u</u>r [U] as *nuclear energy source* (7)=U=URANIUM

last letters

• *Seed* from thes<u>e</u> lon<u>g</u> do<u>g</u> tails (3)=EGG

alternate letters

• *Relative* <u>i</u>n <u>t</u>im<u>e</u> a<u>c</u>t<u>e</u>d every other character (5)=NIECE

or a number of letters

• *Bicycle* used to deliver two letters [T and M] (6)=TANDEM

and, in some cases, the selected letters are written backwards

• *Joy* turned the ends of th<u>e</u> larg<u>e</u> ova<u>l</u> ru<u>g</u> (4)=GLEE

• *Cheerful* at the start, <u>y</u>oung, <u>r</u>ough-<u>r</u>iding, English <u>m</u>aster coming back (5)=MERRY

• *Sailor's* leaders turned to <u>r</u>unning <u>a</u>mok <u>c</u>arrying <u>s</u>words <u>a</u>nd <u>l</u>ances (6)=LASCAR

Usually, selected letters from consecutive words are added together

- *Moulding* Church [C] youth [Y] leaders to a degree [MA] (4)=CYMA

but be prepared to link them with 'and'

- *Sweet* from Church youth leaders [C and Y] (5)=CANDY

Occasionally the selected letters provide a clue to, rather than themselves forming part of, the solution

- Odd characters in Vienna [VEN] identifying its occupant (12)=ARCHDEACONRY (Ven=Venerable, honorary prefix for Archdeacon)

4.2 SELECTED LETTERS/GIVEN WORDS

Letters may be **selected for retention** and combined with **given words**

by **addition**

- Leaders of Conservative [C] ladies [L] offer [O] the [THE] *dress* (6)=CLOTHE

- Starters should [S] take [T] one [ONE] *diamond, perhaps* (5)=STONE

- First signs of elephant [E], leopard [L], and [AND] *antelope* (5)=ELAND

by **subtraction**

- Tripod [TRIP(OD)] losing odds and ends [O, D] in the *fall* (4)=TRIP

- Master [MAST(ER)] missing start of evening recital [E, R] goes *nuts* (4)=MAST

- The first letter [A] to leave P(a)lace *Square* (5)=PLACE

by **inclusion**

- *It refreshed* some teams [TE] during the War [WA-R] (5)=WATER

- Greeting [AV(E)] cut short [=AV] in the city [C-ITY] *hollow* (6)=CAVITY

- *Sound quality* of two bits of bread [BR] in time [TIM-E] (6)=TIMBRE

by **reversal**

- Unfinished grave [TOM(B)] returned [=MOT] to *her* [HER] (6) =MOTHER

- *Set of conditions* Reg [REG] starts. Nobody [N] ever [E] mentioned [M] its [I] rejection [=IMEN] (7) =REGIMEN

- *Life story* of his [HIS] origins. Young [Y] radical [R] openly [O] turns [T] back [=TORY] (7) =HISTORY

Letters may be **selected for elimination** from **given words**

- *Callous* as Marina vis-à-vis Mar(t)ina (9) =HEARTLESS

which may be combined by **addition**

- *He* makes you [YOU] think [TH(INK)] there's no ink [INK] (5) =YOUTH

- *So* cut off the [TH(E)] end before us [US] (4) =THUS

- Drop end of line [LIN(E)] and net [NET] *bird* (6) =LINNET

Selected letters may be changed in given words by **substitution** of other letters

- *He foolishly* has a couple of differences with a bu(r)gl(a)r (7) =BUNGLER

- Replacing one [I] in India [IND(I)A] sailor's [AB] *conference in Africa* (6) =INDABA

- *Foul—* s(i)lly after I become objective (6) =SMELLY (I =subject, me =object)

or by **switching** letters

- Old woman [BELDAM] undergoes change of heart [DL for LD] in *madhouse* (6) =BEDLAM

- Something attractive in oldest one switching first couple [LO for OL] (9) =LODESTONE

- *Situation* of vessels [POTS] which turn tail [ST for TS] (4) =POST or by **merging** the letters of two words

- *Cuts* [CUTS] alternately with one's [ONES] *noble wife*
  (8)=COUNTESS

The substitution may involve another clue

- *Grow* bee [B] and encourage [URGE ON] (7) =BURGEON (clue 10 across)
- *Operator*'s sister [S] succeeds a follower [B] of 10 ac (7) =SURGEON

4.3 SELECTED LETTERS/DERIVED WORDS

Letters may be **selected for retention** for use with **derived words**

by **addition**

- *Gift* of leaders of troops [T] raiding [R] Indonesian [I] island [BUTE] (7)=TRIBUTE

- *In anticipation of* a [A] profit [GAIN] sublet numbers one and six [S, T] (7)=AGAINST

- *Fascinated* by fourth [D] appearance on stage [ENTRANCE] (9)=ENTRANCED

by **subtraction**

- *Number* left when head of legion abandons meal [F(L)OUR] (4)=FOUR

- *Donation* given when first of many [M] English [E] youths [Y] give up wine [(M)ALMS(EY)] (4)=ALMS

- *Carbon, for example,* left after first signs of alcohol [A] lost [L] from spirit [ELEMENT(AL)] (7)=ELEMENT

by **inclusion** of the selected letters in derived words

- *Battered car* starts everything [E] in accident [H-AP] (4)=HEAP

- *A bit of* naughtiness [N] in one night's leave [ABSI-T] on hard [H] *drink* (7)=ABSINTH

63

- *Grievance* arising from head of insect [I] found in cabbage, perhaps [PLA-NT] (6)=PLAINT

or vice versa

- Learner [L] on river [URE] in Surrey boundaries [S-Y] *for certain* (6)=SURELY

- Shed [HUT], to the northeast [NE] with the city limits [C-Y], in a *pickle* (7)=CHUTNEY

- *Address* part [RATIO] in onion skin [O-N] (7)=ORATION

perhaps with the inclusion written as a **reversal**

- *Agree to* head [NESS] returning [=SSEN] in apparent extremes [A-T] (6)=ASSENT

- *Caricature* a girl [DORA] rejected [=AROD] within the bounds of possibility [P-Y] (6)=PARODY

- *A bit of light* thrown on bird [EMU] returning [=UME] in the outskirts of London [L-N] (5)=LUMEN

by **substitution** by replacing letters in the derived words

- Scars [MARKS] fifty [L] not a thousand [M] *birds* (5)=LARKS

- Costly [DEAR] updating coins [P for D] for *fruit* (4)=PEAR

- Note [TENNER] changing direction [S for N] gets *tighter* (6)=TENSER

or by switching letters in the derived word from one position to another

- Take steps [TREAD] to shift direction [E] of *commerce* (5)=TRADE

- One animal [PONY] with another [MOUSE] head-to-tail [=E-MOUS] *with a given name* (9)=EPONYMOUS

- *Study of light* subjects [TOPICS] when the leader [T] is delayed (6)=OPTICS

in some cases, using the device known as a spoonerism

- *Transport from London* Spooner confused with urban [TOWN] sewer [DRAIN] (4,5) =DOWN TRAIN

- Spooner's noticing [MARKING] saint [PETER] *fed by naughty motorist* (7,5) =PARKING METER

Letters may be **selected for elimination** from derived words to leave the solution using

first letters

- Musicians [(P)LAYERS] without leader [P] are found in *bands* (6) =LAYERS

- Coward [(C)RAVEN] who loses his head [C] gets the *bird* (5) =RAVEN

- Churchman [(P)RELATE] who won't begin to *tell* (6) =RELATE

last letters

- Rock [BASAL(T)] without salt ending [T] *at the lowest level* (5) =BASAL

- High-fi set [STERE(O)] lost nothing [O] in *volume* (5) =STERE

- Lose your head [Y] in the hut [BOTH(Y)], *as well* (4) =BOTH

first and last letters

- Not paid so much [(PA)ID LES(S)] — *wastes time* when the old men [PAS] have gone (5) =IDLES (Note the direct clue in the centre)

- *Listen* to the fish [(S)HARK(S)] when the ship [SS] has gone (4) =HARK

- *Fish* mutilated [(M)ANGLE(D)] — had head [M] and tail [D] cut off (5) =ANGLE

other single letters

- Tea, say [T], left mark [S(T)IGMA] in *Greek letter* (5) =SIGMA

• Padre's |CHAPL(A)IN| not in the
end a |A| *funny man*
(7)=CHAPLIN
('In the end' indicates the
omission of the second A, rather
than the first)

• The second one |I| to walk out on
the preacher |MIN(I)STER| in *church*
(7)=MINSTER
('The second one' indicates the
omission of the second I, rather
than the first)

or several letters

• *Study* the devil |DE(MO)N| but not
the doctor |MO| (3)=DEN

• A little bit |S(LIGHT)LY| in the dark
but *cunning* (3)=SLY
('In the dark'=without LIGHT)

• *Cut* way |ST| right |R| out of
imprisonment |(STR)ETCH|
(4)=ETCH

• *Yarn* ignoring the four central
characters in Bentley's verse
|CL(ERIH)EW| (4)=CLEW

Letters may be **selected for
elimination** from derived
words which are then
combined with other words
by **addition**

• Display |PARAD(E)| tailless bull
|OX|. *Absurd but true*
(7)=PARADOX

• Remove sticky substance
|UNGU(M)| cutting tail off almost all
|AL(L)| *of claw* (6)=UNGUAL

• Class |CL| displays |AIRS| dance
|CHACH(A)| without a |A| *harp from
Ireland* (11)=CLAIRSCHACH

or written as **reversals**

• A circle |O| in this *game* would be
a reverse for the Army
|TROOPS=SPO(O)RT| (5)=SPORT
(Note the direct clue in the centre)

• *Lay charge against* soldier
|TROOPER| who returns

[=REP(O)ORT] without a ring [O]
(6)=REPORT

• *Attend to* material [DENIM] that is set back [=MIN(E)D] out East [E] (4)=MIND

or as **inclusions**, with the selected letters inside derived words

• Pipe [H-OSE] round projection [(C)AM] not starting [C] to be *hooked* (6)=HAMOSE

• *Coarse meal* — stomach [G-UT] contains part of fish [RO(E)] with tail [E] cut off (5)=GROUT

• *Sugar-cane refuse* causes embarrassment [M-ESS] when put outside entrance [GA(TE)] without a note [TE] (6)=MEGASS

or vice versa

• Edge [RIM] into prison [C-E(LL)], £50 [LL] missing. *Felony!* (5)=CRIME

• *Moslem student* frequently [OFT] seen in unfinished Indian dress [S-A(RI)] (5)=SOFTA

• *Rock* belonging to him [HIS] fixed [S-(E)T] without energy [E] outside (5)=SHIST

4.4 SELECTED LETTERS/ABBREVIATIONS

Letters **selected for retention** may be combined with **abbreviations**

by **addition**

• Not one [I] unctuous [O(I)LY] politician [MP] on American [US] *mountain* (7)=OLYMPUS

• *Old Muslim* woman [W] will have a [A] shortened garment [HABI(T)] (6)=WAHABI

• Welsh [W] wanted [(N)EEDED] initial name [N] withdrawn — *identified and removed* (6)=WEEDED by **inclusion** of the selected letters inside the abbreviations

- First bits of ignition [I] system [S] in car test [MO-T] are *damp* (5)=MOIST

- Start living [L] in [I] Greece [G] in order [OB-E] to *constrain* (6)=OBLIGE

- Even [E-EN] when you include a Titan's head [T], he was a *giant* (4)=ETEN

or vice versa

- *Material* source of £50 [LL] in one short day [TU-E(SDAY)] (5)=TULLE

- Detectives [CID] in the beginnings of dead [D]-end [E] enquiry [E] *make up their minds* (6)=DECIDE

- Leaders of the cabal [C] are [A] enquiring [E] about company's [BL] *message* (5)=CABLE

5

HIDDEN WORDS

The solution in these cases is obtained from or depends on words actually printed in the clue, but is more or less concealed by phrasing, punctuation and splitting between other words. In some respects, the clues for hidden words are similar to those used in the previous section (Selected letters, Part 1—4) to retain parts of words; the main difference is that the letters which form hidden words will form comprehensible words rather than bits of words that will not stand alone.

Pointers: concealed in, discovered in, evidently, featuring, in, including, ingredient of, in part, items of, not wholly, part of, piece of, seen in, to some extent

The hidden word may be found directly from the clue	• *Throw out* of H/oust/on (4)=OUST
	• *Jury* sto/p an el/ection, to some extent (5)=PANEL
	• *The boy* from Bal/tim/ore (3)=TIM
or it may be used as a further clue to the solution	• Somewhat unr/elia/ble *writer* (7,4)=CHARLES LAMB (Elia=pen name of Charles Lamb)
	• A piece of s/cu/lpture in *metal* (6)=CU =COPPER
	• *President* is st/ron/g to some extent (6)=RON =REAGAN
In a further variation, you are required to deduce the words containing the hidden word which is the solution	• *Man* hiding in the American symbol of freedom (4)=BERT (Statue of Li/bert/y)

- The answer is in the work of David on [ON] *fish* (6)=SALMON (P/salm/ plus on)

- *Monarch* hidden in wife's house (4)=KING (Buc/king/ham Palace)

In some cases, the pointer itself will form part of the hidden word

- Some par/t ext/racted by a preacher from the Bible (4)=TEXT

- Take a litt/le af/ter *tea perhaps* (4)=LEAF

- *Journalist* includ/ed it or/ not? (6)=EDITOR

and, in others, the solution will be a **reversal** of the hidden word

- *Old Norse songs* s/adde/n the heart in retrospect (4)=EDDA

- *Greek hero* held back by unu/sual enem/y (8)=MENELAUS

- In an/y democ/racy, this reflects *the lighter side* (6)=COMEDY

Some hidden words are combined with **derived words**

by addition

- *Watch* the boy from Bal/tim/ore, one with low-grade [E] part [PIECE] (9)=TIMEPIECE

- *Give* man concealed by pseu/don/ym to goddess [ATE] (6)=DONATE

or **inclusion**

- In/draw/n defender [BACK] a *disadvantage* (8)=DRAWBACK

- Watch over [CAR-E] without some com/bin/ation *weapon* (7)=CARBINE

- Some car/din/al in garb [RI-G] for *travelling* (6)=RIDING

- *City-dweller,* part-/own/er in some sort of shirt [T-EE] (6)=TOWNEE

some with **abbreviations**

- *Young maiden* concealed by a/ny MP h/iring a film [ET] (7)=NYMPHET

- *Restrained* editor [ED] following M/r Ein/stein, to some extent (6)=REINED

- Scholar [MA] with part of fre/sh ed/ition is *crushed* (6)=MASHED

and some with **selected letters**

- Partly grown snake [AS(P)] taking bird out of t/he n/est may be *pale* (5)=ASHEN

- Some ca/bin d/oor openings i̲n [I] n̲eo[N]-G̲eorgian [G] *wrapping* (7)=BINDING

- *Happy* to partly untan/gle e/nquiry about fuel [FU(E)L] deficient in energy [E] (7)=GLEEFUL

Occasionally you may be required to import material from another solution

- 1 ACROSS *Missile row* (7)=QUARREL

- *Surviving object* in 1 ACROSS [QUAR/REL] I c/an see (5)=RELIC

6

HOMOPHONES

Homophones may have exactly the same sound (place/plaice; thrown/ throne) or approximately the same sound (whirled/world; lessen/ lesson); they may be composed of only one letter (see/C; you/U), of two letters (cutie/QT; you are/UR), or three letters (effigy/FEG; enemy/NME); they may be one word (doe/dough; son/sun) or two words (knothole/not whole; yew wood/you would), and they may be given or derived words.

In most cases the homophone is used directly as the solution, but in others it acts indirectly to affect the meaning of the clue but does not appear directly in the solution.

Pointers: announced, apparently, auditor (=hearer), I hear, in conversation, it sounds as if, orally, reported, say, so to speak, soundwise, they said, verbally, vocally

Some of the one- and two-letter homophones that may be met are given in the examples which follow; others are listed in A Compiler's Vocabulary, Appendix 4.

A common two-letter homophone is IC =I see, frequently as a word ending

- I see [IC] one [I] queen [ER] is more *frigid* (5) =ICIER

- Island [MONA] saint [ST] I see [=IC] is a *recluse* (8) =MONASTIC

and another is UR =you are

- *Say quietly* Monsieur [M], you are [=UR] double (6) =MURMUR

Even unusual letter combinations can be used for such operations as inclusion

- *Ruler* reported to be cagey [K-G] about partly completed pub [IN(N)] (4) =KING

Three-, four- and even five-letter homophones do exist but are rare in crosswords. A few are listed below:

EEC =easy
FEG =effigy
LEG =elegy
NME =enemy
NTT =entity
YRU =why are you?

APRE =apiary
ICUR =I see you are
LXIA =alexia
RKII =archaise
XLNC =excellency
XPDNC =expediency

Homophones usually relate to whole words, but occasionally the solution requires a homophone for part of a word given as an indirect clue

- *Shrewd* as [AS] some tutors [TUT =TUTE] sound (6) =ASTUTE

- *Goes up* for some prizes [RIZES], we hear (5) =RISES

Combinations of letters and numbers that make up homophones also exist but do not often appear in crosswords. Some samples are listed below:

B9 =benign
B10 =beaten
K9 =canine
U2 =you too

B4U =before you
10SE =Tennessee
XQQ4 =excuse for

6.1 HOMOPHONES ALONE

The **direct form** of homophone sounds like the word derived from the clue

- Sounds like one in need [LACKER] of *a coat* (7) =LACQUER

- *Suitable* as a supporter [PROPPER] (6) =PROPER

- *Want* to work [KNEAD] for an auditor (4) =NEED

while the **indirect form** alters the meaning of the clue but does not appear as part of the solution

- Old Welsh craft [(C)ORACLE] does not start to make a sound *profit* [=PROPHET] (6) =ORACLE

- *Some say Whig* [=WIG] country [PERU] extends to half of Kent' [KE] (6) =PERUKE

- *Fixer* can [TIN] change direction of sale, say [=SAIL] (7) =TINTACK

Two homophones in the clue may yield one word in the solution

- What [=WATT] circular letter [O=EAU] said for *artist* (7)=WATTEAU

- Scotsman's ban [NO, MON] *casts a shadow* (6)=GNOMON

- A prince [GRANDEE=GRANDI] is in debt [OWES=OSE] from the sound of it, *in a big way* (9)=GRANDIOSE

while one word in the clue can yield two in the solution

- *Journey after sunset* for chemical [NITRIDE], say (5,4)=NIGHT RIDE

- *A dandy* fertiliser [BONEASH], they say (4,4)=BEAU NASH

- Plan [INTENTION] said to be *in opposition* (2,7)=IN TENSION

Occasionally homophones will be part-words,

- *It's high* in the V/atic/an, we hear (5)=ATTIC

or use Cockney references to eliminate an H or use colloquial abbreviations

- *Looked* like leather [(H)IDE], the Cockney said [IDE] (4)=EYED

- People will [FOLK'LL] say *where the crew live* (10)=FORECASTLE

and sometimes additions to the homophone are required

- *Turnips* are not just weeds (6)=SWEDES

- Paid, I'm told, not only for *tool* (5)=SPADE

- Sounds not quite right (5)=TRITE

6.2 HOMOPHONES/SYNONYMS

Direct homophones may be combined with **derived words**

by **addition**

- *Model* airborne soldier [PARA] is lost [GONE], we hear [=GON] (7)=PARAGON

- *They're supposed to be funny*
  making appearance [HUE], we hear
  [=HU], with club [MERI]
  (6)=HUMERI

- *On account of* live [BE] bird noises
  [CAWS] I hear [=CAUSE]
  (7)=BECAUSE

by subtraction

- *Rent* for flower-beds [(PAR)TERRE]
  losing equality [PAR], they say
  (4)=TEAR

- *Selected,* say, and allowed
  [(CON)CEDED] no swindle [CON]
  (6)=SEEDED

- *Thy* reported purpose
  [(PLEAS)URE] has no excuses
  [PLEAS] (4)=YOUR

**by the reversal of the
homophone**

- *Painter* on the QE[ER] a few feet
  [ELL] below the rising main [MAIN],
  they say [=MANE=ENAM]
  (9)=ENAMELLER (down clue)

- *Minister* has the opportunity
  [CHANCE] to reverse role [ROLE],
  I'm told [=ROLL=LLOR]
  (10)=CHANCELLOR

- *Tax* on fur [=FIR] in Greece
  [=GREASE=F-AT] is reported to be
  returning (6)=TARIFF

or of the derived word

- *Whip* [CAT] rising [=TAC] artist
  [TITIAN], say [=TICIAN] — *one
  skilled in war* (9)=TACTICIAN

- *Plague* caused by returning spirit
  [RUM=MUR] — check [REIN], it
  appears [=RAIN], is required
  (7)=MURRAIN

- *Glazing material* traveller [REP]
  rejected [=PER] for spectacles
  [SPECS], they say [=SPEX]
  (7)=PERSPEX

by **inclusion** of the homophone inside the **derived word(s)**	• *Fat* for making cover [LI-D] round pastry [PIE], one might say [=PI] (5)=LIPID
	• Workman [HAND], they say, made [=MAID] a small letter [EN] for an *old servant* (10)=HANDMAIDEN
	• Under [SUB] dew [DEW], I'm told [=DUE], an old coin [D] is *put down* (7)=SUBDUED
or vice versa	• *Chain* mail [MAIL], they say [=MA-LE] can [CAN] be coming back [=NAC] in (7)=MANACLE
	• *West Indian drink* provided by station in Paris [Fr. GARE] in middle of European river [SEINE], say [=SAN-E] (8)=SANGAREE
	• Murderer [CAIN], apparently [=CAN-E] holding a [A] little girl [LIZ] will *dig ditches* (8)=CANALIZE
Homophones may sometimes be used with	
given words	• *Makes deduction* in [IN] warm clothing [FURS], we hear [=FERS] (6)=INFERS
	• *Ghost* of tax man [(IN)SPECTOR] dropping in [IN], they say (7)=SPECTRE
	• *Song* can [CAN] amuse [TICKLE], I'm told [=TICLE] (8)=CANTICLE
and such combinations may use homophones of only	
one letter	• *Charging* a [A] couple of hundred [CC] you reportedly [=U] give information [SING] (8)=ACCUSING
	• Met Ber(y)l, perhaps — but why apparently [=Y] disappearing with a *shiver* (7)=TREMBLE

	• See, apparently [=C], socks [HOSE] *selected* (5) =CHOSE
or two letters	• *Not a smart pair of characters* [C, D], we hear (5) =SEEDY
	• I see [=IC] an agent [SP-Y] outside — *very erotic* (5) =SPICY
	• *A brilliant performance* you are heard [=UR] in. Well done, madam [BRAV-A] (7) =BRAVURA (Brava is addressed to a lady, bravo to a gentleman)
Indirect homophones may be used in similar ways	• I [I] heard [=EYE =OP-TIC] about age [ERA] *of musical drama* (8) =OPERATIC

6.3 HOMOPHONES/ABBREVIATIONS

Some homophones may appear in the form of **abbreviations**	• *Impassioned plea* to make agreement [TREATY] on nitrogen [N] verbally [=EN] (8) =ENTREATY
	• Vegetable [PEA], say [=P], which represents its *country* (8) =P =PORTUGAL
	• Bird [JAY], I hear [=J], has some *power* (5) =J =JOULE
sometimes including more than one abbreviation	• Sound examples of it are D [DEE] and X [EXE] both ending in C [SEA] (5) =RIVER
while others are combined with abbreviations	
by **addition**	• Old boy [OB] I would [ID] say [=EYED] *did as he was told* (6) =OBEYED
	• Learner [L] I'll [ILL] say [=ISLE] makes *cotton yarn* (5) =LISLE

• In time [T], Cockney host ['OST],
I'm told [=OAST], will *drink your
health* (5) =TOAST

by subtraction

• *Adroitness* reportedly followed
[TRACKED =T(R)ACT] without
resistance [R] (4) =TACT

• *Agony* for flyer [PLANE] reported
[=P(L)AIN] losing hand [L]
(4) =PAIN

• *Become inefficient* when tied up
[TRUSSED] apparently [=(T)RUST]
without tea [T] (4) =RUST

or by inclusion

• *Provide food* for island [AIT]
reported to be [=ATE] in credit
[C-R] (5) =CATER

• *Fat* insects [BEES] reported [=BES]
in Old English [O-E] (5) =OBESE

• *Carrier* dined [ATE], I hear
[=EIGHT], in French [FR] Queen's
[ER] embrace (9) =FREIGHTER

6.4 HOMOPHONES/SELECTED LETTERS

Homophones may be
combined with **selected
letters**

by addition

• The middle of the [H] cartoon
character [ANDY CAPP], we are told
[=ANDICAP] is a *disadvantage*
(8) =HANDICAP

• *Soberly* waited [STAYED], I'm told
[=STAID], before Leap [L] Year [Y]
initially (7) =STAIDLY

• *Mate* is first Polish [P] successor
[HEIR], I'm told [=AIR] (4) =PAIR

or by inclusion

• A relative [AUNT], I'm told [=ANT],
gets in every other party [P-RY] in
this place (6) =PANTRY

- Row [OAR], apparently [=ORE], between a follower [B] and estate's [DOM(AIN)] three leaders leads to *tedium* (7) = BOREDOM

- *Curbed* image [IDOL] reported to be [=IDLE] inbred [BR-(E)D] and lacking energy [E] (7) = BRIDLED

7

RHYMES

Rhymes, or near-rhymes, are occasionally used in crosswords, as illustrated by these examples:

- *Vexed* by overworked rhyme (5)=IRKED
- Billy's *nonsense* rhyme (5)=SILLY (Note the direct clue in the centre)
- My rhymes may be *used by angler* (3,3)=DRY FLY

The rhyme may sometimes be found in the solution itself rather than between the direct clue and the solution.

- *Nonsense* rhymes (8) =CLAP-TRAP
- *City-centre* rhymes (8) =DOWN-TOWN
- *Feeble* rhymes (10) =NAMBYPAMBY
- *Stew* rhymes(6) =HOTPOT

Another form of rhyme, Cockney rhyming slang, is also used from time to time

- East Ender's apples [APPLES AND PEARS] (6)=STAIRS
- *Watchman* in Cockney butcher's [BUTCHER'S HOOK =LOOK] striking [OUT] (7)=LOOKOUT
- Trouble in Bow [TROUBLE AND STRIFE =WIFE] behind dwelling [HOUSE]. *She runs home* (9)=HOUSEWIFE
- *Have faith* in Cockney's first couple [ADAM AND EVE] (7)=BELIEVE
- Miss Lee [ROSIE LEE =TEA], the tea-girl? (5)=ROSIE

and an Australian version is very similar. Clues would have appropriate pointers such as 'digger's', 'Aussie's', etc.

In a Scottish variant, the Queen may be referred to as Auntie Jean who might be corned beef (deaf, pronounced 'deef')

- *Member* of Australian Warden's Farm (3) =ARM
- *Regard* Australia's discoverer [CAPTAIN COOK] (4) =LOOK
- *Foreigner* from Werris Creek, Australia (5) = GREEK

8

ANAGRAMS

Some crosswords contain many anagrams, the better ones only one or two. In most cases, anagrams required as solutions are formed from given words but, occasionally, they may be formed from derived words.

There are dictionaries of anagrams which list, in alphabetical order, anagrams for words of up to about fifteen letters. The letters of the word or phrase to be anagrammatised are written down in alphabetical order (OWNER HE would be written as EEHMNORW) and this combination can be looked up in the dictionary (answer: NOWHERE). In the absence of such a book, the following may be of some help:

1. If you have decided from the pointer in the clue that the solution is an anagram of, say, nine letters but you cannot immediately see any groups of words in the clue that add up to nine letters, do not be put off. The anagram may be composed of words that are quite widely separated in the clue, it may be composed of parts of given words or it may be made up from a combination of given words and abbreviations or selected letters.

2. First, try to assess from the indirect clue what the form of the solution is likely to be, e.g. a present participle ending in -ING, the past tense of a verb ending in -ED, a noun ending perhaps in -MENT or -TION, an adverb ending in -LY, an adjective ending in -IVE, a word implying 'before', that might start with PRE-, or implying 'again' or 'return', which would probably start with RE-, and so on (*see* Letter Groups, Part 2:28 and Letter Groups, Appendix 1).

3. If such part-words can be identified in the letters forming the anagram, write them down in the form of a word-ending or word-beginning, under the line of letters extracted from the clue, and then see what letters remain to be dealt with. Try rearranging these other letters in the hope of finding a combination that satisfies the clue.

4. If no such part-words can be identified, note the proportion of vowels to consonants. A preponderance of consonants implies that they will be in groups with vowels in between. Look for groups of consonants that go together naturally, such as CH, SH, TH, THR, STR, GH, GHT, etc. (*see also* Letter Groups, Part 2:28 and Letter Groups, Appendix 1). Write these natural groups down with vowels in between and keep rearranging until something clicks.

5. As an alternative, write each letter on a separate scrap of paper and shuffle them around. Scrabble tiles can be used instead. Some people find it easier to write down one letter of the anagram (usually a consonant) and then write the other letters round it, forming a circle, trying to find the solution by letting the eye wander from the centre letter to other letters in the ring.

Pointers: almost any word implying breaking, changing, constituent parts, movement, newness or strangeness, such as the following:

breaking — broken (broken heart =EARTH), crash, mangled, minced (mince pie =IPE or EPI, minced meat =MATE or TEAM), riot, ruined, wrecked
change — altering, arranged, cocktail (gin cocktail =IGN- or -ING), cooking, disturbed, fancy, fashion, melt, mishmash (=SHIM), mixture, ordering, repair
constituent parts — characters in, featuring, ingredients of, letters in, variety
movement — broadcast (<u>outside</u> broadcast =TEDIOUS), curly, dancing, developed, excited, moved, out, resort (re-sort), run, waving
newness — new, fresh, novel
strangeness — anyhow, awful, confusing, crazy, curious, drunken, eccentric, in a mess, oddly, perhaps, possibly, queer (Queer Street =TESTER, etc.), somehow, strangely, troubled, unruly, unusual

There seems to be no limit to the number of words that can be called into service as a pointer to an anagram, so read each clue carefully, looking for anything that seems a little incongruous in the context of the clue.

8.1 STRAIGHT ANAGRAMS

Most anagrams are formed from **given words** which may be single words

• Strange <u>decorations</u> are *all of the same order*
(11)=COORDINATES

	• *Mould* for shaping <u>lamps</u> (5)=PLASM
	• *Spirit* of <u>ripe</u> decay (4)=PERI
two or more consecutive words	• <u>Isn't Ted</u> a smashing *surgeon* (7)=DENTIST
	• Ingredients <u>in tar, say</u>, are *conducive to health* (8)=SANITARY
	• *Air-gauge* in <u>the merry-go-</u>round (10)=HYGROMETER (Note that 'round' is used as a pointer to the anagram, not as part of the words used to form it)
separated words, when each word may have its own pointer	• *Was there* and <u>dead</u> worried [=A-DED] about the damaged <u>tent</u> [=TTEN] (8)=ATTENDED
	• How <u>rust</u> anyhow [=TRUS] pervaded the moulded <u>base</u> [=ABS-E] is *hard to understand* (8)=ABSTRUSE
	• *Creatures,* <u>ten</u> roughly [=ENT], found in the <u>press</u> [=SERP-S] curled up (8)=SERPENTS
or parts of words	• *Search for* change of <u>cours(e)</u>, endlessly (5)=SCOUR
	• Not as <u>blac(k) it</u> might appear, *this sea* (6)=BALTIC
	• *Light and flimsy,* perhaps, as <u>some gras(s)</u> when cut (8)=GOSSAMER
Occasionally two versions will be given for the same solution	• Arranged <u>in e.g. red</u> or <u>green I'd</u> *held sway* (7) =REIGNED • *Dog,* perhaps <u>'e's keeping</u> or <u>pink geese</u> (9) =PEKINGESE
In some cases, the pointer to the anagram will form part of the solution	• *Hurry up* and rearrange [MAKE] <u>heats</u> (4,5)=MAKE HASTE

- *Argument* to change [ALTER] <u>action</u> (11) =ALTERCATION

- *Metallic element* with unusual [RARE] <u>heart</u> (4,5) =RARE EARTH

- Clue for <u>setter</u> *in financial difficulties* (5,6) =QUEER STREET

while, in others, the act of anagrammatisation will form part of the solution

- <u>Bared</u>, possibly [=BREAD], *in* communion service (8,5) =BREAKING BREAD

- <u>Son got in</u>? [=INTO SONG], *Give us a tune, then* (5,4,4) =BREAK INTO SONG

- <u>Nowt</u> [=TOWN] on the map? (3,4) =NEW TOWN

- *Switch from joy to sorrow* is <u>doom</u> [=MOOD], possibly (6,3,4) =CHANGE THE MOOD

In other cases, the direct clue itself may form part of the anagram

- *Kind of <u>tag</u>* [=AG-T] left [L] round end of lac<u>e</u> [E] (5) =AGLET

- This is <u>*routed*</u> *in a different way* (6) =DETOUR

- *Sort of <u>bush</u>* [=SH-UB] hiding monarch [R] (5) =SHRUB

and you may even find a proper name used as a pointer

- The <u>silent Mr</u> Turner is a *musician* (8) =MINSTREL

Occasionally an anagram is required when there is no given word from which to form it

- Pair of anagrams *others play with* (4,4) =TEAM MATE

and sometimes one needs to 'translate' part of the clue that forms the anagram

- *Age* wandering about at one time [=<u>AT I TIME</u>] (7) =IMITATE

85

Some anagrams, known as cognate, have the same meaning as the solution. Some compilers refer to this type as '& lit' clues

- I'm against an *opponent* (10) = ANTAGONIST

- Order to scram is *this?* (9) = OSTRACISM

- *Is not solaced,* maybe (12) = DISCONSOLATE

A few words lend themselves for use as cognate anagrams which can be inferred without additional clues. These are sometimes referred to as inversions

- Dens (4,3) = SEND OFF or SEND OUT
- Kate (4,3) = TAKE OFF or TAKE OUT
- Flow (4,4) = WILD FOWL
- Sore (4,4) = WILD ROSE
- Wolf (4,4) = WILD FOWL

Perhaps the most elegant anagrams are those where not only the words forming the anagram but even the pointer itself describes the solution

- *Where* the last daring break-out of the War occurred (10) = STALINGRAD (The pointer 'break-out' describes what happened at Stalingrad)

- Aide('s) *misconception* (5,4) = WRONG IDEA

- A pure NW Somerset *resort* (6-5-4) = WESTON-SUPER-MARE ('Resort' — which is read as the pointer 're-sort' — also describes the town)

The irony of the last clue is that because of the exact description (resort), the precise geographical location (NW Somerset) and the number and breakdown of the letters in the solution, it can be read as a non-cryptic direct clue, and the solution could be arrived at without the solver being aware of the very neat construction. It does, however, serve to emphasise the point made earlier — the word 'pure' is rather incongruous in the context of the clue and should alert the solver to the anagram.

8.2 ANAGRAMS/SYNONYMS

Anagrams may be combined with **given words**

by **addition**

- *Recipes* for [FOR] a mule, perhaps [=MULAE] (8) = FORMULAE

- *Writ* from man [MAN] <u>Maud's</u> twisted [=DAMUS]
  (8) =MANDAMUS

- *Bird* needs <u>winch,</u> perhaps, [=WHINC] to put on hat [HAT]
  (8) =WHINCHAT

by subtraction

- *Road-making <u>mate(ria)l</u>* without air [AIR] (5) =METAL
  (Note the use of 'material' as a direct clue and also as part of the anagram)

- Excited <u>c(h)att(er)</u> without her [HER] *diplomacy* (4) =TACT

- <u>Pa(in)ter</u> perhaps drops in [IN] to *chatter* (5) =PRATE

by reversal

- *Fox* led [LED] back [=DEL] with <u>due</u> management [=UDE]
  (6) =DELUDE

- *Polish noble* sees rats [RATS] come back [=STAR] to ruined <u>oast</u> [=OSTA]
  (8) =STAROSTA

- Lag [LAG] back [=GAL], somehow <u>slow</u> [=LOWS] to get to the *scaffold*
  (7) =GALLOWS

by inclusion, with the anagram inside the given word

- *Not drinking* <u>is to me</u> out of order [=STEMIO] in a [A] bus [B-US]
  (10) =ABSTEMIOUS

- *Procession* made up of <u>a doctor</u> [=OTORCAD] and me [M-E]
  (9) =MOTORCADE

- *Angry* about the amended <u>list</u> [=ISTL] you bring [BR-ING]
  (9) =BRISTLING

or vice versa

- <u>Clare</u> played [=REC-AL] it [IT] in the *performance* (7) =RECITAL

- <u>Alf's</u> upset [=FLA-S] about me [ME] having *lovers* (6) =FLAMES

• *Imply* not [NOT] in <u>once</u>, perhaps, [=CON-E] (7) =CONNOTE

Anagrams may be combined with **derived words**

by **addition**

• <u>Oil</u> [=OLI] after journey [TRIP] *here* (7) =TRIPOLI

• *Carefully holding* and writing out <u>card</u> [=CRAD] to put on the fish [LING] (8) =CRADLING

• Unusual <u>kids</u> [=SKID] criticise [PAN] *greasy surface* (4-3) =SKID-PAN

by **subtraction**

• <u>S(ore)head</u> extracting mineral [ORE] in Hell, perhaps (5) =HADES

• *Make happy* the poor actor [HAM] quitting a <u>s(ham)bles</u> (5) =BLESS

• *Ruler* has defective <u>g(oats)kin</u> but no pipes [OATS] (4) =KING

by **reversal**

• <u>Let Art</u> out [=RATTLE], side [PART] has returned [=TRAP] in a *decrepit vehicle* (10) =RATTLETRAP

• Behind <u>clear</u> run [=LACER] fix it [NAIL IT] around [=TILIAN] to be *typical of reptiles* (11) =LACERTILIAN

• Unruly <u>wets</u> [=WEST] pull [DRAW] back [=WARD] *in one direction* (8) =WESTWARD

by **inclusion**, with the anagram inside the derived word

• *Streaked like Tom?* Reckoned [MA-DE] without false <u>alarm</u> [=RMALA] (9) =MARMALADE

• <u>Artist</u> possibly [=ISTRAT] in the area [REG-ION] for *making records* (12) =REGISTRATION

• Craft [ART] before [ER-E] carrying crude <u>oil</u> [=IOL] would be a *very small vessel* (9) =ARTERIOLE

or vice versa

- <u>Hit</u> with <u>a mop</u>, perhaps [=OPHT-MIA]? In this, Henry [HAL] makes *a complaint* (10)=OPHTHΛLMIA

- Going round island [SARK] <u>has no</u> new order [=NOAH-S] for *toys* (5,4)=NOAHS ARKS

- *The most sensitive* finish [END] in Queer <u>Street</u> [=T-EREST] (9)=TENDEREST

or inside a derived word written backwards

- *Corrupter* shows colour [RED] return [=D-ER] without <u>life</u> perhaps [=EFIL] (7)=DEFILER

- *Open* to hit [TAP] back [=PA-T] about tangled <u>net</u> [=TEN] (6)=PATENT

- Crazy <u>lice</u> [=ECLI] in earth [LAND] turned [=D-NAL] and *sloping down* (8)=DECLINAL

or vice versa

- *Pompous* fool [NUT] turning [=TUN] into <u>door</u>, perhaps [=ORO-D] (7)=OROTUND

- *Hard taskmaster* is a fool [NIT]. Back [=TIN] in <u>a term</u>, maybe [=MAR-ET] (8)=MARTINET

- *Disease* from bitterness [GALL] which returned [=LLAG] to damaged <u>pear</u> [=PE-RA] (8)=PELLAGRA

Anagrams may also be used with **opposite/negative** solutions

- *No driver* wants to go beyond [PASS] <u>Green</u>, badly [=ENGER] (9)=PASSENGER

- <u>Short tie</u> knotted by *man of action? Not really* (8)=THEORIST

- <u>Toy ball</u>, perhaps, for *short girl? Just the reverse!* (7)=TALLBOY

8.3 ANAGRAMS/ABBREVIATIONS

Some anagrams are formed entirely from **abbreviations**

- *Class* represented by three MA's [MA, MA, MA] and one [I] student [L] (8) =MAMMALIA

- Old railway [LNER] that is [IE] somehow *to renew the inside* (6) =RELINE

- *Rubbish* making no fewer than seven points [NNNSSEE] about love [O] (8) =NONSENSE

others are combined with abbreviations

by **addition**

- Commander [C-IN-C] is <u>true</u> to form [=TURE], displaying *belt* (8) =CINCTURE

- Brown [BR] on top <u>cattle</u> carved up [=ACTLET] *little leaf* (8) =BRACTLET

- *As a reduction,* perhaps, <u>big man</u> retired briefly [RET'D] (10) =ABRIDGMENT

by **subtraction**

- <u>(Ob)serve</u> no old boy [OB], perhaps, in *poetry* (5) =VERSE

- Gunman [RA] left <u>(ra)ptor</u> crazy with *drink* (4) =PORT

- <u>Mira(cu)lous</u>, in a way, to lose copper [CU] and find a *tanner, here* (8) =SOLARIUM

by **inclusion** of the anagram inside the abbreviation

- In training [P-T], a burst of <u>energy</u> [=EER GYN] comes into *play* (4,4) =PEER GYNT

- *The devil of a game* treating <u>a boil</u> [=IABOL] in the same [D-O] (7) =DIABOLO

- *Ambiguous* sort of <u>help</u> [=ELPH] detectives [CID] in their return [=D-IC] receive (7) =DELPHIC

or vice versa

- Unusually <u>active</u> [=CA-TIVE] outside America [USA] *producing effect* (9) =CAUSATIVE

- *Give* one the same again [DO] in a <u>new</u> [=EN-W] wrapper (5) =ENDOW

- A soldier [GI] in <u>nasty</u> fracas [=STY-AN] may well be *gloomy* (7) =STYGIAN

8.4 ANAGRAMS/SELECTED LETTERS

Anagrams may be combined with letters **selected for retention**
using a single letter

- Unusually <u>slim boys</u> [=SYMBOLIS] start to <u>make</u> [M] *representation* (9) =SYMBOLISM

- Shattering <u>noises</u> [=ESSION] at the start of <u>s</u>chool [S] *meeting* (7) =SESSION

- Crazy <u>avenger</u> [=ENGRAVE] took note [D] of *cut* (8) =ENGRAVED

or more

- Most of cold [COL(D)] and broken <u>sepal</u> [=LAPSE] will *break down* (8) =COLLAPSE

- *Looking at* spoiled <u>grain</u> [=ARING] after end of harve<u>st</u> [ST] (7) =STARING

- Drunken <u>Titan</u> [=ANTIT], he [HE] and half-sister [SIS(TER)] in *opposition* (10) =ANTITHESIS

They may also have selected letters **removed by elimination**, in which form they are similar to those made from part-words. The pointers, however, are rather different.

The elimination may be of one letter

- *The language* mangled in <u>Transk(e)i</u>'s not English [E] (8) =SANSKRIT

- *Cutting attack* in endless massacr(e), possibly (7)=SARCASM

- War(i)ly I [I] left [=Y WAL-R] Jake [JA-KE] wandering — *he's a menace on the roads* (3,6)=JAY WALKER

or more

- *Circus equipment* — peg it thro(ugh) with no sign of distaste [UGH] (9)=TIGHTROPE

- *Urbane* Aberdoni(an) is twice detailed [AN] for manoeuvres (8)=DEBONAIR

- Most of fire [(F)IRE] has gone from m(e)teo(ri)c *space traveller* (5)=COMET

- *Detect* removal of middle of core [(C)OR(E)] from broken react(or) (5)=TRACE

and may be combined with **derived words**

- Hair [FUR] blowe(r)s, one side [R] left out [=BELOWS] for making *frills* (9)=FURBELOWS

or **abbreviations**

- King [ER] with endless dutie(s) [=UDITE] to be *learned* (7)=ERUDITE

- *Retaliation* from engineers [RE] non-U t(u)tor, perhaps [=TORT] (6)=RETORT

- *End* of beheaded and mangled (a)nimal [=MINAL] on terrace [TER] (8)=TERMINAL

Occasionally, letters in an anagram may be **substituted**

- *Brought up* a true drum, perhaps [=(M)URTURED], with one end [M] changed (8)=NURTURED

- Crazy daemon [=MOA(N)ED] changing name [N], *surrounded by water* (6)=MOATED

- *Designer* <u>seen in re</u>-capitalisation
  [ENSINEER] (8) =ENGINEER

8.5 ANAGRAMS/HOMOPHONES

Anagrams may be combined
with **homophones**. Usually
the anagram is made

from a **given word**

- I hear new [=NU] <u>clues</u>, perhaps
  [=CLEUS], for *core* (7) =NUCLEUS

- *Mark well,* I am said to know
  [=NO] the <u>beaten</u> characters
  [=TA BENE] (4,4) =NOTA BENE

- *Ringleader* who, they say, few
  [=FU] <u>mangle</u> possibly [=GLEMAN]
  (8) =FUGLEMAN

but occasionally from a
derived word

- *A poem* [AN ODE] you are said
  [=UR] to have composed
  (7) =RONDEAU

9

QUOTATIONS AND ALLUSIONS

Direct quotations are somewhat out of place in cryptic crosswords since they provide no alternative route to the solution, but they do, nevertheless, appear

- 'The . . . and arrows . . .' (Hamlet) (6)=SLINGS
(Anyone who does not know the quotation will be at a loss unless he can deduce the solution SLINGS from letters already filled in or has access to a dictionary of quotations)

Indirect quotations usually have other clues to the solution which can, as a result, be found by anyone who is not familiar with the quotation

- See [LO], live [BE], *part of the loan Antony requested* (4)=LOBE
(Those unfamiliar with Mark Antony's 'lend me your ears' speech can still arrive at LOBE from the indirect clues)

although some are without these additional clues and are just as hard to deal with as direct quotations

- What the moribund say they would do to Caesar (6)=SALUTE
('We who are about to die, salute thee')

Classical references follow the same pattern; some have additional clues

- River-goddess (4)=ISIS
(Even if you do not recognise the Egyptian goddess, you still have a chance with the river in Oxford — if you ignore the punctuation [*see* Punctuation, Part 2:24])

and some do not

- Say, do you know her husband? (7)=JUPITER
('Say' betrays the homophone JUNO ['do you know'], but that doesn't help unless you know that her husband was JUPITER)

It is the same with **literary references**

- *Veronese* in pret/ty Balt/imore collection (6) =TYBALT
  (Even if you have never heard of this character in *Romeo and Juliet* you can still get the solution from the hidden word)

- Swift horse (9) =HOUYHNHNM
  (You may recognise 'Swift' as the author, Jonathan Swift, but you will not get HOUYHNHNM [a race of horses] unless you are familiar with *Gulliver's Travels*)

historical references

- *Martyred bishop* has period [TIME] in Libya [LA-R] (7) =LATIMER
  (You can build up the solution without knowing that Latimer was burned at the stake)

- King with fish-wife? (5) =HENRY
  (You may deduce that the 'fish' is PARR but that is no help unless you know that she [Catherine Parr] was one of the wives of HENRY VIII)

and **Biblical references**

- I moan about Ruth's companion (5) =NAOMI
  (You can get her name from the anagram)

- Father of Hamlet dropping old hindrance (4) =NOAH
  (If you get as far as HAM by 'dropping old hindrance' [LET] from 'Hamlet', you will still not be certain of the solution unless you know that Ham's father was NOAH)

10

COMBINATIONS

Some examples of combinations of various types of clue have been given in the previous sections. As an illustration of the variety of ways of making combined clues, the following list shows some of the ways of making use of a simple word, ESTATE:

- **E** (east) **ST** (saint) **A** (a) **TE** (note)
- **ES** (directions) **TA** (volunteers) **T** (time) **E** (England)
- **E** (English) **S** (second) **TA** (thanks) **T** (sort of shirt) **E** (energy)
- **E** (eastern) **S** (sun) **TAT** (tap) **E** (note)
- **EST** (Fr. 'is') **ATE** (Greek goddess)
- **E** (east) **ST** (street) **ATE** (dined)
- **E** (string) **STATE** (Georgia, for example)
- **E** (key) **STATE** (Fr. 'states' =*états*, reversed)
- **E** (low grade) **S** (bridge player) **TATE** (gallery)
- **ES** (SE [=Home Counties], reversed) **TAT** (middle of st<u>ate</u>) **E** (Spain)
- **E-STAT-E** (makes lace [tats] reversed in the extremes of <u>ea</u>s<u>e</u>)
- **EST** (half of fly [tsetse] reversed) **AT** (at) **E** (universal set)
- **EST** (headless nuisance [(p)est]) **A** (a) **TE** (Fr. 'and' =*et*, reversed)
- **EST** (alcohol compound [est(er)] without hesitation [er]) **ATE** (Greek letter *eta*, reversed)
- **ESTA** (virgin [(v)esta(l)] without head [v] or tail [l]) **TE** (ends of ty<u>pe</u>]
- **ESTA** (headless match [(V)esta]) **TE** (not quite te(n))
- **ESTA** (anagram of <u>seat</u>) **TE** (gun [(S)te(n)] with no ends [S, n])
- **ESTATE** (anagram of <u>tea set</u>)
- **E** (Asian) **STATE** (anagram of <u>taste</u>)
- **ESTATE** (heat controller [thermostat] without heat unit [therm] ring [o] in comfort [ease], say [=EE])

Manipulation of the words in brackets, or similar ones, to form readable clues will give the compiler twenty different ways of indicating the same solution, and the various possible combinations and permutations of these words could provide literally hundreds of ways of providing clues for just one simple word. And the list is far from exhaustive!

11

UNCLASSIFIED

Some clues do not fall readily into categories or they have unusual features worth noting. A selection of such clues is given below:

- **An un-see-through cover would be madness (6)**
  Read 'un-see-through' as UN-C written through 'cover' [L-A-Y] to give LUNACY

- **Part of mountain — return what's been dropped in, etc. (5)**
  'Etc.' is both the clue to the solution and to 'what's been dropped' in it. ETC has been dropped from ET CETERA to leave ETERA which 'returns' to give ARETE =part of mountain

- **A descendant of George III and IV, for example (8)**
  George III =GR, George IV was his son. So 'GR and SON' gives the solution GRANDSON

- **One of those taking risks, possibly turn and turn about (8)**
  Neat use of 'turn and turn about' where 'turn' [VE-ER] is written about 'turn, possibly' [=NTUR] to give VENTURER

- **How do you make an ape point to an antelope? (5)**
  To make 'an ape [APE] point' [APEX] you 'add a X' which gives ADDAX =antelope

- **Mendicant? What an old clown! (5)**
  Mendicant contains both the pointer to an anagram (mend) and the letters which form the anagram (icant), giving ANTIC =clown

- **The diversions of former ages overlapped (8)**
  'Former' [PAST] and 'ages' [TIMES] are written so that the T in each overlaps to give PASTIMES =diversions

- **Oriental festival stricter when overlapping (9)**
  Here the overlapping extends to four letters — 'oriental festival' [EASTER] overlapped with 'stricter' [STERNER] gives EASTERNER

- **Aims which are identical for Europe and America (4)**
  An unusual use of selected letters where the 'identical' items are
  the first and last letters, i.e. the ENDS

- **Unbeliever in Beethoven opera losing maiden (7)**
  A 'maiden' in cricket is one over with no runs which, in a down
  clue, can be translated as 'one' [I] written over O [O]. Deduct IO
  from 'in [IN] Beethoven opera [FIDEL(IO)]' to get INFIDEL

- **Cockney artist's colourful display (7)**
  Neat use of the inferred 'in' [Cockney =IN BOW] to give 'artist' [RA]
  IN BOW, making RAINBOW

- **IV (6,2)**
  Punning homophone of 'four' — get it? FORGET IT

- **Salome's cover — pound insurance? Needs watching! (12)**
  Salome's VEIL with a pound [L] inSUR-ANCE gives
  SURVEILLANCE by using insurance as a 'concealed compound'

- **Three, four or five?   About one or two (4)**
  A neat use of numbers. Three, four or five are par [PA-R] for the
  holes on a golf course and this, written 'about' (=outside) one [I],
  gives PAIR (=two)

- **Lower and upper body garment (6)**
  Lower here is not a complement of upper – it means 'one who
  lows', i.e. a cow, in this case JERSEY.

- **Vulgar slogan - "Bogeys all halved in birdies" (9)**
  A good examples of the use of part-words - vulGAR, sloGAN,
  boGEYS - to give GARGANEYS (=birds)

One feature worth noting is the repetition of words in the clue, often
with different meanings for each use:

- **Heart-to-heart cricket official (6)**
  'Heart' =CORE =middle so CORE goes to the middle of the
  solution which is SCORER

- **Beasts taking sound exercise on river, river, river (3,4)**
  'Exercise on river' [ROW=ROE], the river DEE and the abbreviation
  R give ROE DEER

- **Hydra's home long, long, long time ago (5)**
  'Long' =L; 'long' =yearn; 'long time ago' =old. The 'old' version of
  'yearn' =ERNE which, added to L, gives LERNE (the swamp said
  to be the home of the Hydra)

- **Around, around, around a pound? Get knotted! (7)**
  'Around' is moved 'around' (i.e. anagrammatised) and written
  'around' (i.e. outside) 'a pound' [L] to get 'knotted' =NODULAR

- **Gateshead — fish, fish, fish (8)**
  Gateshead [G] plus one fish [RAY] and another [LING] add up to a
  third, GRAYLING

- **Three coppers arrest one boy shooter (5)**
  Three different ways of indicating copper [CU, P, D] and one [I]
  make CUPID (boy shooter)

- **A way to sit on a horse — a way to sit on a horse (7)**
  A [A] way [ST] to sit on a horse [RIDE] = ASTRIDE, the normal way
  to sit on a horse.

For other uses of repetition *see* Singulars and Plurals, Part 2:26.

Finally, there is the type of clue that constitutes a sort of visual pun,
often met in the word game Dingbats. One such clue is the 'O
(8,6) =CIRCULAR LETTER', mentioned in Definitions and
Classification, Part 1:1. Other examples are:

- **SEGG (9,4)=SCRAMBLED EGGS**
- **Timing tim ing (5,6,6)=SPLIT SECOND TIMING.**

12

THE USE OF 'OUT' AND 'IN'

out
can be used

as a pointer to an anagram

- *After that* <u>one put her</u> out (9)=THEREUPON

- In the <u>line</u>-out [=EL-IN], the fellow [F] looks *mischievous* (5)=ELFIN

- <u>Run Al</u> out [=NU-RAL] and get me [ME] caught for *a certain figure* (7)=NUMERAL

to eliminate letters

- *One's early years* <u>gene(r)ate</u> outright [R] mix-up (7)=TEENAGE
  (Note the use of the compound word 'outright' to mean 'take out R' — *see* Compound Words, Part 2:20)

- *Dig channel* in river [EX-E] without warning [CAV(E)AT] out East [E] (8)=EXCAVATE
  (Note the use of 'without' to mean 'outside' — *see* The Use of 'Without' and 'Within', Part 2:13)

- Pay [SALA(RY)] out of line [RY] for use, *sad to say* (4)=ALAS

to indicate an inclusion

- Peg [T-EE] out right [R] in *box perhaps* (4)=TREE

- He [HE] takes a ship [S-S] out of the country [PERU] — *it was wrecked* (8)=HESPERUS

* *The ability* to spin a <u>rope</u> [=PO-ER] out West [W] (5) =POWER

to indicate a hidden word

* Out of lusciou/s mud ge/ts *soil* (6) =SMUDGE

* *Run* out of ful/1 ope/ra house (4) =LOPE

* *Old coin* dug out of Mount Olympu/s hill in G/reece (8) =SHILLING

or to mean

'abroad'

* *Lose* girl [MISS] abroad [OUT] (4,3) =MISS OUT

'asleep'

* King [R] asleep [OUT] will give *snore* (4) =ROUT

'away'

* *Man in field* starts <u>sc</u>ratching away [OUT] (5) =SCOUT

'dismissed', etc.

* Learner [L] dismissed [OUT], *the boor* (4) =LOUT

* *Fat* saint [ST] fired [OUT] (5) =STOUT

* Dismissed [OUT] group [SET] at *the beginning* (6) =OUTSET

'exceeding'

* *Beginning* to exceed [OUT] six games [SET] (6) =OUTSET

'in error'

* Am I able [CAN I] to run [=INAC] a clergyman [CURATE] *out*? (10) =INACCURATE

'not in'

* *Recording* out [NOT IN] of key [G] (6) =NOTING

(although in some cases 'not in' can imply the elimination of 'in')

* Not in hut [CAB(IN)] or *driver's compartment* (3) =CAB

'square'

* T-square [T-OUT] for *tipster* (4) =TOUT

'strike/striking'
- Striking [OUT] clothes [WEAR] *last longer* (7) =OUTWEAR

'unconscious'
- *Drink* a good man [ST] unconscious [OUT] (5) =STOUT

'unfashionable', etc.
- Unfashionable [OUT] drinks [CIDERS] we hear [=SIDERS] for the *newcomers* (9) =OUTSIDERS

- *Beginning* of old-hat [OUT] film stage [SET] (6) =OUTSET

- Sharp bend [U] and hill [TOR] not acceptable [OUT] in aged [A-E] *highway* (9) =AUTOROUTE

in
can be used

as a pointer to an anagram
- *The attitude* in <u>ascent</u> (6) =STANCE

- <u>Pains</u> and <u>pride</u> in *part of plumbing installation* (10) =DRAINPIPES

to indicate an inclusion
(*see also* Compound Words, Part 2:20, and Split Words, Part 2:21)
- *Recovery operation* for the pound [L] in wild [SA-VAGE] surroundings (7) =SALVAGE

- Way [ST] to love [O] in a bird [HE-N] *in London* (6) =HESTON

- Salesman [REP] in brown [T-AN] *employed by surgeon* (6) =TREPAN

to indicate an addition
- A [A] key [D] churchman [MINISTER] in *control* (10) =ADMINISTER

- *Foreign coin* in Peru [PE], note [SO] (4) =PESO

to indicate a hidden word
- *Cook* put in su/ch ef/fort (4) =CHEF

- *A knot* in stron/g nar/row string (4) =GNAR

| | • *Filed* in the telep/hone d/irectory (5)=HONED |
| to indicate a homophone | • Lincoln's [ABE] Inn, we hear [=IN], two pounds [L-L] *a ticket* (5)=LABEL |

or it can be used to mean

'at home'	• Being at home [IN], the doctor [MO], by the way [ST], is *remote from the outside* (6)=INMOST
'belonging to'	• *Creature* belonging to [IN] a party [SECT] (6)=INSECT
'during'	• *Confluence* during [IN] autumn [FALL] (6)=INFALL
'elected'	• Elected [IN] leaders of <u>L</u>abour [L] <u>e</u>xtend [E] <u>t</u>he [T] *entrance* (5)=INLET
'member of'	• Being member of [IN] party [DO], Lawson's first [L] to show *blue stuff* (5)=INDOL
'wearing'	• Sailor [TAR] — apostle [PAUL] wearing [IN] *waterproof hat* (9)=TARPAULIN
or to mean 'fashionable', etc. (the 'in' thing)	• Fashionable [IN] during tea [CH-A] to provide *porcelain* (5)=CHINA
	• *Position* for sophisticated [IN] and virtuous man [ST], a [A] <u>l</u>ocal leader [L] (6)=INSTAL
	• Voguish [IN] company [CO] got in trouble [=GNITO] *under an assumed name* (9)=INCOGNITO
	• *Instinct* for trendy [IN] schooling [TUITION] (9)=INTUITION
	• Popular [IN] perfume [AROMA] turns up [=AMORA] thanks [TA] to *lover* (9)=INAMORATA (down clue)

Alternative words for 'fashion' (where you might be looking for 'in') are 'ton', 'mode', 'rage', 'à la', or 'forge'

- Black [JET] one's [IS] in fashion [T-ON] to *discard* (8) =JETTISON

- Fashion [TON] <u>a tile</u> roughly [=ALITE] from *Austrian rock* (8) =TONALITE

- *Contemporary* Navy [RN] follows fashion [MODE] (6) =MODERN

- *Attendants* with two points [E, N] leading to [TO] upper-class [U] fashion [RAGE] (9) =ENTOURAGE

- *Startle* in jolly [RM] fashion [ALA] (5) =ALARM

- *Search* for article [A] in fashion [FOR-GE] (6) =FORAGE

'Fashion' can also be used as a pointer to an anagram

- *Vengeance* <u>seems in</u> fashion (7) =NEMESIS

as can 'fashionable'

- *Trends* fashionable in a <u>deist</u> (5) =TIDES

In some cases 'fashionable' does not imply 'in'

- It's fashionable . . . (End of conversation!) (3,4,4) =THE LAST WORD

In many cases, the use of 'in' needs to be inferred from the wording of the clue

- Doctor [MO] preserved by *Athenian misanthrope* (5) =TIMON ('Preserved' =in TI-N)

- *Obvious* that trainee [L] is suffering (5) =PLAIN ('Suffering' =in P-AIN)

- *Charming* sailor [AB] long [L] besotted (7) =LOVABLE ('Besotted' =in LOV-E)

- Request for silence [SH] at work leads to *acrimony* (9) =HARSHNESS ('At work' =in HAR-NESS)

- *Vessel* for every [ALL] potential
customer (7)=SHALLOP
('Potential customer'=in SH-OP)

- *Passing* trouble with <u>rains</u> [=RANSI]
when under canvas
(9)=TRANSIENT
('Under canvas'=in T-ENT)

- Undercover *purpose* (6)=INTENT
('Undercover'=IN TENT;
a similar use but not split)

- Tool [RAKE] bogged down
in Morocco (9)=MARRAKESH
('Bogged down'=in MAR-SH)

- Abstraction [TRANCE] ultimately
gets you *transported*
(9)=ENTRANCED
('Ultimately'=in the EN-D)

- *Fresh* like bather off Cowes
(8)=INSOLENT
('Off Cowes'=IN SOLENT;
a similar use but not split)

- *Raise* one [I] like a parasite
(5)=HOIST
('Parasite'=in HO-ST)

- *Move slowly* among the
congregation (4)=INCH
('Congregation'=IN CH(urch))

- *Dark*, like Fort Knox (4)=INKY
('Like Fort Knox'=IN KY
[Kentucky])

Both **out** and **in** together
with **off** and **on** are terms
used in cricket

- Caught, perhaps [OUT], about [RE]
being *indecorous* (5)=OUTRE

- Batting [IN] again [RE] in big match
[TE-ST] gives *advantage*
(8)=INTEREST

- *Get* duck [O] mishandling <u>bat</u>
[=BTA] at the wicket [IN]
(6)=OBTAIN

- Not an 'in' novelist
  (8) =FIELDING

- *French captain, perhaps,* of side
  dismissed [OFF] by Colder [ICIER]
  (8) =OFFICIER

- *Charge* made by cricket side [ON]?
  Funny thing [LAUGH], in a way
  [S-T] (9) =ONSLAUGHT

although 'off' is sometimes
used as an anagram pointer

- Curta(i)ned off, I [I] dropped *out
  of box* (8) =UNCRATED

and 'out' in the phrase 'out
of' is usually abbreviated
to EX

- *Do better than* get out of [EX]
  what's almost a prison [CEL(L)]
  (5) =EXCEL

- Out of [EX] ten [TEN] say, you [=U]
  take eight [=ATE]? *Underestimate!*
  (9) =EXTENUATE

- One [I] out of [EX] fifty [L] changed
  ends [=LEXI] to study [CON] the
  dictionary (7) =LEXICON

For the use of EX =without

see The Use of 'Without' and
'Within', Part 2:13

For the use of EX =former

see Old Words, Part 2:19

For the use of 'out' in
compound words

see Compound Words, Part 2:20

For other uses of 'in'

see Split Words, Part 2:21

13

THE USE OF 'WITHOUT' AND 'WITHIN'

without
is used in various guises to
indicate an inclusion

It may appear as 'without'

- *Hanging* a malevolent creature [GOB-LIN] without point [E] (7) =GOBELIN

- *Endured* being taken to court [SU-ED] without stigma [STAIN] (9) =SUSTAINED

- Live [EX-IST] without the monster [ORC] *he draws out* (8) =EXORCIST

'outside'

- Father [PA] died [D] after eating meal [L-UNCHING] outside a [A] *missile base* (9,3) =LAUNCHING PAD

- *Blowing up* causes minion [(M)IN-ION] to lose his head [M] outside apartment [FLAT] (9) =INFLATION

- Outside toilet [LOO] priest [F-R] will *knock down* (5) =FLOOR

'round'

- *Here's a loincloth* — pull [LU-G] one [I] round front of navel [N] (5) =LUNGI

- We'll [W-E] go round to cover up [INTER] boundary [BOURN] in an *intermittent spring* (12) =WINTERBOURNE

* *Waders* irritate [G-ALL] round head of R̲ibble [R] — one [AE] on Tay (7)=GRALLAE
(AE='one' in Scots. Note the use of 'Tay' to represent Scotland. *See* Synonyms, Part 1:2.4)

'around'

* *May have sharp edge* [ARRIS] rising up [=SI-RRA] around Spain [E] (6)=SIERRA (down clue)
(Note the direct clue used also as an indirect clue)

* Arranges d̲eft coils̲ [=COD FIL-ETS] around lake [L] *fish* (3,7)=COD FILLETS

* Wine [CLAR-ET] flowing around in [IN] the *instrument* (9)=CLARINET

'out'

see The Use of 'Out' and 'In', Part 2:12

or 'about'

see The Use of 'About', Part 2:14

A frequent use of 'without' is the phrase 'without a . . .' meaning 'outside A'. It is also often used to mean 'omitting A' (*see* below)

* Male [MAN] relative [KIN] without a [A] *dwarf* (7)=MANAKIN

Note that 'outside' does not always imply an inclusion

* *Unconscious* as [AS] fruit outside [PEEL] turned up [=LEEP] (6)=ASLEEP (down clue)

* *Again tell* me to put back [=EM] in the outside [R-IND] (6)=REMIND

and that words such as 'without' can still indicate inclusions when placed after the included word instead of before it

* *Most likely to get a hearing* du̲e to being muddled [=UDE] without being missed [LO-ST] (7)=LOUDEST

without can also be used to mean 'minus', 'omitting' or 'lacking'

* Parts of G̲enev(a)̲ without a [A] *Jewish area* (5)=NEGEV

- *Offshore* in Scotland [(PA)ISLE(Y)] without pay [PAY] (4) =ISLE

- *Measure* a quarter [QUART(ER)] without hesitation [ER] (5) =QUART

and, in this connection, note that many words implying 'lacking' or 'without' have the prefix 'a-' (e.g. apodal =without legs; alogia =lacking speech, etc.) or 'an-' before a vowel (e.g. anaemia =lack of blood)

- A [A] counterfeit [PHONEY], say [=PHONI], before a [A] *loss of speech* (7) =APHONIA

- One [ACE] needs help [AID] to get over [=DIA] *listlessness* (6) =ACEDIA

- *Nervous condition* brought about [RE] in oxygen deficiency [ANO-XIA] (8) =ANOREXIA

If you are without anything you have nothing, so 'without' in some cases is used to indicate 'nothing' =O

- *This is bracing* without [O] a belt [ZONE] (5) =OZONE

and if you have nothing, you are a 'have not'

- Go without [HAVE N(OT)] not finishing the *port* (5) =HAVEN

and 'nothing on' implies a solution ending in -OON

- Light [LAMP] (if you've nothing on) *a squib* (7) =LAMPOON

For other uses of O =nothing

see Numbers, Part 2:23

One of the uses of EX is to stand for 'without'

- *Furthest away* and without [EX] change for <u>meter</u> [=TREME] (7) =EXTREME

The Latin word for 'without' is *sine* and this is sometimes required in the solution; *sine prole* ('without children') also appears as the abbreviation SP

- *Mathematical functions* without [SINE] point [S] (5) =SINES

- Sun-god [RA] without children [SP] will construct *grate* (4) =RASP

Examples of the two uses — 'without' =inclusion and

- *Call* to fasten [SH-UT] without ring [O] (5) =SHOUT

'without'=minus — are shown opposite

- *Close* call [SH(O)UT] without oxygen [O] (4)=SHUT

For 'without' as a compound word

see Compound Words, Part 2:20

within
or its alternatives 'in' and 'inside' are also used to indicate inclusions

- *Noisy* machinery [PLAN-T] having information [GEN] within (8)=PLANGENT

- Let [LE-T] vehicle [VAN] in *the Near East* (6)=LEVANT

- The lady's [SHE-S] been [BEEN] inside these *illegal places* (8)=SHEBEENS

although, of course, 'inside', like any other word, can be used in an anagram

- *What the wild tit* [=ITT] (in)side flying [=D-IES] *sings* (7)=DITTIES (Note that 'tit' acts as part of both direct and indirect clue)

For other uses of 'in'

see The Use of 'Out' and 'In', Part 2:12

For other uses of 'inside'

see Split Words, Part 2:21.

14

THE USE OF 'ABOUT'

about
is often used to mean
'approximately' or 'roughly'
in the form of the
abbreviations C, CA or
CIRC (Lat. *circa*)

• *Old stuff* about ℓcℓ to be included
in new variation ℓ=VI-TORIANAℓ
(10) =VICTORIANA

• *Insouciant* about ℓCAℓ an arbitrator
ℓREF(E)REEℓ who is heartless
(8) =CAREFREE

• *Gannet,* perhaps, roughly ℓCℓ
ensconced in an ℓAℓ isolated pillar
ℓL-ATℓ on the headland ℓRASℓ
(8) =ALCATRAS

• *Write* about ℓCIRCℓ the French ℓLEℓ
ring (6) =CIRCLE

• *Like daring young man* about
ℓCIRCAℓ to turn up round ℓACR-ICℓ
wrecked boat ℓ=OBATℓ
(9) =ACROBATIC (down clue)

but remember that C has
many other uses

see Numbers, Part 2:23;
A Compiler's Alphabet, Appendix 3;
A Compiler's Vocabulary,
Appendix 4

and CA also stands for
(Chartered) Accountant

• *Precise* accountant ℓCAℓ returns
ℓ=ACℓ to priest ℓCURATEℓ
(8) =ACCURATE

or 'cases'

• *Instrument* in refined steel
ℓ=ELESTℓ kept in cases ℓC-Aℓ
(7) =CELESTA

Since 'around' can mean
'roughly' in some cases, this
also appears as C or CA

• Green ℓVERTℓ, one ℓIℓ around ℓCAℓ
fifty ℓLℓ, is *upright*
(8) =VERTICAL

- *Hobble* around [C] in <u>planes</u> after turbulence [=SPAN-EL]
  (7) =SPANCEL

though not always

- *Battle* fought out <u>around Dee</u>
  (9) =OUDENARDE

'Roughly' and 'about' can also be pointers to an anagram

- <u>I act</u> roughly [=TACI] — become [TURN] *incommunicative*
  (8) =TACITURN

- <u>Spot red</u> when about [=TOP DRES] to chant [SING] *'Fertiliser'*
  (11) =TOPDRESSING

and 'about' and 'around' can be interchangeable

- A [A] turn [ROUND] *about*
  (6) =AROUND

about can also mean 'anent', 'concerning', regarding', etc., in which form it is usually abbreviated as RE

- *There's ground* about [RE] a [A] boy [SON] (6) =REASON

- *Apostate* about [RE] entering to eat his words [REC-ANT]
  (8) =RECREANT

- *Clergyman* needs a cushion for sitting [PAD] about [RE]
  (5) =PADRE

- *Economise* in connection with [RE] private home [TRENCH]
  (8) =RETRENCH

and since 'over' can also mean 'concerning' or 'about', it sometimes appears where you might expect to find RE

- *Exaggerate* about [OVER] swindle [DO] (6) =OVERDO

- *Go too far* regarding [OVER] film [SHOOT] (9) =OVERSHOOT

- *Upset* concerning [OVER] change of course [TURN]
  (8) =OVERTURN

while 'concerning' sometimes implies 'on'

- Concerning [ON] a piece [DRAUGHT] *from the cask*
  (2,7) =ON DRAUGHT

re is also used to mean 'again', usually, but not always, as a prefix

- Once again [RE], half a gallon [GAL(LON)] is *fine* (5) =REGAL

- *Stops* again [RE] amid the twinkling <u>stars</u> [=AR-STS] (7) =ARRESTS

- *Bound to* upset us [US=SU] again [RE] (4) =SURE

and it is also the Italian word for 'king'

see Foreign Words, Part 2:22

about is also used to indicate an inclusion

- *Congratulate* when fortune [F-ATE] is about to draw out [ELICIT] (10) =FELICITATE

- *It's grand* when Scotsman [MA-C] is about to joke [JEST] with one [I] (8) =MAJESTIC

- *Revolting* shrew [NA-G] about to handle [USE] a [A] container [TIN] (10) =NAUSEATING

but it may sometimes refer to the preceding rather than the following word

- Always [EVER] sing [S-ING] about *separation* (8) =SEVERING

- *Object to* silly talk [ROT] about plague [P-EST] (7) =PROTEST

- A fool [ASS] about to put money on [B-ET] a *dog* (6) =BASSET

It can also indicate reversal

- Start to <u>enquire</u> [E] about surprise interjection [OCH=HCO] and get *sound reaction* (4) =ECHO

- About time [TIME=EMIT] Edward [TED] *gave out* (7) =EMITTED

- About now [NOW=WON] the German [DER] will *speculate* (6) =WONDER

or in various guises it can be used as a pointer to an anagram

- On return, for instance [EG=GE], <u>learns</u> about [=NERALS] the *officers* (8) =GENERALS

- <u>Peers</u> around the *river* (5) =SPREE

- <u>They plan</u> roughly the *heat content of a substance* (8) =ENTHALPY

15

THE USE OF 'FOR EXAMPLE'

The abbreviation 'e.g.' means 'for example', 'for instance' or 'say'. All are used in crosswords in various ways, some of which are set out below:

to indicate one of a class

- Jeeves, e.g. [SERVANT], would be *watchful* if old boy [OB] were in front (9)=OBSERVANT
  (Note the direct clue in the centre)

- *Man in command,* for example, unidentified [NU] in animal skin [PE-LT] (6)=PENULT
  ('Man' is the penultimate syllable in 'command')

- *It was,* for instance, faulty [IMPERFECT] and strained [TENSE] (9,5)=IMPERFECT TENSE

to indicate a homophone

- Cast, say [THROWN], for *top position in state* (6)=THRONE

- Hughes, they say, *cuts timber* (4)=HEWS

- Ken's [KNOWS] *feature,* I say (4)=NOSE

as synonyms for each other

- *Look* up, for instance [EG=G-E], about hobbles [LIMPS] (7)=GLIMPSE (down clue)

- *Animals spotted* by Riffs, for example [EG] — a [A], strange variety (8)=GIRAFFES

- *'We're about to start',* say [EG] the brave men [HER-OES] outside (4,4)=HERE GOES

or as part of the solution in their own right

- Jeu d'e/sprit, e./g., featuring a *peri* (6) =SPRITE

- *Unconnected figures,* <u>say, tend</u> [=ASYNDET] to confuse one [<u>A</u>] (8) =ASYNDETA

- *Makes advance settlement* for homework [PREP] — revising, <u>say</u> [=AYS] (7) =PREPAYS

and 'exemplary' may be used instead of 'for example'

- *Ingenious* point [E] put by trainee [L] exemplary [EG] worker [ANT] (7) =ELEGANT

16

THE USE OF 'PERHAPS'

'Perhaps', and its equivalents 'possibly' and 'maybe', are used in various ways, some of which are given below:

to indicate an oblique description

- *Sweet fool*, perhaps (10)=GOOSEBERRY

- *Shocking luxury*, possibly, in bed (8,7)=ELECTRIC BLANKET

- *He* makes one cross, maybe (7)=ELECTOR

one of a class

- *Irishman* in league, perhaps [MILES], with Scot [IAN] (8)=MILESIAN

- Possibly 15 [SIDE] poets [B-ARDS] with love [O] in their hearts manufacturing *furniture* (10)=SIDEBOARDS

- *Edentate*, maybe, before [ANTE] and after [A(F)TER] losing key [F] (3,5)=ANT EATER

or an anagram

- Cure me and bend, perhaps, when *burdened* (10)=ENCUMBERED

- Rest once, possibly — *it's quite open* (2,6)=NO SECRET

- Go in this, maybe, when *giving a lift* (8)=HOISTING

116

17

ARTICLES

Compilers, like the writers of headlines, have the knack of reducing sentences to the bare essentials and, as a general rule, articles do not appear in clues. The general form of clue is 'Dog bites man on leg', rather than 'A dog bites a man on the leg'.

Occasionally articles do appear for no good reason

- *Small arms practice* encountered [M-ET] round the river [USK] over the railway [RY] (8) =MUSKETRY

Virtually identical clues can be made to yield different solutions by the use of articles

- *Gather* crowd (4) =MASS

- *Gather* a [A] crowd [MASS] (5) =AMASS

Where articles are deliberately used they are required either to avoid ambiguity

- *Men on the board* get the wind up? (8) =DRAUGHTS
(Without 'the', 'men on board' could have implied 'men on the ship' — *see* use of S-S in Abbreviations, Part 1:3)

or to form part of the solution, using either the whole article

- *She* needs a [A] place to dock [BERTH] (6) =BERTHA

- *She alone* has an [AN] unpleasant task [CHORE] with ships [SS] (9) =ANCHORESS

- *Stock controller* uses pointed stick [GO-AD] going round the [THE] river [R] (8) =GOATHERD

or part of it

- Beginning of t̲he [T] uneven [ROUGH] *groove* (6) =TROUGH

- *Throws* the [(T)HE] headless birds [AVES] (6) =HEAVES

• *Raise* middle of the [H] ring [O] first [IST] (5) =HOIST

or to make up the required number of letters in an anagram

• *Music-maker* — a choir man, maybe (9) =HARMONICA

• *Richard* the Liar? No, that's not right! (4-5) =LION-HEART

• *Scope* of an erg (5) =RANGE

Occasionally the article 'a' will appear as 'alpha'

• A [ALPHA] wager [BET] — *a literal arrangement* (8) =ALPHABET

and 'alpha' may imply 'beginning'

• Expression of surprise [HA] after a [A] record [LP] *beginning* (5) =ALPHA

Another version of 'the' (DE) is sometimes used

• *Coming down,* was Camptown jockey put off it? (7) =DESCENT

• *Writer* of Savage's version of 'The Enemy' (5) =DEFOE

• Man Friday says the [DE] money [CENT] is *quite respectable* (6) =DECENT

Where the word 'article' itself appears in the clue, it may be treated as any other indirect clue from which one can derive A, AN or THE (or a foreign version — *see* below)

• I [I] take advertisements [ADS] to return the article [AN=NA] to those *beautiful women* (6) =NAIADS

• *Greek* produces three articles [A, THE, AN] about six counties [NI] (8) =ATHENIAN

• *Curse* four articles [AN, A, THE, A] written about the musician's leader [M] (8) =ANATHEMA

although sometimes the reverse situation is found where 'a', 'an' or 'the' in the clue is translated to 'article' in the solution

• Perhaps a [ARTICLE] daughter [D] is *bound by written contract* (8) =ARTICLED

• For example, an [ARTICLE] *object* (7) =ARTICLE

• *A very small part* of possibly the [ARTICLE] following page [P] (8) =PARTICLE

'Article' sometimes means an 'object' rather than a part of speech, and any object can be referred to as 'it' or 'thing'

- *Ask* to have the article |IT| written in different <u>vein</u> |=INV-E| (6)=INVITE

- *Sincerely flatter* the article |IT| penned by one |I| friend |M-ATE| (7)=IMITATE

- An article |TH-ING| about ill-considered |RASH| *punishment* (9)=THRASHING

Compilers treat 'a' and 'an' as interchangeable

- A |AN| church |CH| with gold |OR| *hook* (6)=ANCHOR

- An |A| elected representative |MP| the French |LE| regard as *Liberal* (5)=AMPLE

'Of' and 'of the' may have no particular significance in some clues but in others may require the use of an adjective

- Contend |VIE| with quarters |NNESE| *of the city* (8)=VIENNESE

- Look |LA| <u>neat</u> in knitted form |=NATE| *of wool* (6)=LANATE

- Hard |H| to follow the flag |IRIS| *of a Republic* (5)=IRISH

Note that 'a' has many other uses (*see* A Compiler's Alphabet, Appendix 3) including 'type of bomb' (A=atomic)

- *Light shield* to hide |PELT| a kind of bomb |A| (5)=PELTA

Foreign articles appear quite often in clues

in French

'a' or 'one'=UN, UNE

- A French one |UN| guest initially |G| was idle |LAZED| and *dull* (8)=UNGLAZED

- *Convenient* minor work |OP| left |PORT| with one French female |UNE| (9)=OPPORTUNE

'the' =LE, LA, LES

- Mannerism [TRICK] of the French [LE] horse [CHARGER] which *may help driver to start* (7,7) =TRICKLE CHARGER

- Little devil [IMP] receives the French [LA] message [CABLE] which is *inexorable* (10) =IMPLACABLE

- *Disintegrates* like a piece of bread [CRUMB] the French [LES] took off [AWAY] (8,4) =CRUMBLES AWAY

(although, as usual, there are exceptions)

- *Little trouble* to the French (6,8) =ENFANT TERRIBLE

'to the' =AU, A LA, AUX

- To the French [AU], metric measurement [STERE] is *simple* (7) =AUSTERE

- *Battle* in the manner of [A LA] a doctor [MO] (5) =ALAMO

- *Helper* to the French [AUX] moved airily [=ILIARY] (9) =AUXILIARY

'of the', 'from the' =DU, DE LA, DES

- *Mature* article [A] from The French [DU] Lieutenant [LT] (5) =ADULT

- One [A] of the French [DE LA] I'd [ID] encountered initially [E] *in Australia* (8) =ADELAIDE

- *They are learning* from French [DE] dwarfs [STU-NTS] outside (8) =STUDENTS

- *Bravest* of the French [DES] in a rush [BOL-T] (7) =BOLDEST

in German

'a' or 'one' =EIN

- *Checked* one German [EIN] owing money [R-ED] (6) =REINED

'the' =DER, DIE, DAS

- The German [DER], sir [SIR], is returned [=RIS] with *the powder* (6) =DERRIS

- Magnetic force [OD] in the German [DI-E] *valve* (5) =DIODE

- *Frustrate* the German [DAS] h̲othead [H] (4) =DASH

in Italian

'the' =IL

- Can't [CANT] the Italian [IL] girl [ENA] produce a *simple melody*? (9) =CANTILENA

'to the' =AL

- *Warning* to the Italian [AL] member [ARM] (5) =ALARM

in Spanish

'the' =EL, LA, LOS, LAS

- Very warm [HOT], the Spanish [EL] sun [S], so *stay here* (6) =HOTELS

- The Spanish [LA] can [TIN] in a *different language* (5) =LATIN

- *Fence,* most of it [(F)ENC-E] round the Spanish [LOS] (7) =ENCLOSE

- *Statutes* of the Spanish [LA-S] out West [W] (4) =LAWS

or **in combinations**

- *Servant* of the German [DER] after a French [UN] fish [LING] (9) =UNDERLING

- The Spanish [EL] and German [DER] brothers [BRETHREN] *keep lighthouses* (5,8) =ELDER BRETHREN

- The Spanish-French [EL, LA] *girl* (4) =ELLA

Note 'on the Continent' (or similar) may be used rather than the name of a country (*see also* Foreign Words, Part 2:22)

- On the Continent, the [LA] swindle [STING] is *continuing* (7) =LASTING

Moral: assume that any articles in the clue are there for a purpose and expect to use them as given words.

18

SMALL WORDS

Any word printed in the clue may be intended to be used as a given word forming part of the solution. We have already seen in the previous section how this is frequently used in the case of articles and how, because these are such commonplace words, they can easily be overlooked. The same applies to a number of other comparatively insignificant words, mostly prepositions. A further selection of clues, in which such words are treated as given words, is given below to emphasise the point that all words in a clue, however insignificant they may appear, should be given full weight when reading the clue.

and • *Saint* and [AND] king [R] we [WE] look up[=EW] to (6)=ANDREW (down clue)

as • *Out of true* as [AS] a site for the observatory [KEW] (5)=ASKEW

at • *Restrained* anger [TEMPER] at [AT] conclusion of peace [E] (9)=TEMPERATE

by • *Linen* sent by [BY] ship [SS] to America [US] (6)=BYSSUS

for • *Dispatches* for [FOR] key sections [WARDS] (8)=FORWARDS

he • To a [A] degree [D], he [HE] gets revenue [RENT] from a *follower* (8)=ADHERENT

if • Get trustee [TR] if [IF] the French [LE] *dally* (6)=TRIFLE

in • Learner [L] well-versed [UP] in [IN] *botanical subject* (5)=LUPIN

in a • Union [CONCERT] in [IN] a [A] *squeeze* (10)=CONCERTINA

is • *Call* for it [IT] after victory
it • [V] is [IS] achieved (5)=VISIT

me • *Wander* with me [ME] and [AND] the Queen [ER] (7)=MEANDER

no • *Girl* is no [NO] painter [RA] (4)=NORA

not • *Cathedral* not [NOT] concerned [RE] with American woman [DAME] (5,4)=NOTRE DAME

of • Liberal [L] of [OF] rank [TIER] and *of greater stature* (7) =LOFTIER

on • Hat [CAP] on [ON] *chicken* (5) =CAPON

or • Male [MAN] or [OR] *house* (5) =MANOR

to • *Lady* of an age [ERA] to [TO] inspire erotic verse (5) =ERATO

too • *He draws* a vehicle [CAR] too [TOO] and damaged tins [=NIST] (10) =CARTOONIST

In some cases, these small words are used

for **subtraction**

• *This shout is for an American* and [AND] not used by Dutchman [HOLL(AND)ER] (6) =HOLLER

or **inclusion**

• John of England [PRES-TER] imprisoned by [BY] *the elder* (9) =PRESBYTER

• *This sea-area* is [IS] cold [C] in sound [B-AY] (6) =BISCAY

• *Debases* good men [DE-ANS] about me [ME] (7) =DEMEANS

• In my [M-Y] circumstances, unemployment pay [DOLE] is up [=ELOD] in the *air* (6) =MELODY (down clue)

• *Stick* to [TO] during prohibition [BA-N] (5) =BATON

Moral: assume that small words of this sort are printed in the clue for a purpose and expect to use them as given words.

19

OLD WORDS

The word 'old' in a clue can be taken to have any one of several different meanings. The word itself may be old in the sense that it is archaic or obsolete, even if the object it describes still exists (e.g. 'hose' for 'stockings'); the object itself may be old in the sense that it no longer exists, even though the word describing it is still in current use (e.g. 'dinosaur' for 'prehistoric animal'); the thing described as old may be so only in the sense that there is a later version (e.g. 'old' lover='ex'-lover).

The word printed in the clue may be 'old' or any one of several equivalents, such as 'ancient', 'as before', 'former', 'once', 'stale', etc.

Many archaic and obsolete words can be found in dictionaries; the following are a few examples:

BURD=lady, maiden
· *It's ridiculous* to have an [A] old lady [B-URD] excluded by society [S] (6)=ABSURD

DISLOIGN=remove
· *Remove old,* <u>old sign</u> falling about [=DISLO-GN] one [I] (8)=DISLOIGN

EFTSOONS=forthwith
· <u>Soft nose</u> is broken *forthwith* (8)=EFTSOONS
(Note no reference to 'old')

EMMET=ant
· Some of th/em met/ an *old worker* (5)=EMMET
(Note that worker=ant is a frequently used clue)

ENOW=enough
· *Enough* ancient <u>E</u>nglish, <u>N</u>orse, <u>or</u> <u>W</u>elsh leaders (4)=ENOW

EAR or ERE=plough
· Woman's [W] ancient plough [ERE] *used to be* (4)=WERE

ETERNE =everlasting	• Bearing [E] has alloy [TERNE] that's no longer *infinitely durable* (6)=ETERNE
ETHE =easy	• *Clear air* is no longer easy [ETHE] in middle of f<u>ar</u>m [A-R] (6)=AETHER
FLAWN =pancake	• *Stale pancakes* crack [FLAW] — turn tin [SN] over [=NS] (6)=FLAWNS
GAR =spear	• *Indian transport* with ancient spear [GAR] beside one [I] (4)=GARI
GATE =goat	• *Round* lump [LOB] swallowed by old goat [G-ATE] (7)=GLOBATE
ICH =increase	• *Become affluent* once increase [ICH] in rent [R-EN(T)] reduced (6)=RICHEN
NE =not	• Not old [NE] good man [ST] in *comfortable home* (4)=NEST
NIE =near	• *Relative* once near [NIE] church [CE] (5)=NIECE
PEYSE =balance, weight	• *Balance* no longer shows profit [PAYS], we are told (5)=PEYSE
REAL =royal	• Old-fashioned royal [REAL] colour [GOLD] is *valuable* (4,4)=REAL GOLD
RELY =rally	• Rally's dead [RE-LY] and Duke's [D] caught in *bloody fashion* (5)=REDLY
SENNIGHT =week	• Once a *week* (8)=SENNIGHT
SPIAL =observation	• In observation as before [SP-IAL], ape [ORANG] is seen to like *parts of fern* (10)=SPORANGIAL
THY =your	• In addition [TOO], your old [THY] ending is *palatable* (6)=TOOTHY
URE =use	• *Kind of resin* in use before [URE] and accepted [A] (4)=UREA

VIA =way

- An [A] old way [VIA] to a hill [TOR] for a *flier* (7)=AVIATOR

WICK =wicked

- It was once very bad [WICK] in a *country town* (4)=WICK

YE =the

- The old [YE] are [AR(E)] cut in *time* (4)=YEAR

Phrases such as 'the poet said', etc., generally indicate words used by Spenser, Shakespeare, etc., which often have unusual spellings

- *Like birds of South America,* this has brown [TAN] and silver [AG] exterior [RINE=rind], says the poet (9)=TANAGRINE

- *Shakespeare's move in quickly* to stop [END] crafty conduct [ART] (6)=ENDART

- *Spenser's called* people [MEN] back [=NEM] to the point [PT] (5)=NEMPT (=named)

- King's [R] play [NO] making comeback [=ON] last [DURE] for *Shakespeare's Globe* (7)=RONDURE

- *Continent* [AFRIC(A)] as detailed in poetry (5)=AFRIC

- *Repeat*'s shown here — and not [NE] in sorrow [R-EW=rue], according to the oldtimers (5)=RENEW

- *Lazy* poet's grief [DOLE] revealed in modish [IN] books [NT] (8)=INDOLENT

Many words which are themselves regarded as still in current use describe obsolete objects. The following are some examples:

AMBO=desk, pulpit

- *Whence once the preacher's* claim to be [AM] an American chap [BO] (4)=AMBO

ICENI=Celtic tribe

- *Old people* in general want n/ice ni/ghtwear (5)=ICENI

JUTE =Danish invader

• Old tribesman of this fibre
(4) =JUTE

· NEMEAN =lion slain
by Hercules

• Game opponents [N, E] to bad-
tempered [MEAN] *old lion*
(6) =NEMEAN

SHILLING =old silver coin

• Keep [STORE] old coin [S] in *shops*
(6) =STORES

THANE =medieval noble

• *Old landowner* not big enough to
own Kentish Island [THANE(T)]
(5) =THANE

UR =old city

• *Pot* from ancient city [UR] found
in pub [IN-N] (5) =INURN

=primitive

• *Brilliant bird* also [TO-O] carries
primitive [UR] bill [AC]
(7) =TOURACO

When 'old' is used to refer to a former state of affairs, where neither the word itself nor the object it represents is obsolete, the descriptive words 'former', etc., are usually abbreviated to EX.

Pointers: former, once, one-time, past, retired, etc.

Typical examples:

• Former [EX] writers [PENS] I've
[IVE] gathered together, *dear*
(9) =EXPENSIVE

• Once [EX] one stood [POSED] and
revealed (7) =EXPOSED

• *He takes out* one-time [EX] farm
vehicle [TRACTOR]
(9) =EXTRACTOR

• Retired [EX], sounding sad
[TOLLING] and *cracking up*
(9) =EXTOLLING

• *Leave* late [EX] with the <u>tea</u> blend
[=EAT] (5) =EXEAT

• *Makes clear* that no longer [EX] are
certain areas flat [PLAINS]
(8) =EXPLAINS

• *Way out* used to be [EX] the thing
[IT] (4) =EXIT

Note that there are exceptions where EX is not implied

• Former [PAST] article [A] of *Italian food* (5) =PASTA

For the use of EX =out of

· *see* The Use of 'Out' and 'In', Part 2:12

For the use of EX =without

see The Use of 'Without' and 'Within', Part 2:13

old
may occasionally stand on its own feet as 'old', etc.

• One [I] <u>old</u> crook [=DOL] *loved by many* (4) =IDOL

• Strike [THRESH] in front of former [OLD] *entrance* (9) =THRESHOLD

• Grand [G] old [OLD] measure [EN] of very tasty [DELICIOUS] *apples* (6,9) =GOLDEN DELICIOUS

• Have a little time to pass (that's *old*!) (6,4) =SECOND HAND

• Entrance [H-ALL] obstructed by much-used [OLD] *luggage* (7) =HOLDALL

and 'ancient' may have other meanings

• Old Iago, the ensign (7) =ANCIENT
('Ancient' =flag or ensign)

• Ancient [PISTOL] eastern [E] *gold coin* (7) =PISTOLE
(The Shakespearean character 'ancient Pistol')

For some examples of dialect words

see Foreign Words, Part 2:22.

20

COMPOUND WORDS

Compound words, with or without hyphens, can have more than one meaning. Many, particularly those indicating position or direction, have other meanings when they are read as two separate words, thus making them different parts of speech. For example, 'drawback' can be read as a noun and as a verb, to 'draw back', while also having the meaning, from the compiler's point of view, of the word 'draw' back, i.e. backwards. In clues, compound words often need to be read in this way to arrive at the meaning of the derived word or the solution. Some of these are mentioned below:

all-round
read as AL-L round another word

- All round [AL-L] commander [CO] starts hiding old [H,O] *drink* (7) = ALCOHOL

as ALL written in reverse as LLA

- Bad [BA-D] round, all-round [=LLA] *song* (6) = BALLAD

or as ALL plus 'round' (O)

- *Permit* all-round [ALL, O] women [W] (5) = ALLOW

backward
read as WARD back = DRAW

- *Pull out* with [WITH] backward [=DRAW] addition (8) = WITHDRAW

backstreet
street = ST so backstreet = TS

- *Boards* are skilful [ABLE] in backstreet [T-S] (6) = TABLES

begone
read as BE gone, to imply the omission of B and E

- Begone [BE] but still admira(b)l(e) (7) = ADMIRAL

breakdown
read as break DOWN, an anagram

- *Be amazed* at breakdown [=WOND] with queen [ER] (6) = WONDER

129

comeback
read as COME reversed

• *Politician*'s missile [DART] broken [=D-RAT] without comeback [=EMOC] (8)=DEMOCRAT

counteracting
read as 'counter' (BAR) and 'acting' (ON=on-stage)

• Counteracting *joint* (5)=BARON

cutback
read as 'cut'=PARED reversed

• Cutback [PARED=DE-RAP] involving that rickety [=ATH-T] and *dangerous structure* (5-4)=DEATH-TRAP

drawback
read as DRAW back=WARD or, since 'draw'=TIE, drawback=EIT

• *Hindrance* from Ward [=DRAW] (8)=DRAWBACK

• *Too much* sea-foam [SURF] a drawback [=EIT] (7)=SURFEIT

fanlight
read as 'fan' (BLOW) and 'light' (TORCH)

• Fanlight [BLOW, TORCH] *concentrates the heat* (9)=BLOWTORCH

feedback
read as FEED back=DEEF

• *Get report after the event* giving feedback [DE-EF] about broken rib [=BRI] (7)=DEBRIEF

halfback
read as 'half'=SEMI, reversed to IMES

• *The diversions* of a former [PAST] halfback [=IMES] (8)=PASTIMES

heartbroken
read as broken HEART, an anagram

• Heartbroken [THERA] — gets quiet [P], unknown [Y] *treatment* (7)=THERAPY

heavyweight
perhaps a boxer, but often a heavy weight

• *Rock* heavyweight [TON] in the London area [S-E] (5)=STONE

indeed
and other 'in-' words

see Split Words, Part 2:21

interchangeable
read as an anagram of INTER

• Interchangeable *fertiliser* (5)=NITRE

keyring
read as 'key' (music, A to G) plus 'ring' (O)

- Key [G] ring [O] on old vehicle [CART] for *modern one* (2-4) = GO-CART

knockabout
read as PAT written with an inclusion

- It's *obvious*, a little knockabout [PA-T] number [TEN] (6) = PATENT

layabout
read as LAY written outside another word,

- *Finally,* layabout [LA-Y] saint [ST] and learner [L] (6) = LASTLY

as SET written outside another word,

- Layabout [S-ET] we [WE] find is *not tart* (5) = SWEET

or as LAY reversed = YAL

- *Trustworthy* look [LO] for layabout [=YAL] (5) = LOYAL

laidback
read as LAID back = DIAL

- Fussy [PRIM] or [OR] laidback [=DIAL]? No, *original* (10) = PRIMORDIAL

meantime
read as 'mean' = PAR and 'time' = AGE

- *Make little of* the underworld [DIS] meantime [PAR, AGE] (9) = DISPARAGE

miscued
read as an anagram of CUED

- *Cut,* having miscued [=DUCE], the snooker ball [RE-D] on the outside (7) = REDUCED

misterms
read as an anagram of TERMS

- Misterms [=M-STER] the old boy [OB] as the *hoodlum* (7) = MOBSTER

outbreak
'out' and 'break' are both pointers to an anagram so this can imply an anagram of OUT

- *Travelling around* circle [RING] after outbreak [=TOU] (7) = TOURING

or BREAK

- *Reduce speed* of the outbreak (5) = BRAKE

outright
read as 'out right', to imply omission of R

or 'out right', to imply another word written outside R or RT

- *Stop* outright crease [C(R)EASE] (5)=CEASE

  Confront [FA-CE] outright [R] *travesty* (5)=FARCE

- Pay [PA-Y] outright [RT] for the *celebration* (5)=PARTY

outset
read as an anagram of SET

or to imply other words written outside SET

- *Property* of goddess [ATE] after outset [=EST] (6)=ESTATE
- Deep [BAS-S] outset [SET] for *dogs* (7)=BASSETS

outside
read as an anagram of SIDE

or as a straightforward pointer to an inclusion (*see also* The Use of 'Out' and 'In', Part 2:12)

- *Leads* old fiddle [GU] outside [=IDES] (6)=GUIDES
- *Bird* allowed [L-ET] outside the pub [INN] (6)=LINNET

outstanding
read as 'standing outside' for an inclusion

- *Look after* outstanding Old English [O-E] poetry [VERSE] (7)=OVERSEE

overbearing
read as 'over' N, S, E or W in down clues

- Left [L] at [AT] six [VI] with an [AN] overbearing [S] *set of people* (8)=LATVIANS

overdue
read as 'over' DUE, to imply another word written above DUE in down clues

- Half-boarder [RESI(DENT)] overdue [DUE] *remainder* (7)=RESIDUE

overcome
could be read as 'over' COME in down clues, but is more likely simply to mean 'above'

- Capek's robots [RUR] overcome a [A] learner [L] *of the country* (5)=RURAL

overseas
read as 'over' SEAS or

• One French [UN] overseas [SEAS] on [ON] a [A] lake [L] is *ill-timed* (10) =UNSEASONAL

'over' WATER in down clues

• Retire [BACK] overseas [WATER] in *isolated place* (9) =BACKWATER

overweight
read as 'over weight' (e.g. TON) in down clues

• Herb [SIMPLE] is an overweight [TON] *fool* (9) =SIMPLETON

• Teacher [HEAD] with overweight [STONE] *memorial* (9) =HEADSTONE

• *Declare* professional [PRO] bridge player [N] overweight [OUNCE] (9) =PRONOUNCE

precept
read as 'before' CEPT

• *Admit* current [AC] precept [CEPT] (6) =ACCEPT

prepacked
read as 'packed in' PR-E, for inclusion

• (Pr)ovid(e) *this poet* prepacked (4) =OVID

rigout
read as an anagram of RIG

• *Dirty* rigout [=GRI] belongs to me [MY] ($\overline{5}$) =GRIMY

• Rigout [=GIR] student [L], *young female* (4) =GIRL

roundabout
read as 'round, about' (O,RE), giving ORE

• Go slowly [LAG] back [=GAL] to roundabout [ORE] having had *more than enough* (6) =GALORE

or 'round about' (O,C), giving OC

• Queen [ER] and her father [GR] entrap roundabout [OC] *tradesman* (6) =GROCER

or 'round, about' (O,CA), giving OCA

• Transport [BR] roundabout [OCA] of French [DE] *material* (7) =BROCADE

round-up
read as UP reversed =PU

- Round up [=PU] fish [LING], *whining* (6) =PULING

or to imply another word written outside UP

- Round up [UP] Second [S] Army Engineer Regiment [REME] *at the highest point* (7) =SUPREME

or, since 'round' =LAP, to mean LAP reversed in down clues

- *Mean* round-up [=PAL] attempt [TRY] (6) =PALTRY

runabout
read as an anagram of RUN

- Sort of square [T] runabout [=URN] will *twist* (4) =TURN

or as RUN reversed

- Runabout [=NUR] on south-eastern [SE] railway [RY] *training centre* (7) =NURSERY

scatterbrain
read as an anagram of BRAIN

- Scatterbrain *young Scot* (5) =BAIRN

setback
read as SET back =TES

- Setback [=T-ES] about the flapper [WING] causes *pain* (7) =TWINGES

or as a synonym for 'reverse' so that 'bad setback' =DAB, and so on

- *After* tea [T] in real [REAL] setback [=LA-ER] (5) =LATER

set-up
read as SET reversed =TES

- *Swear to* set up [=TES] in a [A] race [T-T] (6) =ATTEST

or, since 'set' =LOT, to mean LOT reversed =TOL, both in down clues

- *Praise* former [EX] set-up [=TOL] (5) =EXTOL

shipwreck
read as 'wrecked' SHIP, an anagram

- The *start of Gulliver's Travels*? Pish! [=SHIP] (9) =SHIPWRECK

stick-up
read as ROD 'up', to give DOR in down clues

- *Approved* of the stick-up [ROD=DOR]; needs to be sorted out [=EN-SED] (8) =ENDORSED

substandard
read as 'below' PAR in down clues

- *E.g. sharp remark* about [RE] substandard [PAR] driving position [TEE] (8)=REPARTEE

sunrise
read as SUN or SOL reversed in down clues

- *Crazy* sunrise [=NU-S] — about time [T]! (4)=NUTS

- *He is beaten* by queen [ER] after sunrise [=LOS] (5)=LOSER

sun-up
read as a synonym of 'dawn' to give SUN reversed (=NUS) in down clues

- *Group* to see George Eliot briefly [GE] at dawn [=NUS] (5)=GENUS

undercurrent
read as 'under current' (AC, DC) in down clues

- *Sharp* undercurrent [AC] to get free from [RID] (5)=ACRID

undergo
read as 'go under' in down clues

- *Chemical* about [RE] to undergo a can [TIN] rise [=NIT] (5)=NITRE

understudy
read as 'under study' (study=CON or DEN) in down clues

- *Adapt* shape [FORM] to understudy [CON] (7)=CONFORM

- *Disown* unknown [Y] understudy [DEN] (4)=DENY

underwrite
read as 'under write' (write=PEN) in down clues

- *Money* to underwrite [PEN] church [CE] (5)=PENCE

uphill
read as TOR reversed=ROT in down clues

- *Run* for a short time [T] uphill [=ROT] (4)=TROT

upholding
read as 'up' meaning reversal in down clues, plus 'holding' which implies inclusion

- *Staff* of the French aristocrat [LE DUC] upholding [=CUD-EL] head of Girondists [G] (6)=CUDGEL

upright
read as 'right' (RT) 'up' to give TR in down clues

- *Follow* upright [=TR] once [ACE] (5)=TRACE

uprising
read as UP written
backwards in down clues

• *Quarrelsome type*'s uprising [=PU]
in faraway [DIS-TANT] situation
(9)=DISPUTANT

upset
read as SET 'up'=TES in
down clues or to imply a
straightforward reversal

• Upset [=TES], for example [EG], at
[AT] *flowers* (7)=TAGETES
(Note the reversal extends beyond
TES)

upturn
read as 'turn' UP=PU

• *South American lion* upturns [=PU]
mother [MA] (4)=PUMA

withholding
read as WITH 'holding' to
indicate an inclusion

• *Ghost* withholding [W-ITH] artist
[RA] (6)=WRAITH

without
read as '. . . with OUT'
(*see also* The Use of 'Without'
and 'Within', Part 2:13)

• Sailor [AB] without [OUT]
following, *almost* (5)=ABOUT

write-up
read as PEN reversed in
down clues

• *Bungling* a write-up [=NEP] in the
thing [I-T] (5)=INEPT

It is perhaps also as well to be aware that you may be called upon to read
a word, which although not a compound word is composed of letters
which conveniently separate into two words, as if it were two separate
words. These are sometimes referred to as **concealed compounds**.
A couple of examples will make the point:

alternate: read as 'alter NATE', to give NEAT

legend: read as 'leg end', meaning 'foot' or 'toe'

For the use of compound
words to select letters

see Selected Letters, Part 1:4

For the use of compound
words as split words

see Split Words, Part 2:21

Moral: keep a lookout for compound words and concealed
compounds and be prepared to read them as separate words.

21

SPLIT WORDS

Almost any word can be split to allow for the inclusion of another word

but some are particularly useful to compilers and a few examples are set out below:

bed
Phrases such as 'in bed', 'between the sheets', 'retired', etc., normally indicate words included in BED, split as BE-D or B-ED

- *Applaud* learner [L] in headgear [C-AP] (4) =CLAP

- *Looked upon* hell almost [HEL(L)] after retirement [BE-D] (6) =BEHELD
- *Filled with the idea* that I'm [IM] u̲pset at first [U] in between the sheets [B-ED] (6) =IMBUED

or in COT, split as CO-T or C-OT

- *Space traveller* put me [ME] in bed [CO-T] (5) =COMET
- A smoke for Hamlet, for example [HERO], when retired [C-OT] (7) =CHEROOT

or in LIT (Fr. 'bed'), split as LI-T or L-IT

- I am [IM] back [=MI] in bed in France [LI-T] in the *end* (5) =LIMIT
- *Allowed* to be in charge [IC] when retired in France [L-IT] (5) =LICIT

but 'bed' can also refer to a garden

- R̲ates for *one in bed* (5) =ASTER

or stand on its own feet as 'bed', 'cot' or 'crib'

- *Discouraged* from taking buns back [=SNUB] to bed [BED] (7) =SNUBBED

137

• *Steak* as an item on the menu
[ENTRE-E] — bed [COT] included
(9)=ENTRECOTE

• *Attribute* to an irregularity in the
<u>sea</u> [=AS-E]-bed [CRIB]
(7)=ASCRIBE

end
is sometimes used as a split
word, as E-ND or EN-D,
to mean 'in the end' or 'in
conclusion'

• *Animal* the French [LA] captured
in the end [E-ND] (5)=ELAND

• In conclusion [EN-D], a challenge
[GAGE] is *taken on*
(7)=ENGAGED

gilded
means covered with gold
(OR) so that anything gilded
has O-R on the outside

• *Different* gilded [O-R] article [THE]
(5)=OTHER

• *He* must be [LIVE] gilt-covered
[O-R] (6)=OLIVER

indeed
translates as 'in DEED' and
means 'inside' DE-ED, or,
less frequently, 'inside'
DEE-D

• Indeed [DE-ED], a fraction [PART]
has *left* (8)=DEPARTED

• *Judged* me [ME], indeed [DEE-D]
(6)=DEEMED

although there are some
exceptions

• Boarding expenses [RENTS] for dog
[CUR] *may indeed be shocking*
(8)=CURRENTS

• *Animadversion* that is indeed
Continental [Fr. 'Indeed!' =
COMMENT] (7)=COMMENT

• Inde/ed I t/ry to *arrange things*
(4) =EDIT

Since 'deed' can mean
'action', 'fact' or 'feat', these
words can be used in the clue
instead of 'deed'

• Action [DE-ED] taken about
discourse [TRACT] being *belittled*
(9)=DETRACTED

• *Recited* by demand [CLAIM] in fact
[DE-ED] (9)=DECLAIMED

and since 'deed' also means 'act', this too can be used, but is usually treated as another split word as AC-T or A-CT, sometimes used to refer to a play

although 'act' can mean BILL, in the legal sense

A further meaning of **deed** is 'document'

although not always as a split word

and 'document' or 'writing' can be abbreviated to MS (manuscript)

Since 'in' is so useful to compilers to indicate an inclusion, it is not surprising that many other words starting with in- are used in the same way as 'indeed', e.g. incite, inflow, etc.

* *Torpedoed* — there could be a story [=STROY] in the feat [DE-ED] (9)=DESTROYED

* *Take* a hundred [C], record [EP] in the act [AC-T] (6)=ACCEPT

* *Change* a very loud [FF] note [E] in the act [A-CT] (6)=AFFECT

* *Damned* dogs [CURS] in play [AC-T] (7)=ACCURST

* Act [BIL-L] about a rate change [=ATERA] *where two parties are involved* (9)=BILATERAL

* *Flattened* document [DE-ED] about papers [PRESS] (9)=DEPRESSED

* *Wrong* documents [DEEDS] I'm [=MI] looking up to (8)=MISDEEDS (down clue)

* *Lots of paper* about [RE] a [A] document [MS] (5)=REAMS

* *Hides* request [ASK] in writing [M-S] (5)=MASKS

* *Salt* will incite [CIT-E] rodent [RAT] (7)=CITRATE

* *Man* to measure [EL] inflow [F-LOW], *no learner* (6)=FELLOW

* Look [RAY] back [=YAR] inland [LAN-D] for *rope* (7)=LANYARD

* *Sweet* with sage, for example [HERB], inset [S-ET] (7)=SHERBET

* *Slip* fifty [L] inside [S-IDE] (5)=SLIDE

* *Apartment* for intent [TEN-T] English [E] soldiers [MEN] (8)=TENEMENT

• Miss Spenlow [DORA] inefficient [A-BLE] but *charming* (8)=ADORABLE

need
can be used as NE-ED or NEE-D

• *Caught* non-drinker [TT] in need [NE-ED] (6)=NETTED

• *Annoyed* by loveless dole [D(O)LE] when in need [NEE-D] (7)=NEEDLED

red
is used as a split word as RE-D or R-ED to signify 'in the red', 'in debt', 'owing money' or 'overdrawn' or 'with an overdraft'

• Country [STATE] in debt [RE-D]. *That's been said before!* (8)=RESTATED

• An [A] abstainer [TT] owing money [R-ED] *deserted* (6)=RATTED

• *Searched minutely* for a [A] king [K] who is overdrawn [R-ED] (5)=RAKED

• The only one [SOLE] with an overdraught [RE-D] *put on a new footing* (7)=RESOLED

but 'owing' or 'debts', as opposed to 'in debt', usually implies an -IOUS ending

• *Irreverent* little devil [IMP] with some debts [IOUS] (7)=IMPIOUS

and 'overdrawn' or 'short of funds' is OD

• *House* short of funds [OD] in Lincoln [AB-E] (5)=ABODE

while **red** can also mean 'Russian' so that RED used in split form can mean 'in Russian'

• *Minister's title* for <u>Verne</u> novel [=VEREN] in Russian [RE-D] (8)=REVEREND

or it can be used, without being split, to mean 'anarchist', 'communist', 'left', 'leftwing', 'revolutionary', etc.

• Anarchist [RED] in city [C-IT(Y)] losing unknown [Y] *distinction* (6)=CREDIT

• *Edit* Communist [RED] decree [ACT] (6)=REDACT

• *Girl* of the soft [MILD] left [RED] (7)=MILDRED

• *Name* of fellow [F] on the left wing [RED] (4)=FRED

- *Exposed* graduate [BA] revolutionary [RED] (5) =BARED

but note that 'revolutionary' can be used to indicate a reversal

- Revolutionary cheesemaker [RENNET] *note* (6) =TENNER

an anagram

- *Completely defeat* counter-revolutionary (7) =TROUNCE

or a real rebel

- *This revolutionary* was not really a master [MA] traitor [RAT] (5) =MARAT

and that **red** can also be used to mean 'flushed'

- *Quiet,* flushed [RE-D], about to treat [SERVE] (8) =RESERVED

'bloody'

- *Knocked down* and bloody [R-ED] when [AS] admitted (5) =RASED

'cardinal' (a red colour)

- *Congenial* to a benevolent [KIND] cardinal [RED] (7) =KINDRED

or just 'colour'

- *Very interested* I [I] examine [VET] coloured cover [R-ED] (7) =RIVETED

or even a snooker ball

- *Was concerned* about [CA] the snooker ball [RED] (5) =CARED

reed
is used as a split word as RE-ED to mean 'in the grass', etc.

- Kind of granite [SHAP] amid grass [RE-ED] *in new form* (8) =RESHAPED

- *Withdrew* in grass-covered [RE-ED] terrain [TRACT] (9) =RETRACTED

although 'in the grass' can have other uses

- Be [B-E] hiding the youth [LAD] in the *grass* (5) =BLADE

- The listeners [EARS] in the grass [H-AY] creating a *rumour* (7) =HEARSAY

and since 'reed' = 'rush' . . .

- Rush [RE-ED] round quantity [SUM] *taken back* (7) =RESUMED

Some abbreviations are used   *see* Abbreviations, Part 1:3
in split form

See also The Use of 'Out' and 'In', Part 2:12

Moral: keep a look out for words beginning with, or phrases which include, 'in' and expect the solution to involve an inclusion.

22

FOREIGN WORDS

Foreign words often appear in clues but they are usually simple words that will be familiar to anyone with a smattering of a continental language. Words taken from 'foreign' versions of English are, ironically, likely to be less well known since many words used by Americans, South Africans, Scots, etc., are unfamiliar to the native Englishman.

The clue may give 'abroad', 'across the Channel', 'on the Continent' or 'foreign' rather than the name of the particular language, or it may use 'translated' to indicate that a foreign version of the clue word is required in the solution.

Some examples of the use of foreign languages are given below:

American

DOVE =dived

- *The flier* dived American style (4) =DOVE

SNAFU =chaos

- Turning of screw [FAN=NAF] in America [U-S] causes *chaos* (5) =SNAFU

THRU =through

- *Loose thread* from one side to the other [THROUGH] of American [=THRU] material's face [M] (5) =THRUM

Australian

CROOK =no good, sick

- Sick Australian criminal? (5) =CROOK

DAMPER =unleavened bread

- *Bread in Australia* is more moist (6) =DAMPER

HUMPY =shed

- In Australian hut [HUMP-Y], the first [T] to take a *seat* (6) =HUMPTY

SKITE =boast

- *Boast* down-under of slight shower [SKIT], note [E] (5) =SKITE

143

French

BAL =dance

• The French dance [BAL] more slowly [LATER] *in Scotland* (8) =BALLATER

BON =good

• *As a hat,* it makes good [BON] trap [NET] (6) =BONNET

BONNE =maid

• English [E] apprentice [L] turns up with French maid [BONNE] *to improve his status* (7) =ENNOBLE (down clue)

CHER =dear

• It's [IT] on the piano [P], dear [CHER], *this jug* (7) =PITCHER

CIE =company
CE =it

• Poles [S-N] about French company [CIE] — in France it [CE] is *common knowledge* (7) =SCIENCE

CRU =vineyard

• *Little bit* of French vineyard [CRU] given to doctor [MB] (5) =CRUMB

DIT =said, it is said

• It is said in Lyons [DIT] to [TO] end *the same* (5) =DITTO
(Note the use of 'Lyons' to represent France. *See* Synonyms, Part 1:2.4)

EN =in

• *Take part* in French [EN] wager [GAGE] (6) =ENGAGE

ET =and

• English dance [BALL] and French [ET] *dance* (6) =BALLET

ETRE =to be

• After a month [DEC], I'm [IM] to be [ETRE] employed as *hand at Longchamps* (9) =DECIMETRE ('Hand' =4 inches =decimetre. Note the use of 'Longchamps' to represent France. *See* Synonyms, Part 1:2.4)

GRAND =big
EST =is

• In France, big [GRAND] is [EST] *biggest* (8) =GRANDEST

ICI =here

• Here abroad [ICI] about [RE] to turn [=ER] *a great deal colder* (5) =ICIER

JE =I

• *Vehicle* — French I [JE] record [EP] (4) =JEEP

MAI =May	• Month's abroad [MAI'S] that is [IE] spent with a *girl* (6) =MAISIE
MAL =bad	• Girl's [DIS] sickness from abroad [MAL] is *depressing* (6) =DISMAL
MER =sea	• A [A] bull [NEAT] in a foreign sea [M-ER] is *a killer* (3-5) =MAN-EATER
MOT =word, saying	• *Grave* saying from French [MOT] returns [=TOM] on British [B] (4) =TOMB
NEE =born (feminine)	• *Wants* to be born in French [NEE] Democrat's [D] society [S] (5) =NEEDS
NON =no	• Is able [CAN] to take no foreign [NON] *weapon* (6) =CANNON
NOUS =we	• We [HE and I =HEI] find French translation [NOUS] *atrocious* (7) =HEINOUS
NU =nude	• Wearing nothing [NU], an [AN] engineer [CE] in the *shade* (6) =NUANCE
NUIT =night	• *Annual payment* some [AN-Y] without a night in Paris [NUIT] (7) =ANNUITY (Note the use of 'Paris' to represent France. *See* Synonyms Part 1:2.4)
ONZE =eleven	• *Buddhist priest* put together black [B] Continental cricket team [ONZE] (5) =BONZE
OU =where	• *Suspicion* where French [OU] replaces English [E] in obligation [D(E)BT] (5) =DOUBT
PAIN =bread	• *Like indigestion* if crammed with French bread? (7) =PAINFUL
QUE =what	• What Parisian [QUE] students [LL] used to *suppress* (5) =QUELL
REINE =queen	• *Forename* of French Queen [REINE], possibly (5) =IRENE

145

ROI =king

• King of France [ROI] entered in [IN] race [T-T] — *we hear this in Church* (7) =INTROIT

SUR =on

• The French on [SUR] Everest, for example [MOUNT], *get to the top* (8) =SURMOUNT

TANT =so much

• *One choosing* to work [OP] so much abroad [TANT] (6) =OPTANT

TERRE =land

• *Flower beds* in average condition [PAR] with French soil [TERRE] (8) =PARTERRE

TRES =very

• *Intrusion* is a very French [TRES] predicament [PASS] (8) =TRESPASS

TU =you

• *Struggles* to get you abroad [TU] on ships [SS]; the [LES] end is foreign, too (7) =TUSSLES

VERT =green

• *Ward off* a [A] foreign colour [VERT] (5) =AVERT

VOUS =you

• Among you French [V-OUS], *he* would become energetic [(V)IGOR(OUS)] (4) =IGOR (Note the direct clue in the centre)

Occasionally you may find an abbreviation for a French word

• *Members of regiment* stop [BAN] retreat [D-EN], having surrounded the French king [SM] (8) =BANDSMEN (SM =Sa Majesté =His Majesty)

and sometimes the solution, rather than the clue, will be in French

• *Confidentially,* the moderate [(C)ENTRE] lack a leader [C] with common sense [NOUS] (5,4) =ENTRE NOUS

• It's liberally sanded *for tennis spectators* (6) =DEDANS (inside)

• *Former* Channel Island [CI] partner of Maskelyne [DEVANT] (2-6) =CI-DEVANT

- *Pontoon* no help in bridge (5-2-2) = VINGT-ET-UN (twenty-one)

- How rifle may be carried [PORTED] back [=DETROP] as *not necessary* (2,4) = DE TROP (superfluous)

- Ill feeling in the main (3,2,3) = MAL DE MER (seasickness)

Note that although 'the king' in French is *le roi,* the clue 'the French King' is more likely to mean 'the French' (LE) 'king' (R)

- <u>Bumf</u> confused [=FUMB] the French [LE] king [R], *a maladroit type* (7) = FUMBLER

see Articles, Part 2:17

while 'queen' in French may be used as a homophone

- Foreign monarch's [REINE] *rule* (5) = REIGN

'The French Connection' will probably mean ET = 'and', used to connect sentences

- *Outstanding* <u>men in</u> disguise [=MINEN] in 'The French Connection' [E-T] (7) = EMINENT

German
EIN = one

- Saint [ST] − one German [EIN] gives *beer-mug* (5) = STEIN

KAPUT = broken, finished (to indicate an anagram)

- Luger kaput? *Punishment* ensues (5) = GRUEL
(Note the direct clue in the centre)

MIT = with

- *Allow* through [PER] with a German word [MIT] (6) = PERMIT

NEIN = no

- *Merciful* hindrance [LE-T] holding up German veto [NEIN = NIEN] (7) = LENIENT (down clue)

UND = and

- British firm [BL] and German [UND] queen [ER] *flounder about* (7) = BLUNDER

Irish
CRATUR = creature

- Dog [C-UR] grabbing another animal [RAT] is an *Irish beast* (6) = CRATUR

PRATIE =potato

- Blab [PRAT-E] about one [I] *vegetable in Cork* (6) =PRATIE (Note the use of Cork to represent Ireland. *See* Synonyms, Part 1:2.4)

Italian
BAMBINO =child

- *A little Italian* fawn [BAMBI] number [NO] (7) =BAMBINO

CONTADINO =peasant

- *Italian peasant* has a [A] racket [DIN] in Portuguese money [CONT-O] (9) =CONTADINO

MONSIGNORE
=an ecclesiastical title

- *Battle* for foreign title [MONS(IGNORE)] — ignore [IGNORE] going (4) =MONS

Latin
AB INITIO =from the beginning

- *From the first,* sailor [AB] in [IN] it [IT] I [I] get a ring [O] (2,6) =AB INITIO

CUM =with

- *Lying* about [RE] with Roman [CUM] criminal connection [BENT] (9) =RECUMBENT

DEUS =god

- *Entreated* Roman god [DEUS] to return (4) =SUED

GENS =tribe

- *Group of ancient families* non-U in class [GEN(U)S] (4) =GENS

HIC =this

- *Sound of drinker* from this Roman [HIC] vessel [CUP] (6) =HICCUP

IBIDEM =in the same place

- I [I] didn't pass [BID] them [EM] *in the same place* (6) =IBIDEM

IDEM =the same

- Same Roman [IDEM] content in heroic work [EP-IC] seems to be *prevalent* (8) =EPIDEMIC

LEX =law

- <u>Era</u> in confusion [=A-ER] about Roman law [LEX] and [AND] *Macedonian king* (9) =ALEXANDER

SED =but

- *Exercised* but once [SED] after university [U] (4) =USED (For the use of 'once' =former, in this case Roman, times see Old Words, Part 1:19)

QED (*quod erat demonstrandum*) =which was to be proved

- 'Quite elementary' displayed initially [Q.E.D.] as *coda to the proof* (4,4,13)=QUOD ERAT DEMONSTRANDUM

Scots
ANE =one

- *Tree* — require flat [PLAT] one in the Highlands [ANE] (7)=PLATANE

AIN =own

- Ian's *own*? (3)=AIN

AWA =away

- Get off [AWA], man [KEN]. *Come to!* (6)=AWAKEN

CLEUCH =valley

- Beside river [R] in the Highland valley [CLE-UCH], I'd [I] have a [A] *Greek style allotment* (9)=CLERUCHIA

CRAIG =cliff

- First bit of climbing [C] equipment [R-IG] to get a grip on a [A] *Scottish cliff* (5)=CRAIG

DEIL =devil

- Scot's demon [DE-IL] will hold up military movement [OPS=SPO] to *go on the rampage* (7)=DESPOIL (down clue)

JO =sweetheart

- One close to Scot's [JO] way of working [modus operandi=MO] with a *cow* (4)=JOMO

LUM =chimney

- *Sapwood* to incinerate [BURN] in a [A] chimney for Jock [L-UM] (8)=ALBURNUM
(Note the use of 'Jock' to represent Scotland. *See* Synonyms, Part 1:2.4)

ORRA =casual

- Sailor [AB] at Leith casual [ORRA] lifting *weight from Spain* (6)=ARROBA (down clue)
(Note the use of 'Leith' to represent Scotland. *See* Synonyms, Part 1:2.4)

PANEL =accused person
- *Put on jury,* see me [ME] upset [=EM] over the accused in Scotland (7) =EMPANEL (down clue)

PROO =a call to cattle
- A hybrid is <u>poor</u> *Scots call to cattle* (4) =PROO

QUINE =girl
- English [E] girl of Scotland [QUINE] or *of the shires* (6) =EQUINE

RIT =score, scratch
- Celtic score [R-IT], letting nothing [O] in — *a great success* (4) =RIOT (Note the use of 'Celtic' to represent Scotland. *See* Synonyms, Part 1:2.4)

SIST =stay, stop
- *Maintain* during [IN] stay in Scotland [SIST] (6) =INSIST

SOWANS =dish from oat husks
- *To Scots, jellied husks* are colourless [WAN], limited in appeal [SO-S] (6) =SOWANS

SPULYE =plunder
- Leaders of <u>s</u>ome [S] <u>p</u>easant [P] <u>u</u>prising [U] <u>l</u>atch [L] on to the old [YE] *Scottish plunder* (6) =SPULYE

TRON =marketplace
- *Marketplace up North* that's right [R] in fashion [T-ON] (4) =TRON

TAISH =apparition
- Somehow <u>it has</u> to appear before death, says Mac (5) =TAISH

WEAN =child
- The Scottish infant put on the bottle (4) =WEAN

South African
LAER =laager =fortification
- What's healthy [BONNY] about [C] blacks [BB] penetrating Boer defence [LA-ER]? *Clots in it are soured* (12) =BONNYCLABBER

SJAMBOK =whip
- *Whip* son [S], squeeze [JAM] boy [B], right [OK]? (7) =SJAMBOK

Spanish
ADIOS =goodbye
- *A farewell* gets <u>Ida so</u> upset (5) =ADIOS

GUERRA =war

- Sick [ILL] in Spanish war [GUERR-A]? This is *irregular* (9) =GUERRILLA

HOMBRE =man

- Spaniard [(H)OMBRE] loses his head [H] at *cards* (5) =OMBRE

OLE =exclamation of approval

- The usual [PAR] cry of delight [OLE] on *release* (6) =PAROLE

QUE =that, what

- *Weaver bird* that in Spain [QUE] is seen on pasture [LEA] (6) =QUELEA

Combinations
French/South African

- Part of Anfield [KOP] I discovered abroad [Fr. 'I' =JE] by *the hill* (5) =KOPJE

French/German

- *Board* of Franco-German agreement ['yes' =Fr. OUI, Ger. JA] (5) =OUIJA

Dialect
Dialects are not, of course, foreign languages but they may be unfamiliar to some ears. A few examples are given below:

CHE =I

- Once in the West of England I [CHE] could have days [DD] beside a [A] river [R] *gorge* (7) =CHEDDAR

ENOW =presently

- Weak [W] individual [ONE] will bounce back, *presently* (4) =ENOW

STITCH =ridge of land

- *Local ridge of land* [STITCH] about [RE] to be turned over [=ER] for *sewer* (8) =STITCHER

TATH =dung

- Covered with *i/t* at h/ome, roses will thrive (4) =TATH (Note the direct clue in the centre)

UN =one

- *On nail, everybody* [AL-L] *carries one* [UN] — universal [U], if you look round (6) =LUNULA

One particular form of dialect, Cockney rhyming slang, is referred to in Rhymes, Part 1:7.

23

NUMBERS

Numbers, often referred to as figures in clues, feature prominently in many crosswords, and Roman numerals, being written as letters, are particularly useful to the compiler. A list of these, together with other numbers, is given in A Compiler's Vocabulary, Appendix 4.

If you were asked to write down 'one hundred' as a Roman numeral, you would probably write C; when the compiler refers to 'one hundred', he probably means it quite literally as 'one' (I) 'hundred' (C) and you should write IC, although IC also means 99 and functions as a homophone (IC=I see), which is often used as a word-ending (*see* Homophones, Part 1:6).

Pointers: few, figure, numeral, number, many, some, etc.

Most examples use **Roman numerals** combined with **derived words**

by **addition**	• A hundred [C] not concealed [OVERT] *hidden* (6) =COVERT
by **subtraction**	• Four [IV] leaving the development [NEGAT(IV)E] will *have a nullifying effect* (6) =NEGATE
by **reversal**	• *Unemotional* when 501 [DI] items for sale [LOTS] are put up (6) =STOLID (down clue)
by **inclusion**	• Swimmer [E-EL] about ninety [XC] will *be superior* (5) =EXCEL
by **substitution**	• Free [RID] to replace fifty [L] in the city of Paris [I(L)IUM] for *this metal* (7) =IRIDIUM (Note that 'city of Paris' =Paris's city =Troy =ILIUM)

or with **anagrams**

while others have solutions composed entirely of Roman numerals

Some clues use Roman numerals to indicate a number which gives not the solution direct but a means of arriving at it

while others have to be translated into their Arabic equivalents before being included in the solution

and some require the opposite translation

Clues such as 'hundreds', 'number', 'figure' or 'many'

• <u>Rum</u> three-D [III, D] analysis of *this element* (7) =IRIDIUM

• *Sort of dignitary* is 104 [CIV], I see [IC] (5) =CIVIC

• Three figures [C, I, D] for *leader* (3) =CID

• *Very angry* at getting fifty [L] for say [=FOUR =IV], I [I] should get five hundred [D] (5) =LIVID

• MCC XI needing another four to time *this historic declaration* (5,5) =MAGNA CARTA (MCC =1200 plus XI =11 plus 4 =1215, the date of Magna Carta)

• *Part of county* represented by its leader [C] (7) =HUNDRED

• 1200-200 (10) =MARYLEBONE (1200 =MCC =Marylebone Cricket Club)

• *It's* almost standard [STOC(K)] on rapacious fellow [KI-TE] wanting to hold up X [TEN =NET] (11) =STOCKINETTE (down clue)

• *Christian* X [IO] taken in by doctor [D-R], *designing* (4) =DIOR

• *Host* in midsummer [MM] (9) =THOUSANDS

• An 'ell [L] of an *age* (5) =FIFTY

• Doublecross [X, X] representative of *so many* (6) =TWENTY

• *Sham* 1000-to-1 [M, I] shot doubled [=MI, MI] and then some [C] (5) =MIMIC

• *Saw* half-a-dozen [VI] sheep [EWE], then hundreds [D] (6) =VIEWED

often indicate the use of one of the larger Roman numerals

- *Shuts down* on a number [CL] of current units [AMPS] (6) = CLAMPS

- Not getting a false [=REAL] figure [M] for *the region* (5) = REALM

- *Just average* and not [NOR] many [M] (4) = NORM

whereas 'several', 'some', etc. often refer to the smaller Roman numerals

- Several [V] diamonds [ICE] show a *blemish* (4) = VICE

- Chatters [PR-ATES] about some [IV] *soldiers* (8) = PRIVATES

sometimes two at once

- *Minor* gets four [IV] or six [VI] in test [TR-I-AL] (7) = TRIVIAL

CL normally means 150

- One hundred and fifty [CL] animals [ASSES] in these *biological divisions* (7) = CLASSES

but can also mean 'about fifty'

- *Potato stores* have about [C] fifty [L] electrical units [AMPS] (6) = CLAMPS

C can be 'sea' or 'see'

- Speed of light [C]? They say [=SEA] fifty [L]. *Close!* (4) = SEAL

- See [C] the old people [AGED] *in prison* (5) = CAGED

and CC can be 'seas' or 'sees'

- Cubic centimetres briefly [CC] — *a lot of water* (4) = SEAS

- *Looks at* the county cricket club [CCC] (4) = SEES

or 'two hundred'

- *Bird* needs 200 [CC], OK [OK]? (4) = COCK

Ordinary (i.e. Arabic) **numbers** can be used in the same way as Roman numerals but only I, IO and II can be substituted for 1, 10 and 11

- Gold [OR] wise men [MAGI] returned [=IGAM], one [I] concludes, in *Japanese art* (7) = ORIGAMI

- Ready [PAT] at ten [IO] in *court* (5) = PATIO

- *Bones* of king [R] over 1978 years ago [ADII] (5) = RADII (down clue)

In most cases, ordinary numbers in clues are combined with **derived words**

by addition
to derived words

- *Floor* meant for particular apartment [FLAT 10] (7)=FLATTEN
- Pair [TWO] stage [STEP] *dance* (3-4)=TWO-STEP

or to selected letters

- *Tie* one [UNIT] rope's end [E] (5)=UNITE

by subtraction

- *Personalities* – one [I] missing from flight [STA(I)RS] (5)=STARS

by reversal

- Crushing defeat [TEN-NIL] setback for *bird* (6)=LINNET

or by **inclusion**
of a derived word in a number

- *Means to see* the crew [E-IGHT] about an agreement [YES] (8)=EYESIGHT
- Muscovite [MICA] in one-goal result [I, NI-L] is *hostile* (8)=INIMICAL

of a number in a derived word

- Soccer authority's [FAS] one short of a team [XI-I=TEN] – Ed's [ED] *tied up* (8)=FASTENED

or with **anagrams**

- Novel dame [=ADEM] in one [AC-E] *university* (7)=ACADEME
- *Character found in Genesis,* chapter [CH] one? Wrong (5)=ENOCH

They can also appear as **homophones**

- Oxford and Cambridge [EIGHT], we hear [=AIT], *pass it during the Boat Race* (3)=AIT

In many cases, indirect clues combine to form a number in the solution

- *Number* of Poles [S-N] getting round a woman [EVE] (5)=SEVEN

• *A period* that could be described as OE [NAUGHT E], say [=NAUGHTY] (8)=NINETIES

but sometimes numbers in the clue combine to form a solution which is not a number

• One [I] in a hundred thousand [LA-C] *of the people* (4)=LAIC

• No. 200 got [NO, TWO HUNDRED GOT] mislaid *completely* (4,2,3,6)=DOWN TO THE GROUND

The use of 'some', 'figure' or 'number' implies the use of a numeral

• Some [TEN] haven't finished training [DRIL(L)] *for assisting climbing* (7)=TENDRIL (down clue)

• *Revolutionary* figure [NINE] taken up [=ENIN] by student [L] (5)=LENIN (down clue)

• A cat [REX] lives [IS] recurrently but *this counts for less than his number* (5)=SIXER (Six is 'less than' nine lives)

although 'figure' may imply 'statue'

• Figure [STATU-E] out the letter [T] of the *law* (7)=STATUTE

'shape'

• *Ice figures* (8)=DIAMONDS

or 'figure of speech'

• *Figure* of fifty [L] I [I] carry [TOTE] to start of s̲um [S] (7)=LITOTES

and 'large number' may not be a numeral at all

• *Cuckoo*'s born [B] wanting a large number [ARMY] (5)=BARMY

'Number one' is usually abbreviated to No. 1 (NOI), often reversed as the word ending -ION

• No single [NOI] story [TALE] sent up causes such *high spirits* (7)=ELATION (down clue)

although it can also refer to the first mate on a ship

• *Adam or Eve?* (6,3)=NUMBER ONE

whereas 'I' can be ONE

• Act [DO] I [ONE] for *a novel family* (5)=DOONE

'single' can be ONE

- *Heavy blow* for single [ONE] king [R] (4) =ONER

'one' can be I or A or ACE

- *Even* one [I] in design [PLA-N] (5) =PLAIN

- One [A] member [MP] to the French [LE] is *sufficient* (5) =AMPLE

- *Resist* loud [F] one [ACE] (4) =FACE

and 'ace' can mean 'winner' or 'expert'

- *White* is soft [P] drink [ALE] and loud [F] winner [ACE] (8) =PALEFACE

- *Expert* needing only one shot (3) =ACE

Where 'one' is used in 'everyone' it usually means ALL or 'anybody'

- *Superficial* display [SH-OW] includes everyone [ALL] (7) =SHALLOW

- *Liable* to be a bit prim [PR(IM)] with anybody [ONE] (5) =PRONE

but can sometimes mean EACH

- *Instructor* for everyone [EACH] in short school period [T-ER(M)] (7) =TEACHER

which may be abbreviated to EA

- Everyone [EA] is wearing plain [OVER-T] *stuff* (7) =OVEREAT

Some clues are phrased so that 'one' appears to mean 'oneself' when it really means 'a'

- Fighter [(B)OXER] guillotined makes one *jump* (4) =OXER

The possessive 'one's' =IS

- One's [IS] country [LAND] is *surrounded by sea* (6) =ISLAND

A zero (O) =nil, no, nothing, nought, ought

- Sort out target zero [O] and *finish off* (7) =GAROTTE

- *Spoke like Brutus,* not qualifying for VAT? (6) =ORATED (No VAT =zero-rated)

- No [NIL] return [=LIN] to eastern [E] time [AGE] for *ancestry* (7) =LINEAGE

• Silent God? (4)=ODIN

• *Suppose* there is nothing |O| long [PINE] (5)=OPINE

• Countryman [HOB] will come to nought |O| — the *tramp* (4)=HOBO

• *Simple* pub [INN] ought [O] to get money [CENT] (8)=INNOCENT

or, in tennis, LOVE

• The dog [CUR] I [I] love |O| is *a rare item* (5)=CURIO

• *Lose heart* and agree with [FALL IN] nothing [LOVE] (4,2,4)=FALL IN LOVE

• *Introduce* one [I] to good man [ST] in love [N-IL] (6)=INSTIL

although 'love' can have other meanings

• Possibly <u>ready</u> for *'love'* (5)=DEARY

In cricket, O means 'no score', 'duck'

• Duck [O] a [A] half-sister [SIS(TER)] in *waterhole* (5)=OASIS

and a batsman who gets two ducks is said to 'get a pair of spectacles'

• Wicked sister [REGAN] wears spectacles [O-O] *for cooking with* (7)=OREGANO

Anything which has 'nothing in it' or which is 'hollow', 'vacant' or 'empty' will contain O

• *Jump* dam [B-UND] with nothing [O] in it (5)=BOUND

• *Measure* the pole [RO-D] which is hollow [O] inside (5)=ROOD

• *Due* to getting a vacancy [O], fly [WING] (5)=OWING

• *Weight* of an empty [O] vegetable-shell [PO-D] (4)=POOD

Since O=love, a word from which O is eliminated will be 'loveless' or 'without love'

see Selected Letters, Part 1:4

For other uses of O=nothing

see The Use of 'Without' and 'Within', Part 2:13

For the many other meanings of O

see A Compiler's Alphabet, Appendix 3

Ordinal numbers as well as cardinal numbers appear in clues, with 'first' frequently appearing as -IST, a word ending, or as NO1 (No.1)

- *Material* for the fourteenth verse (5)=LINEN
  (Line N; N=14th letter)

- *Affected* twice as much as Daisy's admirer (5)=CRAZY
  (He was 'half-crazy')

- *Health-worker* joining the [THE] strike [RAP] first [IST] (9)=THERAPIST

- The first [NO1] man [TOM] backs [=MOT, ION] the *proposal* (6)=MOTION

and there are some cases where multiplication is involved

- Two-by-two [=FOUR] — *very firm and solid* (4-6)=FOUR-SQUARE
  (Four=square of two)

- *Increases* for members of the choir (7)=TREBLES

- Relating to [OF] a sort of table [TEN TIMES]? *Frequently in the past* (10)=OFTENTIMES

and, sometimes, division

- 1/100 [ON-E divided by C] *formerly* (4)=ONCE

Some cases use fractions in the clue

- *Number* one in a quarter [¼], for example (9)=NUMERATOR

- *Type size* is $^{22}/_{7}$ [PI], approximately [CA] (4)=PICA

- *Isolated* half of London [LON(DON)] city [ELY] (6)=LONELY

or in the solution

- *A fraction* behind medal winners (6)=FOURTH

- Henry [HAL] strong [F] in *part* (4)=HALF

- Not a full-size footballer (5-7)=THREE-QUARTER

but remember that 'quarters' can also mean 'directions'

- *A piece let in* — it [I-T] covers three quarters [NSE] (5)=INSET

see Abbreviations, Part 1:3

159

Percentages (decimal fractions) are sometimes used

- *He does an examination* getting 70% in hall [AUDITOR(IUM)] (7) = AUDITOR

- 60% crude [=CRU(DE)] *wine from this* (8) = VINEYARD

Occasionally, deliberate use is made of cross-references to other clue numbers

- What can a/il 1Ac/? *Part of hip-bone* (5) = ILIAC

- 10 to 1 on an *operatic slave* (4) = AIDA (In this case, 10 across was AID, so 10 to 1 = AID to A = AIDA)

- No 1Dn in formation *dance* (8) = CHACONNE (1 down in this case was CHANCE, giving <u>no chance</u> = CHACONNE)

- 8 . . . a few [SOME] stagger [REEL] at *dance* (9,4) = EIGHTSOME REEL (The clue number, 8, is incorporated in the solution)

- 20. Half [TEN] go bust [FOLD] *a number of times* (7) = TENFOLD (The clue number, 20, is used with 'half' to give TEN)

Groups of numbers may include

  2 bi-, bis, brace, couple, di-, duad, dual, duo, pair, twain

  3 ter-, tern, tri-, triad, trio

  4 quartet (-ett, -ette, -etto), tetrad

  5 quintet (-ett, -ette, -etto), pentad

  6 sestet (-ett, -ette) sextet (-ett, -ette)

- *Tropical plant* has to be twice [BI] cut [AX] back [=XA] (4) = BIXA

- Twice [BIS] reacting [=SIB] in anger [RI-LE] is *ludicrous* (7) = RISIBLE

- *Resembling some nobles* caught [C] in a double [DU-AL] bind (5) = DUCAL

- *So nice* to spend a couple of days [WEEK-END=WE] in the group [S-ET] (5) = SWEET

7 heptad, septet (-ett, -ette)

8 octet (-ett, -ette), ogdoad

9 nonet (-ette, -etto), ennead

10 decad

but 'double' in ancient Egyptian religion =KA

and can also imply a look-alike or alternative

Note that 'number' sometimes means the abbreviation NO.

or the indefinite number 'n'

and occasionally means 'that which numbs', e.g. 'anaesthetic' or 'knockout'

In the plural, 'Numbers' can refer to the Old Testament book

and numbers may refer to time on the clock

Number/word combinations often appear, the number in the clue requiring the associated word as the solution, or vice versa

1 Kelly's eye

• Sound attempt [TRY=TRI] — total [ADD=AD] *three* (5) =TRIAD

• *Get three* if you transpose [TR] one [I] class [SECT] (7) =TRISECT

• *Involving four* in the courtyard [QUAD]? Right [R] — riding [UP] with the French [LE] (9) =QUADRUPLE

• British [B] first-class hotel [RITZ] wants double [KA] *open carriage* (7) =BRITZKA

• Pantomime sweetheart's [COLUMBINE] double found in bed (9) =AQUILEGIA

• *Time* for writing number [NO] on [ON] the main movement [TIDE] (8) =NOONTIDE

• *Boat,* one famous for record runs [C-OE] loaded with a [A] great quantity [N] (5) =CANOE

• One [I] in the number [E-THER] — *one or the other* (6) =EITHER

• Back number (8) =EPIDURAL

• Count of ten, perhaps, for this *knockout* (6) =NUMBER

• *Figures* inscribed by Moses? (7) =NUMBERS

• *Be there* at [AT] the time [TEN] and the day [D] after (6) =ATTEND

• Kelly's eye unit (3) =ONE

2 Lily-white Boys • Exceptionally clean couple? (4-5,4) =LILY-WHITE BOYS

3 Blind Mice *see* Selected Letters, Part 1:4

Coins in the Fountain • Three found under water at Trevi, perhaps (5) =COINS

Fates: Atropos, Clotho, Lachesis • Undue delay [LACHES] is [IS] *one fate* (8) =LACHESIS

Furies: Alecto, Megaera, Tisiphone • *Fury* at being caught [CT] in a drink[ALE]-ring [O] (6) =ALECTO

Graces: Aglaia, Euphrosyne, Thalia • *Grace,* wi/th a lia/son, disguised (6) =THALIA

Harpies: Aello, Celaeno (or Podarge) Ocypete • *Harpy* in river [PO] raged tumultuously [=DARGE] (7) =PODARGE

Musketeers: Aramis, Athos, Porthos • *Third rifleman* aims badly [=A-MIS] about gunners [RA] (6) =ARAMIS

Rs in education • *Wrong* note [E] nothing [O] in basic education [RR-R] (5) =ERROR

Wise Men (Magi): Balthasar, Gaspar, Melchior • Graduate [MA] American [US] stands on each side of grand [G] *soothsayer* (5) =MAGUS

4 Estates of the Realm: clergy, commons, lords, press • Press forth, say [=FOURTH] (6) =ESTATE

Freedoms: fear, speech, want, worship • Oration [SPEECH], *one of four* (8) =FREEDOMS

5 Famous Five (Magnet comic) • Renowned [FAMOUS] victory [V =FIVE] recorded attractively in *this periodical* (6) =MAGNET

Pentateuch (first five books of the Old Testament): Genesis, Exodus, Leviticus, Numbers, Deuteronomy • Eugene's [GENE] little sister [SIS(TER)] is *leader of the First Five* (7) =GENESIS

Senses: hearing, sight, smell, taste, touch

• Incomplete t(e)a-set broken — *one of five* (5) =TASTE

Towns (Arnold Bennett's novels): Burslem, Hanley, Longton, Stoke, Tunstall

• Asiatic quarter of Hanley, perhaps (9) =CHINATOWN

6 Counties (of Northern Ireland): Antrim, Armagh, Down, Fermanagh, Londonderry, Tyrone

• A [AN] tidy [TRIM] *part of Northern Ireland* (6) =ANTRIM

over (cricket)

• Six [OVER] arrived [CAME] and *conquered* (8) =OVERCAME

six-footer (insect)

• Sort of soldier, a six-footer (3) =ANT

sixth sense (ESP)

• *Liveliness* of telepathic gift [ESP] right [R-T] outside one [I] (6) =ESPRIT

7 Deadly Sins: anger, covetousness, envy, greed, lust, pride, sloth

• Initially, North Vietnam [NV] is reported [=ENVY] to be *one of these* (6,4) =DEADLY SINS

Heptateuch (first seven books of the Old Testament): as the Pentateuch, plus Joshua and Judges

• *Trumpeter* who blew 'The Tumbling Walls' (6) =JOSHUA

Magnificent Seven (film)

• Superb [MAGNIFICENT] film *number* (5) =SEVEN

Sages: Bias, Chilon, Cleobulus, Periander, Pittacus, Solon, Thales

• Unfinished farewell [SO LON(G)] to *sage* (5) =SOLON

Seas: Antarctic, Arctic, North Atlantic, South Atlantic, Indian, North Pacific, South Pacific

• Musical ocean? (5,7) =SOUTH PACIFIC

Senses: as the five senses, plus speech and understanding
• One in seven delivers *oration* (6) = SPEECH

Stars (of Pleiades or Great Bear)
• *Ear* of Great Bear (6) = PLOUGH (For 'ear' *see* Old Words, Part 2:19)

Wonders of the World: Colossus of Rhodes, Hanging Gardens of Babylon, Mausoleum at Halicarnassus, Pharos (lighthouse) at Alexandria, Pyramids of Egypt, Statue of Zeus (by Phidias) at Olympia, Temple of Artemis at Ephesus
• *Babylon wonder* exhibiting [HANGING] layers [BEDS=GARDENS] (7,7) = HANGING GARDENS

year itch
• *Restlessness* after one under the eight? (5-4,4) = SEVEN-YEAR ITCH

8 crew
• *Cargo* of French [FR] crew [EIGHT] (7) = FREIGHT

figure of eight
• Number [FIGURE] of [OF] crew [EIGHT] make a *design on ice* (6,2,5) = FIGURE OF EIGHT

pieces of eight
• *Pieces of eight,* perhaps, or [OR=GOLD] money [COINS] (4,5) = GOLD COINS

9 days' wonder
• Does Stevie [WONDER], perhaps, stay *so long* (4,4) = NINE DAYS

lives of a cat
• *Attribute of cat* perhaps <u>enlivens</u> [=NINE L-VES] one [I] inside (4,5) = NINE LIVES

Muses: Calliope, Clio, Erato, Euterpe,
• Time [ERA] to [TO] *muse* (5) = ERATO

Melpomene, Polyhymnia, Terpsichore, Thalia, Urania
• One of nine [MUSE] retired [in BE-D] *stupefied* (7) = BEMUSED

one over the eight	• Bird [PIE] watched [EYED] *one over the eight* (3-4) =PIE-EYED
points of the law	• A number of points of law (4) =NINE

10 Commandments
• Grown-up [ADULT] queen [ER], young leader [Y], forbidden to commit *this* (8) =ADULTERY

Downing Street
• Address given by PM? (6,3) =NUMBER TEN

Green Bottles
• *Number* of new [GREEN] wine containers [BOTTLES] (3) =TEN

11 legs (Bingo)
• *Members* of bingo game (4) =LEGS

side/team (FA)
• XI × XI − *close together* (4,2,4) =SIDE BY SIDE

12 Apostles: Andrew, Peter (also called Simon Peter), James the Great, John, Philip, Bartholomew (also called Nathanael), Matthew (Levi), Thomas (doubting Thomas), James the Less, Judas (also called Thaddeus, brother of James), Judas Iscariot (replaced by Matthias), Simon Zelotes
• *One of twelve* used to prison [STIR] (7,5) =APOSTLE SPOON

Days of Christmas: 1 partridge, 2 turtle doves, 3 French hens, 4 calling birds, 5 gold rings, 6 geese, 7 swans, 8 milkmaids, 9 ladies, 10 lords, 11 pipers, 12 drummers
• One of seven given for a Christmas present (4) =SWAN

EEC members: Belgium, Denmark, France, Great Britain, Greece, Ireland, Italy, Luxembourg, Netherlands, Portugal, Spain, West Germany

• *Member of community* in south-western [SW] garden [EDEN] (6)=SWEDEN

Glorious Twelfth (12th August)

• Shot on the 12th [GROUSE] day [D] and *moaned* (7)=GROUSED

signs of the Zodiac: Aquarius, Aries, Cancer, Capricorn, Gemini, Leo, Libra, Pisces, Sagittarius, Scorpio, Taurus, Virgo

• *Sign* in small capitals [SC] found in pies [PI-ES] (6)=PISCES

13 unlucky

• Cross [X] two [I, I] with one [I] — *unfortunate number* (8)=THIRTEEN

15 side/team (RU)

• *Team* leaders of French international forum take early evening nap (7)=FIFTEEN

18 majority

• Age of the Cross? (8)=EIGHTEEN

19 nineteenth hole

• Score [20] one under [20-1=19] *the bar, ordinarily* (8)=NINETEEN

20 20-20 vision

• Score twice [20-20] — what *good vision!* (6-6)=TWENTY-TWENTY

22 Catch 22

• *Unexpected difficulty this,* with two XI's [=22] causing absurd situation (5)=CATCH

27 books in the New Testament

• American [US] following bird [TIT] — only *one of twenty-seven* (5)=TITUS

39 books in the Old Testament

• *Work* for one in thirty-nine (3)=JOB

Steps (John Buchan's novel)

• The novel 39? (5)=STEPS

40 Thieves

- *Robbers* for tea, say [=FORTY]
  (7) =THIEVES

50 States of America

for list *see* A Compiler's
Vocabulary, Appendix 4. *See also*
Abbreviations, Part 1:3

70 age of man

- *Allotted span* of Sunday [S] sports
  meeting [EVENT] unknown [Y]
  (7) =SEVENTY

    speed limit

- Even [EVEN] in the enclosure
  [S-TY] there's a *speed limit*
  (7) =SEVENTY

100 century/ton

- *A hundred* sent you, they say
  [=CENT U], lines [RY]
  (7) =CENTURY

- *Diamond, perhaps* for a hundred
  [TON] in the Home Counties [S-E]
  (5) =STONE

600 Light Brigade/Balaclava

- *At Lords,* they outnumber the
  Light Brigade by two to one
  [600×2 =1200 =MCC]
  (10,7,4) =MARYLEBONE
  CRICKET CLUB

- *Type of helmet* worn by six
  hundred (9) =BALACLAVA

24

PUNCTUATION

The **possessive apostrophe** will not, of course, appear in the solution. Where it appears in the clue, it is sometimes treated in the normal way

- Foreigner's wife [FRAU] and daughter [D] together in *crime* (5)=FRAUD
- *Spenser's shady retreat,* the lady's [HER] place to tipple [BAR] (6)=HERBAR
- *Relation* finds reference to Mozart's work [K] in [IN] text [MS] returned [=SM] with article [AN] (7)=KINSMAN

though, quite often, the apostrophe is ignored but the following 's' is retained

- Poor <u>Joan's</u> *hero* (5)=JONAS
- <u>See term's</u> work for *university course* (8)=SEMESTER
- *Gambolled* with Diana's [DIS] unwanted [DE TROP] backing [=PORTED] (9)=DISPORTED

or both are ignored

- Rifle's [GUN] bullet [SHOT] *range* (7)=GUNSHOT
- Poor <u>goop Harry</u>'s *description of mountains* (9)=OROGRAPHY
- *Gilbertian peer*'s opportunity [CHANCE] to bring list [ROLL] back [=LLOR] (10)=CHANCELLOR

The alternative possessive form, 'of' or 'belonging to',

- *Husband* of Eva [EVAS] returns (4)=SAVE

may be given in the clue, requiring the use of the apostrophe S but with no apostrophe in the solution

- *Hairy* refuge [HAVEN] belonging to international organisation [UN'S] (8) = UNSHAVEN

and an apostrophe in the clue may require 'of' in the solution

- Fence's *crime* (7) = OFFENCE
- River's *refuse* (5) = OFFAL

As an alternative to the apostrophe, one can use a possessive adjective (e.g. Norway's trees = Norwegian trees) and this construction is sometimes required in the solution where the apostrophe appears in the clue

- *Emperor's* taking of southern [S] region [AREA] in French city [CAE-N] (9) = CAESAREAN
- *Blooms'* origins <u>f</u>rom [F] <u>L</u>iberia [L] it is said [ORAL] (6) = FLORAL
- *Philosopher's* energy [E] in being [HUM-AN] (6) = HUMEAN

The sound of the possessive apostrophe may indicate a homophone

- Hawthorn blossom's [MAYS] is said to be fit for *animal feed* (5) = MAIZE

Note that 'the lady's' is usually translated as HER, even if the apostrophe is one of omission rather than possession

- The lady's [HER] got most of the rent [REN(T)] among the *Germans* (6) = HERREN

but 'her' may also be treated as a given word

- Bird [C-OOT] conceals her [HER] *smoke* (7) = CHEROOT

The **apostrophe of omission** also will not appear in the solution and where it appears in the clue it may be treated in the normal way

- There's a little girl [DI] in the boat [PUN-T], *he's learned* (6) = PUNDIT
- *She* doesn't get top-grade [B] for bringing an instrument [LYRE] back [=ERYL] (5) = BERYL
- <u>N</u>eil's first [N] to receive good reception [OVATION] — that's *something new* (8) = NOVATION

though, quite often, the apostrophes are ignored but the letters are retained

- A [A] prophet [MOS(ES)] 'e's [ES] abandoned for *another* (4) = AMOS

• Pistol's [GUNS] turning up [=SNUG] for *another Shakespearean role* (4)=SNUG (down clue)

• I'm [IM] one under treatment [PATIENT], *showing irritability* (9)=IMPATIENT

or both are ignored

• He's back [=E-H], Bill's [AC] in, *everyone* (4)=EACH

• To a professor [PROF], it's [IT] *gain* (6)=PROFIT

• Bird's [TIT] on horseback [UP] to *canter* (5)=TITUP

In other cases, the apostrophe is used to eliminate unwanted letters in the clue

• After a breather [LUNG], 'e [(H)E] makes a *thrust* (5)=LUNGE

• Fellow [MAN] challengin' [DARIN(G)] *bureaucrat* (8)=MANDARIN

• *The bullet* for Jack's first [J] 'elicopter crash (10)=PROJECTILE

in others, it needs to be inferred to obtain the right derived word for the solution (*see also* Abbreviations, Part 1:3)

• *Stay* in Lincoln [AB-E], I would [I'D=ID] (5)=ABIDE

• *Flower* I have [I'VE=IVE] planted between two more [R-R] (5)=RIVER

• Are [ARE] right [R] she is [SHE'S=SHE-S] outside with the *farm-workers* (8)=SHEARERS

• I [I] cannot [CAN'T=CANT] drink [AL-E] outside *in Spain* (8)=ALICANTE

and, in others, the apostrophised word needs to be expanded to the full expression

• *Stomach ache* — it's [IT IS] following depression [COL] (7)=COLITIS

Note that the compiler often makes no distinction and may use the apostrophe of omission as if it were the possessive

- *Joseph's home,* <u>Maria! Heat</u> goulash (9) =ARIMATHEA

Quotation marks sometimes indicate homophones

- 'Hang on' [WAIT], you say, with some *importance* (6) =WEIGHT

- Sounds like 'apprehend' [SEIZE] but it 'apprehends' (4) =SEES

and are normally used for direct quotations

- '. . . as false as dicers' . . .' (Hamlet) (5) =OATHS

but, more often than not, they are misleading, frequently disguising anagrams

- 'Extremely <u>valuable</u>' [VE], <u>he said,</u> 'curiously *sticky*' (8) =ADHESIVE

- *Sings* out '<u>Oscar</u> [=CARO-S] is about fifty [L]' (6) =CAROLS

- The reference is to a man [AL] 'a <u>soul in</u> torment [=LUSION]' (8) =ALLUSION

and other forms of clue

- Everyone [A-LL] is about to [TO] read *'Coral Island'* (5) =ATOLL

- *'It's very cold',* you sing [HUM]. 'Get inside, silly man [IN-ANE]' (8) =INHUMANE

- Give 'Love [O] Divine [DD]' a second [S] *chance* (4) =ODDS

Even where the quotation marks do indicate a homophone, they can be misleading

- Say 'Stop running round the room' (6) =FRIEZE
  (You might expect the five words in quotes to be read as one sentence. Read as: Say 'Stop!' [FREEZE] plus 'running round the room')

The **question mark** is usually a pointer to an opposite/ negative, a double meaning or a pun

- A handsome sum? (4,6) =FAIR AMOUNT

- Nice surroundings? (7) =RIVIERA

- Underpinned?
  (3,6)=ONE-LEGGED

- Sub-aqua clothing?
  (9)=UNDERWEAR

but, just as often, it is misleading

- Wreckage from reef? Try *searching persistently*
  (7)=FERRETY
  (The ? and separation into two sentences disguise the anagram)

- One island [MAN]? Why [WHY], I hear [=Y], it's *a great number*
  (4)=MANY
  (The ? and separation into two sentences disguise addition)

The **hyphen** can make a considerable difference to a clue

- Have not [NOT] indeed [DE-ED] *signified* (7)=DENOTED

- Have-not, we hear [LACKER], in *Japan* (7)=LACQUER

but the compiler will happily ignore this if it makes his task easier and yours more difficult

- Get up for charlady?
  (3-4)=TEA-GOWN
  ('Get-up' would have made the solution easier)

- One-nil away, Liverpool's transferred *too many people*
  (9)=OVERSPILL
  (The hyphen disguises the real meaning of 'one nil' [i.e. one of the Os] taken away from 'Liverpo(o)ls', which gives the anagram OVERSPILL)

- Something like a horse-shoe
  (4)=MULE
  (Not 'like a horse-shoe' but 'like a horse' =MULE which is also a form of shoe)

- Number caught up in tree-climbing *exercise* (5)=EXERT (down clue)
  (Not 'tree-climbing' but 'number' [X] in 'tree climbing' [=E-ERT])

• Mince-pies a *brown colour*
(5) =SEPIA
(Not 'mince-pies'; 'mince' is a
pointer to the anagram of <u>pies a</u>)

• One of those things that are
sometimes recovered before they
are lost (8) =UMBRELLA
(Impossible? Not if you read 'recovered' instead of 'recovered')

• *Heart*-broken uncle, Uncle Sam
(7) =NUCLEUS
(Not 'heart-broken' but broken
<u>uncle</u> [=NUCLE] with US)

Accents, whether in the clue or the solution, are ignored

• City [EC] hiding place [LAIR] for
cake (6) =ECLAIR (Fr. éclair)

• *Entrée* of little piece [ORT] broken
[=TRO] in bringing in [IN-DUCTION]
(12) =INTRODUCTION

Brackets are sometimes used to mislead

• *Sleeveless coat* in army [TA]
(Shakespeare) [BARD]
(6) =TABARD
(The brackets lead one to think
the clue is a quotation when it is
not)

Other punctuation marks can make a considerable difference to phrasing and hence to the meaning of the clue

see Phrasing, Part 2:25

Moral: assume that punctuation is designed to mislead rather than to help; ignore the given punctuation and repunctuate as necessary.

25

PHRASING AND PRONUNCIATION

Some words, particularly adjective/noun and noun/noun combinations, go together so naturally that it is easy to overlook the fact that,
in a clue, they are often intended to be treated as completely separate
words:

- **Head I had gift-wrapped (9)**
  One naturally reads 'gift-wrapped' as one descriptive phrase; read
  as '*head* — gift [PRES-ENT] — wrapped round I had [ID]' to give
  PRESIDENT (=head)

- **Southern Irish lake or bog (6)**
  No use looking for the name of a lake in Southern Ireland; read as
  'southern [S] — Irish lake [LOUGH]' to give SLOUGH (=bog)

- **Lowdown woman in Switzerland (6)**
  Do not search for a word meaning 'a Swiss harlot'; read as
  'lowdown [GEN] — woman [EVA]' to get GENEVA

- **Famous Venetian painter will do this (4)**
  Not 'famous Venetian painter' nor even 'Venetian painter'; read as
  'famous Venetian [Othello=MOOR] — painter will do this' to get
  MOOR (painter =rope used to tie up [moor] a boat)

- **Wine for drinking haunts an accountant (6)**
  Not 'wine for drinking'; read as '*wine*-drinking haunts [BARS] — an
  accountant [AC]' to give BARSAC (=wine)

- **Grand Canyon, the heart of bucolic America (8)**
  Grand Canyon must surely be read together? Not so; read as
  '*grand* — canyon [GORGE] — the heart of bucolic [O] — America
  [US]' to give GORGEOUS (=grand)

- **Set off outside, free to walk (6)**
  Not 'set off' nor 'free to walk'; read as 'set off [=ST-E] written
  outside free [RID]' to give STRIDE (=walk)

- **No, no. Not having sense, he's a fool (4)**
  Read as '(no)t with no 'no' [T] — sense [WIT]' giving TWIT (=fool)

- **Gains this country eastern decoration from Japan (7)**
  Not an 'eastern decoration'; read as 'gains [NETS] — this country [UK] — eastern [E] — *decoration from Japan*' to give NETSUKE

- **Go upriver in lightweight material (7)** (down clue)
  Neither 'upriver' nor 'lightweight'; read as 'go [GO] up [=OG] — river [R] — in light weight [GR-AM]' to give GROGRAM (=material)

- **A cough-mixture up in Argentina (6)**
  Not 'cough-mixture' but a mixture (anagram) of '<u>a cough</u>' to give GAUCHO, who is 'up' (=riding) 'in Argentina'

- **A Frenchman, without character and lacking education (10)**
  No 'Frenchman' here. Read as 'a French [UN] man [ED] without (=outside) character [LETTER]' to give UNLETTERED

- **E.g. Buckingham <u>Palace men</u> in revolution (5,4)**
  The anagram gives the PLACE NAME, Buckingham

Very occasionally, the compiler may indicate that the phrasing is not to be taken literally, as in

- **Blackwood taken apart** [BLACK WOOD]? **It's very hard (5)**=EBONY
  Here you are invited to separate 'blackwood' into two parts

- **Speed well, in a word** [=SPEEDWELL], **the saint of the bullring (8)**=VERONICA
  Here you are invited to add 'speed' and 'well' together to get VERONICA which is not only the name of the Speedwell genus of plants and the name of the patron saint of the bullring, but also the name of a manoeuvre used by a bullfighter

- **Join a shy** [=ASHY] **motion picture** [CINE] **artist** [RA] **on the line** [RY] **(8)**=CINERARY
  Here you are invited to join A and SHY to get ASHY =CINERARY

Sometimes the solution will contain the same letters, in the same order, as the words derived from the clue but split up in a different way to form a new phrase:

- Male [HE] sheep [TUP] obviously *agitated* (3-2) =HET-UP

- Adores [LOVES] Mr Right [TORY]. That's *novel* (4-5) =LOVE-STORY

- Numb [DEADEN] daughter [D] *with no prospects for promotion* (4-3)=DEAD-END

- Deals competently with [COPES] sound [TONE] *finishing touch* (4-5)=COPE-STONE

- *Put back in office* to control [REIN] government [STATE] (9)=REINSTATE

- *Aged relative* showing dreadful <u>rage</u> [=GREA] over a jibe [TAUNT] (5-4)=GREAT-AUNT

- *Slip* provides the least true [FALSEST] record [EP] (5,4)=FALSE STEP

- Confessing to foolishness [AM ASS] when you *make a pile* (5)=AMASS

- Artist [RA] has suspicion [TRACE] *this competition's fierce* (3-4)=RAT-RACE

- *Fairy* can [TIN] edge [KERB] some distance [ELL] (6,4)=TINKER BELL

- Mother [MA] spoils [DEFACES] what's *mowed* (4,5)=MADE FACES (mow=grimace)

- *Begin* with brilliant [STAR] tipster [TOUT] (5,3)=START OUT

- Daily's [GUARDIANS] joint [HIP] *responsibility for ward* (12)=GUARDIANSHIP

- <u>Later</u> upset [=REAL T] getting away from [OFF] *a good sort* (4,4)=REAL TOFF

- *Get on* a Caribbean island [H(A)ITI] without a [A] bean [TOFF] (3,2,3)=HIT IT OFF

- *Shout* 'An evil [SIN] and a disease [GOUT]' (4,3)=SING OUT

- Racecourse [REDCAR] favourite [PET] *often given a walkover* (3,6)=RED CARPET

- Person [HUMAN] had [<u>HAD</u>] resolved [=DHA] to *shilly-shally* (3,3,2)=HUM AND HA

- *Initial advantage* makes minds [HEADS] sharp [TART] (4,5)=HEAD START

- Told an untruth [LIED]? Then admit [OWN] the *rest* (3,4)=LIE DOWN

- Look for [SEEK] beer [ALE], say, and find *vegetable* (3-4)=SEA-KALE

Compilers do not allow themselves to be bound by the normal rules of pronunciation which seem to be ignored as long as the required letters are provided to make up the solution:

- *Measuring device* **encountered by Cockney girl (5)** =METER
  Encountered =MET (short e) plus Cockney girl =(H)ER, giving METER (long e). The dropping of 'h' in this example is typical of clues referring to Cockney speech (*see* 4: Selected Letters)

- **Get rid of black marks for** *tyrant* **(6)**=DESPOT
  De-spot (long e) =DESPOT (short e)

- **Transgress again, by** *gum***! (5)**
  Re-sin (long e and s sound) =RESIN (short e and z sound)

In everyday speech we tend to shorten words (see also Abbreviations):

- **The French (LE) not hurried (N'T) but fast (4) =LENT**

Foreigners often pronounce words differently and some Asians have difficulty with 'r' which comes out as 'l'

- **Chap who's pronounced penniless [BROKE] in China (5) =BLOKE**

Speech defects which result in mispronunciation include

—stuttering with duplication of the initial letter
- *Push* P'pole [P'ROD] (4) =PROD

- *Shout* at r-rower [R-OAR] (4) =ROAR

- A [A] q'quarrel [R'ROW]? A *quarrel!* (5) =ARROW

- *Need* w-worker [W-ANT] (4) = WANT (*see also* p62)

— lisping with 'th' substituted for 's' or 'ss'
- Imperfectly greet [KISS] *relative* (4) =KITH

— and the inability to pronounce the letter 'r' which becomes 'w'
- Imperfect box, perhaps, [TREE] is *small and pretty* (4) =TWEE

Similarly, a drunken person often uses slurred speech

- *Hair style* for the individual [SINGLE], if drunk (7) =SHINGLE

- *Collapsing* drunkard's thinking (7) = SINKING

- Same when drunk. *Disgrace!* (5) =SHAME

One of the most frequently used examples of the way in which pronunciation is ignored occurs in the use of 'flower' to mean 'river' or something that flows:

- **Give flower to Scot, a** *flower found in America* **(7)**=POTOMAC
Flower, usually considered as rhyming with 'power', needs to
be read as rhyming with 'mower' to give 'flower [PO] to [TO]
Scot [MAC] '=POTOMAC (=river in America)

- **I found abroad yellow** *flower that's divine* **(5)**=ICHOR
Not a yellow flower, nor any other flower. 'I found abroad'
[Ger. 'I'=ICH] plus 'yellow' [OR] gives ICHOR which flows in the
veins of mythical gods — even though ICH is properly pronounced
'eekh'.

This type of logic allows the compiler to regard 'birdy' as 'bird+y' and so we get:

- **Cricketing birdy? (5)**=GULL+Y =GULLY

Changing the emphasis often helps towards a solution.

- **A man with lots to offer (10)**
Shift the emphasis from 'man' to 'lots' and it immediately becomes
clear that he is an AUCTIONEER.

Even the alphabet is not safe in the hands of some compilers:

- *Strike* **a follower [=B] with tree [ASH] (4) =BASH**
which defines B as follower of A may be reasonable enough but

- *Win* **when work initially is halved (7) =VICTORY**
where work initially (W) is halved to give V =victory is perhaps a
bit much!

see also Compound Words, Part 2:20

Moral: ignore the given phrasing and rephrase the clue in as many
different ways as you can until you see the solution.

26

SINGULARS AND PLURALS

Some words are 'plural' — for the purpose of crosswords — in the sense that they may end with 's' (which may be an 's' with the apostrophe ignored — *see* Punctuation, Part 2:24) or may be made up of repeated syllables (e.g. tom-tom), but are, nevertheless, singular.

'Plural' clues may require a singular solution

- *Sailor* beside himself with tooth trouble [TAR(TAR)] (3) =TAR

- *Mistake* to offer half a comfit [BON(BON)] to Queen Bess [ER] (5) =BONER

- *Chant* twice in American prison [SING(-SING)] (4) =SING

A word which is truly plural in the clue may require a singular word used twice in the solution

- *He persecutes* people [MEN] in the hills [TORS=TOR-TOR] (9) =TORMENTOR

- Coloured [RED] plus-fours [IV's=IV, IV] America [US] *resuscitated* (9) =REDIVIVUS

- One [I] among forwards [ON's=ON-ON] *familiar to the expert* (5) =ONION

- *University* has two scholars [MA's=MA, MA] in turn [AL-TER] (4,5) =ALMA MATER

- *Trumpet sound* for sailors [TAR's=TAR-TAR] with articles [AN-A] (9) =TARANTARA

• Both halves fit [WELL]? *You do surprise me!* (4,4) =WELL WELL

• Small firms [CO's=COCO] go forward [ON] in this *case* (6) =COCOON

or a word which is singular in the clue may be required to be used twice in the solution

• *Goddess*'s double life [IS] (4) =ISIS

• Preserve [CHOW] one of two *dogs* (4-4) =CHOW-CHOW

• Performing [ON] twice [ON-ON] without one [I] *vegetable* (5) =ONION

• *A lemur* is always [AYE] set on reproduction (6) =AYEAYE

• Eliot initially [TSE] twice duplicated this *fly* (6) =TSETSE

• *Unmentionable* whist [HUSH] pair (4-4) =HUSH-HUSH

• *Turn up one's nose* at bear [POOH] twice (4-4) =POOH-POOH

• *Killer* creature [ASS] twice on the spot [IN] (8) =ASSASSIN

• *Say* 'Drink [RUM] up [=MUR]' repeatedly (6) =MURMUR (down clue)

• The twin boys [ALF, ALF] are given a [A] *plant* (7) =ALFALFA

and the same device may be used with homophones

• *Skirt* for lily-white boys number [TWO], say [=TU] (4) =TUTU

• *Disease* apparently affected by fruit [BERRY=BERI] and more fruit (8) =BERIBERI

• *African dish* causes expressions of surprise [COO's], apparently [=COUS], to be repeated (8) =COUSCOUS

or abbreviations

- Joe's [GI] copy [GI] of a *film*
  (4) =GIGI

- *Absurdity* no [NO] three-quarters
  [NSE] must repeat [NSE]
  (8) =NONSENSE

- *Tree* about [CA] to add another
  [CA] ring [O] (5) =CACAO

- *Stop* a couple of streets
  [ST AND ST] ? Difficult! [ILL]
  (10) =STANDSTILL

Occasionally you may find
that a plural clue requires a
solution which uses the
singular in two different
forms

- Two pounds [LI and QUID]; *easily
  convertible* (6) =LIQUID

- One way [ST] and [AND] another
  [A, RD] poor side's [=ISED] *made
  par* (12) =STANDARDISED

- Different actions [SUIT, CASE]
  taken by holidaymaker
  (8) =SUITCASE

and some clues relate to
singular and plural letters

- *Garment* seen in Qatar but not in
  Quetta (7) =SINGLET (single T)

Another device is to clue a
pair or group of which only
one is required in the
solution

- *Partiality* for one novel weakness
  (9) =PREJUDICE
  (Pride and Prejudice, a novel)

- Apparently eats [CHEWS] with *pick*
  (6) =CHOOSE
  (Pick and choose)

- *Worry* third member of an
  undistinguished trio (5) =HARRY
  (Tom, Dick and Harry)

For the plurals of some
abbreviations

see Abbreviations, Part 1:3

Moral: since the compiler plays fast and loose with his singulars and
plurals, you might as well do the same.

27

PROPER NOUNS

Many nouns double as proper nouns, starting with a capital letter, and common nouns, starting in lower case. Where a common noun is placed at the beginning of a clue, and therefore starts with a capital letter, it is not easy, at first glance, to determine whether a proper or a common noun is required in the solution. The following pairs will serve to illustrate the point:

- *China* could become a region of France [BEAUNE], we hear (4) =BONE
- *Fine china* for a dog's dinner (4) =BONE

- Job description — '*long suffering*' (7) =PATIENT
- I am [IM] like Job, *reckless* (9) =IMPATIENT

- *Fletcher's case* will shake (6) =QUIVER (fletcher =arrowmaker)
- *Shake* fletcher's case (6) =QUIVER

Sometimes a proper noun is used in the clue when a common noun is required in the solution

- *Most generous* is Ken [KNOW], we hear [=NO], and happy [BLEST] (7) =NOBLEST
- *Garden* in China [(C)ROCKERY] short of carbon [C] (7) =ROCKERY
- Daily [CHAR] Telegraph's initial [T] *horoscope* (5) =CHART

or vice versa

- Not long [SHORT] before the house [=COMMONS] finishes *meagre fare* (5,7) =SHORT COMMONS
- *Politician* is a safe [PETER] stroller [WALKER] (5,6) =PETER WALKER
- Raise sailor (4) =JACK

Personal names come into the category of proper nouns and some compilers make frequent use of them

Sometimes the solution is arrived at by the combination of two or more personal names

- *Foreign* chap [AL] in girl's [M-AY] embrace (5) = MALAY

- *Grand* pair of boys [ROY, AL] (5) = ROYAL

- *Treachery* of a girl [BET] and two boys [RAY, AL] (8) = BETRAYAL

- *Calmness of temper* leads to nothing [O] between boy [PHIL] and girl [SOPHY] (10) = PHILOSOPHY

perhaps with other letters added

- *Language* two boys [D-AVID, IAN] used about redhead [R] (9) = DRAVIDIAN

- *Capital cover* for Gordon initially [G], then two other chaps [LEN, GARRY] (9) = GLENGARRY

or by the **addition** of **personal names** to **derived words**

- With a girl [EVA], chatter [P-RATE] about love [O] and *disappear* (9) = EVAPORATE

- Sailor-man [TAR, PAUL] wearing [IN] *canvas* (9) = TARPAULIN

- Country [PERU] lad's [KE(N)] not finished *piece of thatching* (6) = PERUKE (= wig)

or to **given words**

- And [AND] there's a girl [VER-A] outside on the *terrace* (7) = VERANDA

or to **abbreviations**

- Girl [IRIS] is hot [H] and in *a temper* (5) = IRISH

- Mark [ANTONY] getting married [M]? *Just the opposite* (7) = ANTONYM

- Ring [O] a non-U girl [PA(U)LINE] *of milk-white complexion* (7) = OPALINE

183

or by **subtraction**	• Fellow [DON] leaving London [LON(DON)] with one [I] needed to get *back* (4) = LOIN
or by **inclusion**	• *Sends out* boy [DE-S] to get a drink [PORT] (7) = DEPORTS
	• *He sculpted* a man [RO-N] embracing a woman [DI] (5) = RODIN
	• Girl [CHLO-E] carrying free [RID] *bleaching powder* (8) = CHLORIDE
Sometimes the required solution is an **anagram**	• Dicky, <u>Sue</u> and <u>Sam</u> are *to take over* (6) = ASSUME (Dicky = anagram pointer)
or a **homophone**	• *Lively* lady [ANNIE = ANI] got married [MATED], we hear (8) = ANIMATED
	• *Operatic spectacles* devised for Handel, we hear [= HANDLE] (9) = LORGNETTE
	• *Jack* can do this, says Philip [= FILLIP] (4) = LIFT
In some clues, the name appears in the clue as a **given word**	• Charles [CHAS] <u>sent</u> out [= TENS] with *moderates* (8) = CHASTENS
	• *He* makes Ian [IAN] a foreigner [RUSS(IAN)] (4) = RUSS
	• Give Ronald [RON] your votes [ELECT] *just a bit* (8) = ELECTRON
and in others the name appears as the solution to an **oblique description**	• One of the Great names (5) = PETER
	• *This chap* goes in circles, in the main (4) = EDDY
or as the result of a **reversal**	• I [I] grumble [MOAN] back [= NAOM] to the *girl* (5) = NAOMI
	• *He* is [IS] back [= SI] in the <u>lab</u> maybe [= BA-L] (5) = BASIL

184

or arising from an **anagram**	• *Languish* troubled by <u>daily</u> suitors (5) =LYDIA
or other combinations	• *He*'s always [EVER] difficult [(H)ARD], says the Cockney (7) =EVERARD
	• *He* has to change his <u>suit</u> [=ITUS] on the tee [T] (5) =TITUS
Some **foreign names** are also used	• *Make a fresh start*, taking a French name [RENE] and going to the west [W] (5) =RENEW
	• *She* is the one [I] with the French name [RENE] (5) =IRENE
'miss' sometimes indicates a girl's name	• *Face* little Miss [VI] Wiseman [SAGE] (6) =VISAGE
but can mean 'girl'	• Girl [MISS] with raw skin [PELT] having *literally erred* (8) =MISSPELT
or 'lose'	• Miss [LOSE] after a name [N] in the City [E-C]? *Shut up!* (7) =ENCLOSE
Occasionally you will find that a 'personal name' is really a common noun or a verb given a capital letter in the clue	• *Entreaty* by Copper [P] field [LEA] (4) =PLEA
	• Assistant to Doctor Foster (5) =NURSE

Note: 'old man of Paris' is not *vieux* (Fr. 'old man') but Paris's father =PRIAM
'a girl from Australia' =SHEILA
'Merchant of Venice' may be Antonio but may well be POLO (Marco)
'a couple' could be EVADES (Eva plus Des)

Moral: capital letters do not always indicate a proper name and you can be sure the compiler will make improper use of both common and proper nouns.

28

LETTER GROUPS

Certain letters of the alphabet frequently occur in well-known groups (e.g. PRE-, -ING, -OUGH, etc.) and these can be very useful in the solution of clues. Even when you cannot immediately spot the solution, it is often possible to pencil in some parts of it in the hope that they will be confirmed as other letters are obtained from other solutions intersecting.

Any clue involving

able
will include CAN, probably at the beginning

• Is able [CAN] once more [CAN] to *dance* (6) =CANCAN

admitting/claiming/ confessing/declaring
will probably start with AM-, IM- or IAM-
(*see also* Abbreviations, Part 1:3)

• I claim [AM] small piece [BIT] of *circuit* (5) =AMBIT

• Admission [IM] of one [I] by gallery [TATE] to *take as model* (7) =IMITATE

• *Measure* for confession [IAM] of bishop [B] (4) =IAMB

against
will probably start with CON-

• *Strengthen* against [CON] the company [FIRM] (7) =CONFIRM

at home
will include IN, probably at the beginning

• At home [IN], firm [CO] got in trouble [=GNITO] *using a false name* (9) =INCOGNITO

can
will include TIN

• Can [TIN] sell [SEL(L)] almost *anything gaudy* (6) =TINSEL or perhaps end in -ABLE

- Observation [REMARK] can [ABLE] be *singular* (10) =REMARKABLE

cane
will perhaps end in -ANCE

- *Pierces* side [L] with broken <u>canes</u> [=ANCES] (6) =LANCES

cannot/unable
will include CANT,

- Cannot [CANT] even [EEN] *box for cutlery* (7) =CANTEEN

usually as an ending, -CANT

- London area [SE] unable [CANT] to *function* (6) =SECANT

church
will use the letters CE, CH or RC, with C-E and C-H often used as the first and last letters of the solution

- That man [HIM] in the church [C-E] will *agree* (5) =CHIME

- For each [PER] church [CH] once in the North [ANCE], *perhaps* (9) =PERCHANCE

- Main [SEA] church [RC] hard [H] to *explore* (6) =SEARCH

debts/owing
will end in -IOUS

see Split Words, Part 2:21

Diana/Diana's
will probably start with DI- or DIS-, though sometimes 'the girl' or 'the girl's' or 'Princess' is used instead

- Diana's [DI] form [VERSION] of *amusement* (9) =DIVERSION

- Diana's [DIS] disposition [TEMPER] is *dog's indisposition* (9) =DISTEMPER

- Put pressure [STRESS] on the girl [DI] and *cause pain* (8) =DISTRESS

- The girl's [DIS] operation [PLAY] will *show* (7) =DISPLAY

- Princess [DI], traveller [REP], the Queen [ER] and the Italian [IL] in *grave danger* (4,5) =DIRE PERIL

doctor
will include DR, GP, MD or MO

- Doctor [DR] has one [I] penny [P], the *twerp!* (4) =DRIP

- Doctor [G-P] goes round a [A] *fissure* (3) =GAP

187

- Doctor [M-D] embraces first-class [A1] *servant* (4) =MAID

- Nearly all [AL(L)] doctor's [MOS] shirt [T] — *nearly* (6) =ALMOST

editor/journalist
will start or end with ED

- *Order* journalist [ED] one [I] carat [CT] (5) =EDICT

- *Taught* process [TRAIN] to editor [ED] (7) =TRAINED

Edward
will probably end with -ED, -NED or -TED

- *Reproved* for spreading Ed's cold (7) =SCOLDED

- *Wise* King [LEAR] Edward [NED] (7) =LEARNED

- *Left* Edward [TED] feeling poorly [under PAR] (6) =PARTED (down clue)

fish
will perhaps end in -LING

- *Allowing* curtailed existence [ENTIT(Y)] to fish [LING] (9) =ENTITLING

former/one-time, etc.
will start with EX

see Old Words, Part 2:19

gin cocktail/gin sling
will start with IGN-

- *Unaware* splashing gin [=IGN] on gold [OR] worker [ANT] (8) =IGNORANT

or end with -ING

- Carry [BEAR] gin cocktail [=ING] in *a certain direction* (7) =BEARING

but note that -ING endings can be achieved in other ways

- *Dawdling* with Beatrix [POTTER] in [IN] Gateshead [G] (9) =POTTERING

head
will end in -NESS (Note loch =NESS sometimes)

- *Vacuity* of empty [BLANK] head [NESS] (9) =BLANKNESS

hesitation
will imply the use of ER or UM, often as word endings

- *Boy* takes cat, perhaps [=PET], with hesitation [-ER] (5) =PETER

188

- King [R], with hesitation [UM], has *drink* (3) =RUM

I have
will end in -IVE
(*see also* Abbreviations, Part 1:3)

- Out of [EX] sulphur [S], say [=EXCESS], I've [IVE] *more than enough* (9) =EXCESSIVE

intended/meant/understood
will end in -MENT

- Yielding [SUPPLE] intended [MENT] *supply* (10) =SUPPLEMENT

- Key [F]-ring [O] intended [MEANT], I'm told [=MENT], to *foster* (6) =FOMENT

in the East
will end in -INE

see Abbreviations, Part 1:3

king/queen
will include K or R
(Rex=king, Regina=queen)
or ER (Edward or Elizabeth),
often as an ending

- Scotsman [MON], king [K] and *friar* (4) =MONK

- *Trademark* of king [R] in orchestra [B-AND] (5) =BRAND

- *Encouraging shout* from revolutionary [CHE] monarch [ER] (5) =CHEER

marine/jolly
will include RM (Royal Marine)

for which Jolly is the nickname

although 'jolly' can mean 'very' as in a 'jolly good idea'

- Marine [RM] always [A-Y] outside the *battle-group* (4) =ARMY

- *Foolish* but jolly [RM] in cove [BA-Y] (5) =BARMY

- Jolly [VERY] following fifty-one [LI] in *uniform* (6) =LIVERY

motorway
usually refers to M1 =MI

but sometimes uses M alone

- *Ape* caught [C] following two motorways [MI, MI] (5) =MIMIC

- *Demonstrate* motorway [M] bridge [ARCH] (5) =MARCH

note
can include any letter from A to G (the most frequent

see Selected Letters, Part 1:4

use is to imply E at the end
of the solution)

but it can also mean 'fiver',
'tenner', etc.

- *Note* cross [X=TEN], not old [NE],
king [R] (6) =TENNER

race
will end in -NATION

- Modify [ALTER] the race
[NATION] by *changes in turn*
(11)=ALTERNATION

or include -TT-

see Abbreviations, Part 1:3

Scot
will include MAC

- Scot's [MAC] English [E] *club*
(4)=MACE

or end in -IAN

- Scot [IAN] following County
[DEVON] *geological system*
(8)=DEVONIAN

study
will start with CON-

- Study [CON] knowledge [SCIENCE]
of *moral sense*
(10)=CONSCIENCE

or include DEN

- *Testimony* of study [DEN] in
Eastern [E] depravity [VI-CE]
(8)=EVIDENCE

or READ

- Study [READ] clothes [DRESS] and
send on (2-7)=RE-ADDRESS

tea-blend/kind of tea, etc.
will end in -ATE

see Abbreviations, Part 1:3

underworld
will start with DIS-

- *Talk* of underworld [DIS] lectures
[COURSE] (9)=DISCOURSE

Perhaps the most important letter groups are those that occur at the
beginning and end of words since they are the most useful in helping
one to recognise the solution for partly-completed entries. Some of
the most common are listed below, including, for completeness,
examples mentioned in other sections

Beginnings include:
AM- =admitting/confessing

- *Magistrate* admits [AM] to being a
male [MAN] (5) =AMMAN

CON- =study

* Graduates [MAS] study [CON] *area of high gravity* (6) =MASCON

DE- =of French

* *Longing* of French [DE] father [SIRE] (6) =DESIRE

DIS- =devil

* *Breaks up* the Devil [DIS] and his gang [BAND] (7) =DISBAND

Diana's/girl's/ princess's underworld

* *Food* in girl's [DIS] hospital [H] (4) =DISH
* *Distribute* underworld [DIS] coins [PENCE] say [=PENSE] (8) =DISPENSE

EN- =in French

* *Delights* in French [EN] songs [CHANTS] (8) =ENCHANTS

ENT-=speciality (ear, nose and throat)

* *Complete* anger [IRE] after medical speciality [ENT] (6) =ENTIRE

tangled net

* *Fast* learner [L] has tangled net [=ENT] (4) =LENT

IGN- =gin cocktail/sling

* *Takes no notice of* gin cocktail [=IGN] and minerals [ORES] (7) =IGNORES

IM- =admitting/confessing

* *Taxes* on admitting [IM] Poles [POSTS] (7) =IMPOSTS

IMP- =I am quiet

* I am [IM] quiet [P] and have no [O] right [RT] to *imply* (6) =IMPORT

one Member

* *Charge* Indian [UTE] following one [I] member [MP] (6) =IMPUTE

one policeman

* *Suggests* one [I] policeman [MP] does not tell the truth (7) =IMPLIES

one politician

* One [I] politician [MP] has painting [ART] to *bestow* (6) =IMPART

PAR- =average

* *Average* [PAR] weight [TON] of *particle* (6) =PARTON

norm(al)

* *Deflect* normal [PAR] lines [RY] (5) =PARRY

PARA- =airborne soldier/
trooper

PER- =by/through

A frequently used word-
ending is -AL and this can
be achieved in a variety of
ways

- *Most important* trooper [PARA]
  has horse [MOUNT] (9)
  =PARAMOUNT

- *Allow* through [PER] with German
  [MIT] (6) =PERMIT

- Terribly <u>prim</u> [=IMPR] conduct
  [AC.] one [I] has to reckon [CAL(L)]
  almost wholly *unrealistic*
  (11)=IMPRACTICAL

- One who objects [CO] to mass [M]
  lopping of all [AL(L)] *of forest tops*
  (5)=COMAL

- *Publication* put in charge of [IC]
  motherless dancing girl [AL(MA)]
  after a time [PERIOD]
  (10)=PERIODICAL

- *Shoot* Capone [AL] after — not
  now [LATER] (7)=LATERAL

- *Book* for girl [MISS] on the A50
  [AL] (6)=MISSAL

- *Funny* commander [COM] in
  charge of [IC] centre-h<u>al</u>f [AL]
  (7)=COMICAL

- *Including all* the drink [TOT], one
  [A] pound [L] (5)=TOTAL

- Obese [FAT] man [AL] is *mortal*
  (5)=FATAL

- According to [PER] America [US],
  almost all [AL(L)] *study*
  (7)=PERUSAL

- Country [PERU] girl [LAS(S)] not
  quite up [=SAL] to *examination*
  (7)=PERUSAL (down clue)

- *Study* country [PERU] girl [SAL]
  (7)=PERUSAL
  (The last examples show three
  ways of writing the clue for the
  same solution)

other word endings include:

-ABLE =can

- Can [ABLE] bone [T] be *fish*? (5) =ABLET

-ALLY =all unknown

- Shut up [INTERN] everything [ALL] unknown [Y] *on the inside* (10) =INTERNALLY

    friend

- European [FINN], say [=FIN], has a friend [ALLY] *at last* (7) =FINALLY

-ANCE =broken <u>cane</u>

- *Country* friar [FR] has broken cane (6) =FRANCE

-ATE =a note

- Many [D] take a [A] note [TE] of *fruit* (4) =DATE

    at East(ern)...

- German [G] at [AT] east [E] *en-trance* (4) =GATE

    at English...

- Beginner [L] at [AT] English [E] is *dead* (4) =LATE

    <u>tea</u> blend/mixture

- *Detest* hard [H] <u>tea</u>-mixture [ATE] (4) =HATE

-ATED =wrong <u>date</u>

- *Married* many [M] on the wrong <u>date</u> [=ATED] (5) =MATED

-ATION =breaks/turns <u>into</u> a

- Norway [N] turns into a [=ATION] *state* (6) =NATION

-CANT =cannot/unable

- Engineers [RE] cannot [CANT] *withdraw* (6) =RECANT

-ED =editor/journalist

- *Urged* newspaper [PRESS] editor [ED] (9) =PRESSED

    Edward

- *Minded* little Edward [ED] behind the vehicle [CAR] (5) =CARED

-ENT =specialism (ear, nose, throat)

- *Meaning* fashionable [IN] bone [T] speciality [ENT] (6) =INTENT

    tangled <u>net</u>

- *Fast* learner [L] has tangled <u>net</u> (4) =LENT

-ER =king/queen/monarch

- *Provide for* animal [CAT] and monarch [ER] (5) =CATER

-ETIC =call [CITE] back

- *Contemptible* way [PATH] to call [CITE] back [=ETIC] (8) =PATHETIC

-FUL =almost complete	• *Horrible* headgear [HAT] (English[E]) almost complete [FUL(L)] (7) =HATEFUL
not quite satisfied	• *Unhappy* when ration [DOLE] not completely satisfied [FUL(L)] (7) =DOLEFUL
-IAN =I have an	• Girl [SAL] and I [I] have an [AN] *ancient tribe* (6) =SALIAN
in a spin/whirl	• *Man* <u>in a</u> [IN A] spin [=IAN] on the railway [BR] (5) =BRIAN
Scotsman	• The normal [PAR] Scotsman [IAN] makes *porcelain* (6) =PARIAN
-IC =I see	• Church [CH] I see sounds [=IC] *very smart* (4) =CHIC
in charge	• The male [MAN] in charge [IC] is *mad* (5) =MANIC
one about	• Joke [PUN] - one [I] about [C] *ancient language* (5) =PUNIC
one cold...	• Fashion [TON] one [I] cold [C] *drink* (5) =TONIC
-ICAL =I state	• "Green [VERT]", I [I] state [CAL], "is upright" (8) =VERTICAL
-INE =in East(ern)	• Eat [SUP] in [IN] the East [E], *lying on back* (6) =SUPINE
-ING =<u>gin</u> cocktail/sling	• *Desiring* <u>gin</u> cocktail after dance [HOP] (5) =HOPING
in <u>G</u>ateshead	• *Walking* for a month [MARCH] in [IN] <u>G</u>ateshead [G] (8) =MARCHING
in <u>G</u>erman capital	• *Being* fifty-four [LIV] in [IN] <u>G</u>erman capital [G] (5) =LIVING
in the middle of the night	• *Fetch* lines [BR] in [IN] the middle of the night [G] (5) =BRING
-INGS =in G and S	• *Gate money*, thanks [TA] to king [K] in [IN] G and S (6) =TAKINGS

-ION =No.1 comes back	• No.1 [NOI] comes back [=ION] after taking test [MOT] and makes a *proposal* (6) =MOTION
one leg	• Pet [CAT] with one [I] leg [ON] produces *charged particle* (6) =CATION
-IOUS =debts	• *Peculiar* low type [CUR] has debts [IOUS] (7) =CURIOUS
owing	• Penny [P] owing [IOUS]? *Good!* (5) =PIOUS
-ISE =is Eastern	• King [R] is [IS] given Eastern [E] *lift* (4) =RISE
-ISH =his break/broken	• *White-faced* friend [PAL] takes his break (6) =PALISH
-ISM =is married	• *Belief* that Scotsman [MON] is [IS] married [M] (6) = MONISM
-IST =first	• *Duke* is first [IST] after fellow [F] (4) =FIST
is square	• Angle [L] is [IS] square [T] in *border* (4) =LIST
premier	• The [THE] premier [IST] is *one who believes in God* (6) =THEIST
-ITE =I note	• *Bird* takes potassium [K] I [I] note [TE] (4) =KITE
one note	• Queen [Q] you say [=U] has one [I] note [TE]? *Yes* (5) =QUITE
-IVE =I have	• The lump [MASS] I have [IVE] is *huge* (7) =MASSIVE
-LED =was ahead	• *Crumpled* when animal [BUCK] was ahead [LED] (7) =BUCKLED
was first	• Bird [TIT] was first [LED] to be *named* (6) =TITLED
-LING =fish	• Fish [COD], fish [LING] and *little fish* (7) =CODLING

-MENT =intended/meant/ understood	• *Dirge* the French [LA] understood [MEANT] I hear [=MENT] (6) =LAMENT
soldier's shirt	• *Fix* soldier's [MEN] shirt [T] behind engineer [CE] (6) =CEMENT
workers in front of square	• *Agony* of hill {TOR]-workers [MEN] in front of square [T] (7) =TORMENT
-NATION =break/turn <u>into an</u>	• *Condemnation* of mother [DAM]-race [NATION] (9) =DAMNATION
race	• Motor [CAR]-race [NATION] is a *bloomer* (9) =CARNATION
-NESS =head	• *Importance* of big [GREAT] head [NESS] (9) =GREATNESS
-OON =with nothing on	• *Swell* dance [BALL] with nothing [O] on [ON] (7) =BALLOON
-OUS =nothing to America	• Newton [N] takes nothing [O] to America [US]. *Common sense* (4) =NOUS
nothing to us	• Shout [CALL] "Nothing [O] to us [US]". *Brutal!* (7) =CALLOUS
round America	• I [I] am in run [RU-N] round [O] America [US]. *Very destructive!* (7) =RUINOUS
-TION =changes/turns <u>into</u>	• Time [MO] changes <u>into</u> [=TION] *movement* (6) =MOTION
turns it on	• English [E] and the French [LA] turn it [IT=TI] on [ON] *in high spirits* (7) =ELATION

Always note the form of the direct clue to see if it is singular or plural, noun or adjective, comparative or superlative, past or present, and so on, since:
—plural nouns will probably end in -S (though -A, -AE, -I, etc. are possible)
—many adjectives end in -AL or -IVE
—comparative adjectives usually end in -ER or -IER

—superlative adjectives end in -EST or -IEST
—many forms of the past tense of verbs end in -ED
—present participles end in -ING
—adverbs usually end in -LY
These endings can often be pencilled in to advantage.

You may sometimes see answers to parts of the clue without being able immediately to see the full solution. In such cases, it may help with other solutions if you pencil in those parts of the clue that you do recognise. The following examples illustrate the point:

- **Cunning occupation joined by one head (10)**
  The phrase 'joined by' points to 'occupation' and 'one head' as indirect clues making up a word which means cunning. Since it is not difficult to spot 'one' =I and 'head' =NESS, you can pencil in -INESS even if you have to wait a little before recognising that 'occupation' =CRAFT to give CRAFTINESS ='cunning'

- **Well-known talker can in drink, making a proposal (10)**
  The pointer 'making' indicates 'proposal' as the direct clue. You may well recognise 'can' =TIN and, if you already happen to have T, I or N in the grid, you can pencil in _ _ _ _ _ _ TIN _ and then, with some confidence, add G. Alternatively, the grid may show _ _ M _ N _ _ _ _ _ from which you may recognise 'well-known talker' =MINA and enter _ _ MINA _ _ _. Recognising 'drink' =NOG to give the full solution, NOMINATING, may take a little time, but the part solutions you enter may well help you with other solutions

- **One's lover is said to be an American dancer (7)**
  The construction of the clue makes it fairly obvious that the required solution is the name of an American dancer. Even if you do not know the name, you should see that 'one's' =IS and be able to pencil in the first two letters. 'Said to be' clearly indicates a homophone for lover (ADORER =ADORA) to give ISADORA (Duncan)

  Similarly, you may spot just a single letter of a solution which can then be pencilled in — it all helps towards the solution of other clues. The following examples illustrate the point:

  - **Vice ring repelled girl (5)**
    'Ring' is almost certainly O and, since 'repelled' indicates a reversal, the girl's name will then begin with O. From there it is easy to see 'vice' =EVIL which, reversed with the O, gives OLIVE

• **Posh decoration by novice, this flower cluster (5)**
'Novice' will surely be L (learner), so you can try this as the last letter of the solution even if you have to wait a little while before you appreciate that 'posh' (U) and 'decoration' (MBE) added to L gives UMBEL

• **Pledge nothing in Californian city (10)**
Nothing will be O. 'In' might mean that O is written inside the name of the 'city' to make 'pledge' but, when you recall the Spanish influence in California, you can be reasonably sure that the O will be the last letter in the solution which is SACRAMENTO (pledge + O)

Solutions are quite often in the form of two or more words and it is good practice, when you are reading through the clues, to mark off the grid into the appropriate letter groups so that they are not overlooked if you have to leave a clue and come back to it later. It is very frustrating to spend time looking for a 10-letter word when the solution required is 2,3,5.

In solutions that have several words
—a single letter between two other words will almost certainly be A
—a two-letter word between two other words will probably be IN, OF or OR
—a three-letter word between two other words is likely to be AND or THE
—a sequence of two- and three-letter words between others will probably be OF THE, IN THE or TO THE
It is useful to pencil in such part solutions.

It is also the case that some letter groups, far from being easily recognisable, are so unfamiliar as to lead you to think you may have made an error in an earlier solution which intersects with the word you are trying to find. It is not easy to imagine words that begin with BD-, DZ-, MPR-, ZH-, etc., words containing CTZ or a Q without a following U, or a word ending with -OTL, but they all exist. When the indirect clue points to a solution with a strange letter group, do not reject it as impossible, check with the dictionary.

The following are a few examples of words with unfamiliar letter groups:

axolotl	gytrash	mpret	sgraffito	yttrium
bdellium	hoactzin	ngaio	tsotsi	zhomo
caatinga	iynx	ogdoad	Uzbeg	
dzo	jymold	Pnyx	vraic	

ewghen	kgotla	Qoran	wowf
fylfot	lherzolite	rhabdus	xyster

The following cases illustrate how you may be led to think that you have made an error in earlier solutions when unfamiliar letter groups appear:

- **Ligature used in shocking case (4)**

  The pointer 'shocking' indicates an anagram which must be of 'case', the only likely four-letter word in the clue. It follows that 'ligature' is the direct clue. But what four-letter word meaning 'ligature' can be made from the letters CASE when you already have C as the last letter, derived from another solution? Perhaps that C is wrong? It is not; check possible anagrams of CASE with the dictionary and you will find AESC (a ligature in phonetics)

- **Plant producing oil for week initially in a month (5)**

  You are faced with a grid that shows _ J _ _ _. 'Week initially' will obviously be W and it appears that this has to be written 'in a month'. The J in the grid indicates 'a month' as A-JAN or A-JUN. Where does the W fit in? The letter group -AWN- is familiar from such words as 'lawn', 'pawn', etc., so you may opt for AJAWN, shunning the unfamiliar AJW combination. In fact, the solution is AJWAN, an oil-producing plant

See also Letter Groups, Appendix 1.

Moral: look out for familiar letter groups and even single letters that can be pencilled in to help with other solutions but never be put off by unfamiliar letter groups.

29

DOUBLE-CHECKING

The importance of checking that your solution not only fits the grid and any letters that may already be entered in it, but also satisfies both the direct and the indirect clues, has already been touched on in the Introduction.

You may think you know the solution from the direct clue and be content to enter this solution, even though the relevance of the indirect clues may not be immediately apparent, in the hope that the meanings of the indirect clues will occur to you later. They may not — and if they do, they may well give you a different answer. Consider the following examples:

- **Man involved in plundering Mediterranean for eucalyptus (6)**
  There is no clear indication as to whether the solution will be a form of pirate or a form of eucalyptus but, either from direct knowledge or from an inference from letters already entered in the grid, you may settle for MALLEE, a form of eucalyptus, even though the connection with 'plundering' is not clear. Further help from letters from other clues may cause you to look up SALLEE which is not only a form of eucalyptus but also a Moorish pirate

- **Written Indian teaching to beat backward influence of magic (6)**
  Again there is no clear guide as to the direct clue, although the probability seems to be that it is 'written Indian teaching'. You may get to the stage _ _ N _ RA and, remembering that another word for 'magic' could be 'art', realise that ART 'backward' (=TRA) would fit nicely at the end to give _ _ NTRA. That will almost certainly remind you of MANTRA, which the dictionary will tell you is 'a Vedic [i.e. Hindu] hymn . . . a sacred text. . . .' If you settle for that, ignoring the indirect clue 'to beat', you will be wrong. 'To beat' is TAN, and TANTRA is also 'a written Indian teaching'

- **Echidna concealed in a plantation (8)**
  'Concealed in' invariably means a hidden word. Or does it? Look at the word 'plantation' and you will find ANT concealed in it so

you would be justified in regarding 'pl/ant/ation' as an 'ant-eater', which is exactly what an echidna is. But, although 'ant-eater' has the required eight letters, in some dictionaries it is a 3-5 hyphenated word — not quite what is called for — so, if you enter 'ant-eater' you will be wrong. The correct solution is an anagram of 'echidna' and 'a', HACIENDA, a plantation, ranch, etc.

- **Foreigners you'll see this year among ones coming to English capital (10)**
The grid may show S _ N _ _ _ LESE and the obvious solution may appear to be SENEGALESE, which may well satisfy the grid in that it is compatible with intersecting clues. 'England's capital' is obviously the final E, but what about 'this year' and 'the ones'? They are, respectively, HA (Lat. *hoc anno*='this year') and SING-LES, giving SINGHALESE

It is occasionally possible to get to the stage where you have a solution that fits the grid, matches the letters that link with intersecting clues and satisfies the clue, only to find that it does not quite fit with other solutions solved later. Take the following example:

- **Keep causing jam (8)**
The grid may show _ _ _ S _ _ VE, and you may conclude that the solution is PRESERVE which satisfies both 'keep' and 'jam'. It is only when you find that the first E does not suit the intersecting clue, which you are trying to solve after entering PRESERVE, that you realise that the correct solution is CONSERVE

In the section on Articles, Part 2:17, compilers are credited with the ability to write clues without wasting words. Enough has now been said in this section to make the point that if you arrive at a solution which does not take full account of *all* the words in the clue, the chances are high that it will be the wrong solution.

The importance of reading clues simply as a collection of words, treating each one separately as a freestanding entity and ignoring the compiler's tricks with compound words, punctuation, phrasing, etc., cannot be too strongly emphasised. If you accept 'Waterloo Station' as a railway terminus instead of two words meaning 'battle' and 'position'; if you interpret 'heavyweight' as a boxer when it really means 'a heavy weight' (TON); if you take 'indeed' to mean 'certainly' instead of an indication of another word written inside DE-ED, then you are sure to have difficulties with cryptic crosswords.

Moral: always re-interpret each word, trying out all possible meanings; rephrase and repunctuate as necessary; take account of all the words in the clue, not just those that seem significant; and *never* take the clue as meaning what it appears to mean.

30

MAKING A START

1. Use a good dictionary. A pocket or concise dictionary is not likely to contain many of the alternative meanings that so many words in the language are capable of bearing. A crossword dictionary listing words from two to about fifteen letters is also useful; it may have few, if any, definitions but it is useful for finding words that fit the grid and letters that are already entered, leaving the meanings to be checked in a standard dictionary. To help with many of the problems set by compilers, try the author's *Crossword Dictionary*, also published by Collins.

2. Remember that there are no hard and fast rules. What you have always regarded as a pointer may turn up as a direct clue, so be flexible in your thinking.

3. You may decide to tackle all the Across clues before trying the Down clues, but it is often easier having completed, say, 1 Across to use the letters of 1 Across that constitute the first letters of some Down clues to have a go at these. If you are lucky with these Down clues, you will then have some letters in place for the Across clues that come lower in the grid. You can often build up a complete corner in this way and then work outwards.

4. Read each clue carefully:
   —looking twice at words that have several possible meanings (*see* Definitions and Classification, Part 1:1)
   —noting the presence or absence of articles (*see* Articles, Part 2:17)
   —noting those small words that may be significant (*see* Small Words, Part 2:18)
   —noting the compound words and the split words (*see* Compound Words, Part 2:20 and Split Words, Part 2:21)
   —looking for pointers to the solutions (*see* notes on pointers throughout Parts 1 and 2)
   —ignoring punctuation and repunctuating (*see* Punctuation, Part 2:24)
   —ignoring phrasing and rephrasing (*see* Phrasing, Part 2:25)

—looking for likely letter groups (*see* Letter Groups, Part 2:28).

5. If the solution contains more than one word, mark off the grid appropriately (*see* Letter Groups, Part 2:28).

6. Determine, if possible, which is the direct clue and underline it, and, if you think the solution involves an anagram, put brackets around the word or letters likely to be involved.

7. Do not waste time and effort struggling to find a solution to each clue at the first reading; pass on to the next. Entering all the solutions which you can see at first reading will give you letters for other clues and make their solution easier.

8. If you think you see a solution at first sight, check that it meets all the requirements of the grid, any letters already entered and all parts of the clue; if it does, you can enter the solution with some confidence (but *see* Double-Checking, Part 2:29); if it meets some of the requirements but you are not certain about the others, enter the solution in pencil for later revision, if necessary.

9. If you do not see a solution at first reading, see if you can get any idea as to parts of the solution, particularly beginnings and endings (*see* Letter groups, Part 2:28). Enter these, if only single letters, for later confirmation. Never commit yourself to a positive solution until you have double-checked (*see* Double-Checking, Part 2:29).

10. Check the grid occasionally to see if you can spot any familiar letter groups in what you have completed so far and pencil in any letters that seem to fit with existing letters to make up a commonly used letter group (*see* Letter Groups, Part 2:28).

11. Remember that many words have alternative spellings, so if you think the answer to a clue involving 'rope' is 'lanyard' but find it does not quite meet the case, check the dictionary; you may well find that 'laniard' is what you want.

12. Finally, remember that crosswords are just that — words. The compiler is using words as a collection of letters to fill a grid in a certain pattern; he is not much concerned with the facts behind the words. When he talks about a 'theatre movement', he is not in the least concerned with any particular school of acting but only with the 'movement' of the letters in the word 'theatre' to form the anagram THEREAT.

And, thereat, we will leave the subject!

APPENDIX 1

LETTER GROUPS

The letters shown in the white squares are those most likely to be found with the letters shown in the shaded squares.

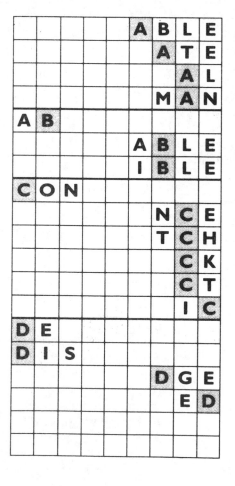

Left grid:

D	I	S				
M	I	S				
				I	A	L
				I	A	N
				I	N	G
		A	T	I	O	N
				I	S	E
				I	S	T
				I		C
A	D	J				
S	K					
				C	K	
				L	K	
				N	K	
				S	K	
			A	B	L	E
					A	L
				F	U	L
M	I	S				
			M	E	N	T
			M	A	N	
U	N					
C	O	N				
			N	C	E	
				I	N	G
			M	E	N	T
			M	A	N	
		A	T	I	O	N

Right grid:

C	O	N							
				O	U	G	H		
					O	U	S		
				A	T	I	O	N	
P	E	R							
P	R	E							
A	P	P							
S	P								
U	P								
I	M	P							
					S	C	O	P	E
					S	H	I	P	
Q	U								
E	Q	U							
S	Q	U							
						Q	U	E	
R	E								
P	E	R							
							E	R	
						E	S	S	
						I	S	E	
						I	S	M	
						I	S	T	
						T	C	H	
						A	T	E	
						I	T	E	
						G	T	H	
						M	E	N	T

Cultivate the habit of testing letters to fit vacant squares in the grid, particularly at the beginnings and ends of words. These tables cover the more usual combinations but others are possible; if none of those given meets your case, test other letters.

U	N						
O	U	T					
Q	U						
S	Q	U					
					U	A	L
					U	R	E
					F	U	L
					O	U	S
					Q	U	E
O	V	E	R				
					I	V	E
						W	L
						W	N
E	X						
				T	R	I	X
P	H	Y					
P	S	Y					
					A	R	Y
					I	T	Y

To illustrate the use of letter groups and part-words, consider the specimen crossword below and assume that you are unable to solve a single clue at first sight.

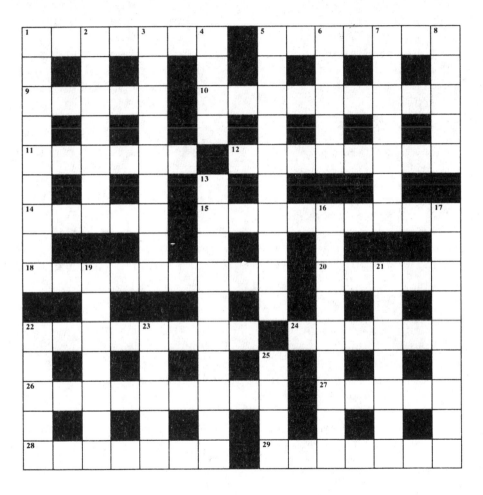

Across

1 Batting with one inside the limit for intervening period (7)
5 Confer against eastern ruler without an end (7)
9 End as broken chair (5)
10 She studies bone and broken cane (9)
11 Glamorous former love has time in charge (6)
12 150 are almost indeed stated (8)
14 Composer who threw one they say (5)
15 Burial in the early Roman origins intended (9)
18 Moving curate nor storyteller (9)
20 Almost fear street festivity (5)
22 Has tea in London, for instance, in moderation (8)
24 Country sounding fat (6)
26 Capable of taking in sailors or grass (9)
27 I admit period likeness (5)
28 Graduate theologian (Fr.) is most crazy (7)
29 Give directions to thymus perhaps in this country (7)

Down

1 Fashionable spirit say, for supervisor (9)
2 Boring and unruly youth has debts (7)
3 Representation of tear — no one comes back after it (9)
4 Rodents found in church on motorway (4)
5 Forecast will work magic without shock treatment (10)
6 Two little boys from part of Africa once (5)
7 Weaken international organisation's strength (7)
8 Rated broken step (5)
13 Teams negotiate we hear, in minor road (4,6)
16 Judge making a mistake in submitting (9)
17 Document called 'Origins of English Epidemic Diseases' (5,4)
19 Methodically arranged about fifty to fool journalist (7)
21 State in the style of graduates (7)
22 Church has a jolly entrance (5)
23 Short trees chopped up (5)
25 A way to the old eyesore (4)

From the hints given in these notes, you should be able to pencil in some parts of the solutions (bold letters), as follows:

Across

1 Batting =IN
5 Against =CON
10 Studies =CONS;
   broken cane =ANCE
11 Former =EX; in charge =IC
12 Indeed =in DE-ED
15 Intended = -MENT
20 Street =ST
26 Sailors =ABS
27 I admit =IM
28 Superlative = -EST
   (confirmed by '(Fr.)
   is' =EST)

Down

1 Fashionable =IN
2 Debts =IOUS
3 No one comes back =-ION
4 Motorway =MI; church =CE
7 Universal organisation =UN
16 Present participle = -ING
19 About =C; fifty =L;
   past tense =ED
21 In the style of =ALA
22 Church =CE or CH − try C;
   jolly =RM
25 A way =ST; the old =YE

Looking back over the grid, you can then, with some confidence, pencil in the following additional letters (light letters):

Across

10 T to complete
   CONSTANCE
11 T to complete EXOTIC
12 CL for 150 in DE-ED
28 A and D to complete
   MADDEST
29 N for the other 'direction'
   between E and G

Down

5 O between C and N
19 AS to complete CLASSED
22 H to complete CHARM

As a result, the grid now looks like this:

It gives you a very good start on the crossword, which you should be able to complete without too much difficulty. The full solution is given overleaf.

Across

1 Batting [IN] with one [I] inside the limit [TER-M] for *intervening period* (7) = INTERIM

5 *Confer* against [CON] eastern ruler [SULT(AN)] without an [AN] end (7) = CONSULT

9 End as broken *chair* (5) = SEDAN

10 *She* studies [CONS] bone [T] and broken cane [=ANCE] (9) = CONSTANCE

11 *Glamorous* former [EX] love [O] has time [T] in charge [IC] (6) = EXOTIC

12 150 [CL] are almost [AR(E)] indeed [DE-ED] *stated* (8) = DECLARED

14 *Composer* who threw [TOSSED] one [I], they say (5) = TOSTI

15 *Burial* in [IN] the early Roman origins [TER] intended [MENT] (9) = INTERMENT

18 Moving curate nor *storyteller* (9) = RACONTEUR

20 Almost fear [FEA(R)] street [ST] *festivity* (5) = FEAST

22 Has [HAS] tea [T] in London, for instance [C-ITY], in *moderation* (8) = CHASTITY

24 Country [GREECE] sounding *fat* (5) = GREASE

26 *Capable of taking in* sailors [ABS] or [OR] grass [BENT] (9) = ABSORBENT

27 I admit [IM] period [AGE] *likeness* (5) = IMAGE

28 Graduate [MA] theologian [DD] (Fr.) is [EST] *most crazy* (7) = MADDEST

29 Give directions [E, N] to thymus perhaps [GLAND], in *this country* (7) = ENGLAND

Down

1 Fashionable [IN] spirit [SPECTRE] say [=SPECTOR], for *supervisor* (9) = INSPECTOR

2 *Boring* and unruly youth [TED] has debts [IOUS] (7) = TEDIOUS

3 *Representation* of tear [REND] — no one [NOI] comes back [=ION] after it [IT] (9) = RENDITION

4 *Rodents* found in church [CE] on motorway [MI] (4) = MICE

5 *Forecast* will work magic [CONJ-URE] without shock treatment [ECT] (10) = CONJECTURE

6 Two little boys [NAT, AL] form *part of Africa once* (5) = NATAL

7 *Weaken* international organisation's [UN] strength [NERVE] (7) = UNNERVE

8 Rated broken *step* (5) = TREAD

13 Teams [SIDES] negotiate [TREAT], we hear [=TREET], in *minor road* (4,6) = SIDE STREET

16 Judge [REF] making a
mistake [ERRING] in
submitting
(9)=REFERRING

17 *Document* called [TITLED]
'Origins of English Epidemic
Diseases' [EED]
(5,4)=TITLE DEED

19 *Methodically arranged* about
[C] fifty [L] to fool [ASS]
journalist [ED]
(7)=CLASSED

21 *State* in the style of [ALA]
graduates [BA, MA]
(7)=ALABAMA

22 Church [CH] has a [A] jolly
[RM] *entrance* (5)=CHARM

23 *Short* trees chopped up
(5)=TERSE

25 A way [ST] to the old [YE]
eyesore (4)=STYE

APPENDIX 2

PERSONAL NAMES

Frequently used names:
Male: AL, ED, DES, DON, LES, RON, TED
Female: ANN, ANNE, DI, ENA, IDA, SAL, SUE, UNA, VERA,VI

The following are largely 'compiler's definitions' of some personal names. Most names also have literal meanings (eg: Agatha =good) which can be found in standard dictionaries

MEN

AARON	AA man
	high priest
ABE	LINCOLN
ABEL	[able]
	ADAMSON
	third man
ACHATES	Bill doesn't like
	trusted friend
ACTAEON	cuckold
	hunter
ACTON	historian
ADAM	architect
	BEDE
	first mate
	front runner
	furniture designer
	gaoler
	leading man
	race leader
	SMITH
ADAMSON	ABEL
	CAIN
	SETH
ADONIS	beau
	dandy
ADRIAN	MOLE
AIDAN	NADIA<.DIANA

AL	CAPONE
	gangster
ALAN	from New Ze/alan/d
ALBERT	two boys
	watchchain
—Albert's place	HALL
ALEC	smart(ypants)
ALEX	a Roman law
ALEXANDER	a Great name
ALF	is from S/alf/ord
ALFRED	a Great name
	almost (h)alf
	Communist
	cake-burner
ALGY	in hospit/al gy/m
	LG, say
ALI	boxer
	CLAY
ALVIN	[anvil]
AMOS	Andy's partner
	bookmaker
	OT book
ANANIAS	liar
ANDREW	Apostle
	fisherman
	may [wander]
	merry fellow

ANDY	Amos's partner
	CAPP
with us *in* spirit (br/andy/)	
ANSELM	bishop
	theologian
ANTHONY	ADVERSE
	smallest pig in litter
ANTON	is a heavyweight
ANTONIO	Merchant of Venice
ANTONY	MARK
APOLLYON	destroyer
ARCHIE	AA gun
	RICE
ARCHY	
	Mehitabel's biographer
ARISTOTLE	philosopher
ARKWRIGHT	NOAH
ARNE	composer
ARNOLD	BENEDICT
	headmaster
	[ROLAND]
	[RONALD]
ARTHUR	lived at Camelot
ATKINS	private
	soldier
	TOMMY
ATLAS	giant
	map-book
	mountains
ATTILA, *say*	a ploughman
AUTOLYCUS	plagiarist
	thief
BACON	rasher
	philosopher
BALDWIN	simple victory
BALTHAZAR	wise man
BARKER	dog
BARKIS	carrier
	is willing
BARNABY	RUDGE
BASIL	BRUSH
	dislodged [bails]
	herb
BEN	big man
	big timer

	HUR
	peak
BENJAMIN	gum benzoin
	overcoat
	youngest son
BERT	*has some* li/bert/y
BERTIE	WOOSTER
BERTRAND	RUSSELL
BILL	AC
	account
	act
	ad
	poster
	tab
BILLY	brother
	BUNTER
	can
	companion-in-arms
	goat
	teapot
BILLY's	boy kid
—wife	nanny
BOANERGES	noisy preacher
	shouting
	orator
BOB	shilling
	your uncle
BOBADIL	
	swaggering boaster
BOBBY	PC
	policeman
BOOTH	assassin
jeer at most of th(e)...	
	stall
BORIS	is good enough
	(Goudenov)
BOTTOM	weaver
BRIAN	*scatter*[brain]
BROWN	capability
	tan
BROWNE	SAM
BRUCE	ROBERT
	spiderman
BUD	American friend
	FLANAGAN

BURGESS	freeman	DAI	Welshman
	treacherous guy	DAMON	*returning* nomad
BUTLER	RAB		RUNYON
	RHET	DAN	black belt man
CAIN	ADAMSON		dangerous
	(first) murderer		desperate
	tribute		*in some* /dan/ger
CARL	churl		judo expert
	husbandman		MCGREW
	niggard	DANIEL	bookmaker
CARLO(S)	[CAROL(S)]		lion-tamer
CASCA	conspirator		OT book
CATO	censor		wise judge
CECIL	fried meat-ball	DANTE	*made* [a dent]
CELLINI	hole-in-one		poet
CHARLES	Bonny Prince	DAVID	giant-killer
	Chas		his work, Psalms
	LAMB	DENIS	is *after* a room
CHARLEY/			*is* [snide]
CHARLIE	gullible fool		the man [I send]
	inefficient person	DENNIS	fell back
	moustache		sinned
	night watchman	DENRY MACHIN	card
	small beard	DICKENS	BOZ
CHARON	ferryman	DIOGENES	tubby man
CHRISTIAN	Milton's man	DON	assume
CHRISTOPHER	KIT		dress
	SLY		Fellow
CLARENCE	carriage		riverman
	diligence		Spanish noble
CLAUD	[ducal]	DONALD	duck
CLAUDE	painter	DORIAN	*makes* [inroad]
CLEMENT	mild man	DOUGLAS	fir
	Pope		his pet, Manx cat
CLIVE	man of India		Man's man
COLIN	quail		Manxman
COLLINS	letter of thanks	DUNCAN	ISADORA
CONSTANT	LAMBERT	DUNNE	done, *say*
CRAIG	*rolls* [cigar]		poet
CRISPIN	shoemaker	DUSTY	MILLER
CROMWELL	NOLL	EBENEZER	chapel
	Protector		meeting-house
CUTHBERT	shirker		memorial stone
CYRIL	*writes* [lyric]	EDDY	goes in circles
CYRUS	Persian king		NELSON

EDGAR	*makes the* [grade]		important to be
	[raged] *wildly*		*sounds* sincere
EDISON	*has* [no side]	ESAU	hunter
	inventor	ETTY	artist
EDWARD	confessor	EVAN	Welsh John
	potato	EZRA	bookmaker
	king		OT book
EDMUND	Ironside		poet
ELGAR	compositions		POUND
	[glare]	FELIX	cat
	[lager]	FLASHMAN	bully
	[large]	FLETCHER	arrowmaker
	[regal]	FOX	TOD
ELI	priest	FRANK	franc, *say*
	Samuel's teacher		open
ELIA	LAMB		sincere
	unr/elia/ble writer		stamp
ELIAS	*in the* [aisle]	FRED	KARNO
ELIOT	poet	GABRIEL	archangel
	TS	GANYMEDE	cup-bearer
ELISHA	prophet	GARIBALDI	biscuit
	[SHEILA]		Italian hero
ELVIS	*changed* [lives]	GARY	state railway
	destroyed [evils]	GASPAR	wise man
	PRESLEY	GENE	item of make-up
EMIL	*makes* [lime]	GEORGE	automatic pilot
	running [mile]		BOY
ENOCH	Ayli's mate		ELIOT
	priest		SAND
ERASMUS	[masseur]		sandboy
	philsosopher	GERALD	[glared] *wildly*
ERIC	a fine boy	GIBBON	historian
	blood money		monkey
	cooks [rice]	GILBERT	composer
	Central Am/eric/an		WS
	gradually	GILES	farmer
	Red Norseman	GOLDSMITH	or mighty
	[rice] *pudding*		man
ERNIE	bondsman	GORDON	general
	number chooser		riots
	WISE	GRANT	allow, give
	upsets [IRENE]		general
ERNEST	EARNEST, *say*		tank
	HEMINGWAY	GREGORY	PECK
			pope

GRIMES,	Mr sweep
GUS	large store
	theatre cat
GUY	anchorman
	FAWKES
	helps with
	camp upkeep
	supporter
HADRIAN	wall-builder
HAL	HENRY
comes from	
	/Hal/ifax
HAMLET	great Dane
upset [THELMA]	
	village
HANK	skein
HARPAGON	miser
HARRY	harass
HECTOR	badger
	bully
	Trojan hero
HENRY	female line
	navigator
HENRY FORD's	
bunk	history
HENRY, Sir	WOOD
HERB	simple
HERCULES	Labour man
HERMAN	*bit of a*
	fis/herman/
HERBERT	AP/APH
HILARY	term
HIRAM	employs people
HOMER	pigeon
	poet
HUGH	hew or hue, *say*
HUME	philosopher
HUMPHREY	bogey/bogie
IAN	FLEMING
	one and one
	Scot
IBSEN	ghost-writer
INGE	dean
INIGO	in I go, *say*
	JONES

IRA	*captured by* p/ira/tes
	terrorists
ISAIAH	bookmaker
	OT book
	prophet
ISHMAEL	*makes a mess*
	of [his meal]
	outcast
IVAN	Russian
HENRY	*might be* [vain]
	terrible man
IVOR	*is from* L/ivor/no
IXION	fiery revolutionary
JACK	AB
	American detective
	breadfruit tree
	car lifter
	card
	defensive coat
	fellow
	flag
	FROST
	hearty
	honour
	house builder
	in the box
	Jill's boy
	knave
	knife
	nave, *say*
	nob
	ripper
	sailor
	salt
	SPRAT
	tar
	term of contempt
	union
	weight-lifter
	wood (bowls)
	young pike
JACK KETCH	hangman
	suspender
JACOB	ladderman
JAKE	good fellow

JAMES	baked sheep's head	JOHN	AUGUSTUS
	bookmaker		bookmaker
	crowbar		BULL
	homely fellow		DOE
	NT book		EVAN (Welsh)
	overcoat		GAUNT
	WATT		IAN (Scottish)
JASON	Argonaut		lavatory
	[JONAS]		NT book
	looks both ways		PEEL
JASPER	stone		PRESTER
JAY	bird		SEAN (Irish)
	J, *say*		simpleton
	walker	JOHNNY	latecomer
JEEVES	manservant		WALKER
JEHU	road-hog	JONAH	bookmaker
JENKINS	society reporter		OT book
	toady		whale-food
JEREMIAH	bookmaker	JONAS	[JASON]
	OT book	JONATHAN	American
	prophet of doom		(people)
JEROME	boatman		apple
	KERN		SWIFT
	writer	JONES	riding-coat
JERRY	builder		standard-setter
	can-man	JOSEPH	coloured coat man
	chamber-pot		dreamer
	German		woman's
JESSE	candlestick		riding-coat
	church window	JOSHUA	bookmaker
	genealogical tree		OT book
JIM	CROW		trumpeter
	lucky	JOSHUA, Sir	PRA
JOB	bookmaker		REYNOLDS
	OT book	JUDAS	notorious kisser
	patient one		spyhole
JOCK	Scot		traitor
JOE	GI	JUDE	bookmaker
	sweetheart		OT book
	threepenny piece	JULIUS	CAESAR
	US soldier	KELLY	Man's man
JOEL	bookmaker		Manxman
	OT book	KIM	Kipling character
JOEY	kangaroo	KINGSLEY	his friends
	roo		are AMIS

KIT	CHRISTOPHER	MAL	degree student
	outfit	MARCEL	*could be* [calmer]
LAMB	CHARLES	MARCO	POLO
	ELIA	MARIO	LANZA
	Mary's follower		March 10th
LANCE	pierce	MARK	ANTONY
	spear		bookmaker
	weapon		German coin/DM
LANG	archbishop		imprint
LAUD	archbishop		NT book
	praise		scar
LAWRENCE	DH		TWAIN
	ROSS	MARK TWAIN	two fathoms
	TE	MARTIN	bird/birdman
LEANDER	hero-worshipper		LUTHER
LEE	general	MATTHEW	bookmaker
	student's quarters		NT book
	tank	MAX	*makes* master cross
LEN	student's quarters		maximum/most
LEO	lion	MELCHIOR	wise man
	man of pride	MICHAEL	angel
	sign of Zodiac		archangel
	the *French* circle	MICK	Irishman
LEON	[NOEL]	MICKEY	FINN
LEONARDO	top drawer		gets taken
LES	student's quarters		MOUSE
LEW	student's quarters	MILES	knight
LEWIS	CARROLL	MILL	economist
	gun		factory
	island		fight
	metal cramp	MILLER	dusty
LIAM	[mail] *order*		GLENN
	from [Mali]		grinder
LINCOLN	ABE	MONTAGUE	ROMEO
LIONEL	young lion	MORGAN	pirate
LLOYD	[DOLLY]	MOSES	lawgiver
	MARIE		prophet
LOTHARIO	lover	MR *TURNER*	RM
	rake	MURPHY	potato/spud/
LOUIS	coin		tuber
LUKE	bookmaker	NAPOLEON	brandy
	NT book		pig
	physician	NAT	insect impersonator
LUTHER	MARTIN		*sounds*+ fly
MAC	Scot	NED	*half* sto<u>ned</u>

219

NEDDY	donkey		moor
	economic council		NOLL
NEIL	*from the* [Nile]		orphan
	kneel, *say*		Roland's friend
NELSON	admiral		warrior
	arm-lock	OMAR	*comes from* [Roma]
	EDDY		*may* [roam]
NERO	emperor	ONEGIN	singular spirit
	fiddler	ORIGEN	theologian
NEWMAN	cardinal		*may* [ignore]
NEWTON	ISAAC	OSCAR	film award
	force		statuette
	[not]		large vehicle
	physicist		WILDE
NICK	Devil		zero mark
	notch	OSWALD	assassin
	prison		MOSLEY
	steal	OTHELLO	black lead
NOAH	ARKWRIGHT		Moor
	boatbuilder		Venetian
NOEL	Christmas	OTTO	emperor
	COWARD		German
	[LEON]		perfume
NORMAN	and not male		race *in* circles
	conqueror		to *turn* to<
	standard article	PABLO	sailor in P-LO
	windlass bar	PADDY	is Irish
	WISDOM		rage/temper
NYE, Nicholas	ass		rice-field
NYM	Falstaff's henchman	PARIS	kidnapper
	corporal	PAT	butter
OBERON	fairy king		glib
	from [Borneo]		is Irish
	has [no robe]		light blow
	honoured name	PAUL	Pope
	is [no Boer]		PRY
OG	King of Basham		REVERE
OLAF	*sliced* [loaf]		silver coin
OLD BILL	police		tentmaker
OLD BOB	shilling	PAUL REVERE	rider
OLIVER	biscuit	PECKSNIFF	hypocrite
	duck liver	PEDRO	fisherman
	forge-hammer	PERSHING	general
	hungry boy		missile
	[or evil]		tank

PETER	a Great name	REYNOLDS, Sir	JOSHUA
	Bishop of Rum-ti-foo		PRA
	Blue boy	RHET	butler
	bookmaker	ROBERT	BRUCE
	dwindle away		BURNS
	fisherman		peeler
	flag		policeman
	makes sham fabric	ROBIN	ADAIR
	NT book		GOODFELLOW
	PAN		is sometimes round
	RABBIT		HOOD
	safe		hob
	some trum/peter/s	ROGER	acknowledgment
PETER PAN	child's play		jolly fellow
PHIL	fluter		pirate flag
PHILIP	fillip, *say*		OK/understood
	PIP		well received
	sparrow	ROLAND	[ARNOLD]
PICKWICK	clubman		Oliver's mate
PISTOL	ancient		RAT
	braggart		[RONALD]
PLATO	philosopher	ROLLO	has bread-round
POLO	Merchant of Venice	RON	*something of*
POOTER	nobody		an ast/ron/aut
PROCRUSTES	strecher	RONALD	[ARNOLD]
PUNCH	tight-fisted character		[ROLAND]
RABBIE	BURNS	RUDOLPH	reindeer
RALPH	imp	RUSSELL	AE
	sacred river (R. Alph)		BERTRAND
RAMON	[NORMA]	SAM	BROWNE
	[Roman]		missile
RAPHAEL	archangel		Uncle
	artist		together
RAVEL	*in* t/ravel/ogue		WELLER
	tangle	SAMUEL	bookmaker
RAY	bright boy		OT book
	fish		PEPYS
	is from [Ayr]		PICKWICK
	light	SANDY	gritty character
	sunny chap		Scot
	X		two characters
REG	*man from* O/reg/on	SCROOGE	miser
	short regulation	SERGE	candle
RENE	DESCARTES		cloth
	Frenchman		Russian

SETH	ADAMSON	TELL	archer
	fourth man		hill
SHERMAN	general		utter
	tank	TERENCE	old dramatist
SILAS	*alias* [alias]		RATTIGAN
	makes [sails]	TERRY	towelling
SILVER	AG	THEO	KOJAK
	pirate		man in the ring
SIMON	PURE		the love...
	Saint	THOMAS	AQUINAS
	TEMPLAR		doubter
	simple(ton)	TIM	*is from* Bal/tim/ore
SLY	tinker		is tiny
SMITH	ADAM		tim(e) *without end*
	besieged Lady	TIMON	Athenian
	FE		misanthrope
	forger	TIMOTHY	bookmaker
	mighty man		grass
SNUG	joiner		OT book
SOLOMON	bookmaker	TITUS	bookmaker
	OT book		NT book
	song-writer		OATES
	wise man	TOBIAS	has some prejudice
SOLON	wise man		SMOLLETT
STAN	*is in the*	TOBY	BELCH
	di/stan/ce		highway robbery
STEPHENSON	RLS		Irish road
STEVENSON	rocket		jug
	designer		Punch's dog
STEVEN	outcry		Scottish stop-cock (cover)
	voice	TOM	BOWLING
*STRANGE*LOVE	[vole]		(he-)cat
SULLIVAN	Gilbert's		fool
	partner		peeper
SWIFT	JONATHAN		piper's son
	screecher		queen's mate
SYDNEY	CARTON		THUMB
	city boy		TIDDLER
TACITUS	historian		uncle
TAFFY	flattery		with Dick and Harry
	is Welsh	TOM EAST	HECATE
	sweet	TOMMY	ATKINS
TED	can make hay		gun
TEDDY	bear		soldier
	ROOSEVELT	TONY	theatrical award

Name	Clue
TREE	actor
TURNER	painter
	spit
	wheel
WHITTINGTON	
TWAIN	[a twin]
	author
	pair/two
ULYSSES	GRANT
	Greek hero
URIAH	HEEP
VALENTINE	gentleman
	of Verona
	tank
VA/LEN/TINO's name	LEN
VICTOR	HUGO
	winner
WALKER	JOHNNY
	leg
WALTER	bridegroom
	MITTY

Name	Clue
WALTER, Sir	SCOTT/Scot
WAT	TYLER
WATT	engine man
	power unit
	what, *say*
WEBSTER	spider
WELLER	boots
	SAM
WHITE	chalky
	paleface
	part of egg
WHITTINGTON	TURNER
WILL	bard
	inclination
	man of determination
	poet
	scarlet
	testament
WILL's	companion way
WRIGHT	early flier
	right, *say*

WOMEN

ABIGAIL	has a large drink, *say*
	Lady Masam
	lady's maid
	takes a lot of trouble
ADELAIDE	Australian girl
	city girl
	state capital
AELLO	Harpy
AGATHA	CHRISTIE
	crime writer
AGNES	Miss Wickfield
	takes some m/agnes/ia
AIDA	opera
	slave girl
AILSA	*may be* [alias]
ALECTO	Fury
ALICE	Australian town
	Carroll's girl
	[CELIA]
	city girl
	band
	Miss Liddell
	Wonderland girl
ALMA	dancing girl
	essense/soul
	mother of AL
AMELIA	claims to be Lamb
	Miss Scoley
AMI	an /ami/able girl
	French friend
AMY	[MAY]
	steeped in inf/amy/
ANITA	LOOS
ANNA	coin
	King's associate
	royal governess
ANNE	*from* the Ch/anne/l
ANNIE	gun girl
	orphan
	sharpshooter
APHRODITE	*is* [atrophied]
ATROPOS	Fate

AVA	Miss Gardner
AYESHA	she
BARBARA	ALLEN
	Major
BEATRICE	BEA/BEE
	thresh grain
BEATRIX	POTTER
BECKY	sharp girl
BELLA	Miss Wilfer
BERTHA	bed *with* a...big gun
	falling collar
	is a [bather]
	out of [breath]
BERYL	gem
	sparkling girl
BETTY	burglar's jemmy
	man doing housework
BEULAH	land of rest
BLANCHE	white
CALLIOPE	Muse
	tank
CARMEN	opera girl
CAROL	[CARLO]
	Christmas girl
	makes [coral]
CAROLE	*works* the [oracle]
CARRIE, *say*	BEAR
	TOTE
CASSANDRA	accountant's girl
	prophetess
	unbelievable female
CATHARINE	*makes* [a nicer hat]
CATHERINE	ARAGON
	fireworks girl
	Great name
CATHY	*makes a* [yacht]
CELAENO	Harpy
CELESTE	sky-blue
	soft pedal
CELIA	[ALICE]
CHARLOTTE	sweet girl
CICELY	chervil
	growing girl

CLARA	BUTT	DORA	Defence of the
	makes de/clara/tion		Realm Act
CLARE	college girl		Miss Spenlow
	in the [clear]		Mrs Copperfield
CLEMENTINE's	father		[road]-*builder*
	Forty-niner	DORIS	some drink
	lived in cavern	DOROTHY	bag
	miner	EDITH	CAVELL
CLEO	caught *by* lion		Mrs Dombey
CLIO	Muse		nurse
CLOTHO	Fate	EFFIE	FE, *say*
CONSTANCE	lady of Lake	ELEANOR	queen
CORAL	[CAROL]	ELECTRA	complex girl
	[CARLO]		tragic woman
DAISY	flower girl	ELIZA	Higgins's girl
	girl cyclist		Shaw's girl
	growing girl	ELIZA's	aim aspiration
DAPHNE	growing girl	ELIZABETH	ER
	in a shrubbery	ELLA	two-letter girl
DEBORAH	prophetess	ELLEN	LN, *say*
DELIA	has daughter		one measure
	by Lamb		after another
	[I lead] *astray*		TERRY
	is [ideal]	ELSA	lioness
DELILAH	courtesan		*in* [sale]
	Samson's girl	ELSIE	[ELISE]
	temptress		LC, *say*
DELLA	*uses* [ladle]	EMILY	BRONTE
DIANA	[AIDAN]		*could be* a [Limey]
	huntress		PANKHURST
	[NADIA]		suffragette
	sort of [naiad]	EMMA	HAMILTON
	princess		letter M
DINAH	diner, *say*		MA, *say*
	might/dynamite		Miss Woodhouse
	nobody finer		Nelson's woman
DOLLY	carries a camera		two-letter girl
	easy catch	EMMY	ME, *say*
	laundry aid/peg		TV award
	[LLOYD]	ENA	is a girl *of*
	PARTON		m/ena/ce
	rivet-holder	ENID	*taken to* [dine]
	truck	ERATO	Muse
	VARDEN	ERICA	growing girl
DOLORES	*has* [old rose]		heather

	[I care] *about*		ling
	is from Am/erica/n stock	HECUBA	tragic woman
	ling	HEL	queen of the dead
ESTHER	bookmaker	HELEN	girl from Troy
	OT book		he-man
ETHEL	ancestral land		ship-launcher
EU/GENIE/	girl with spirit	HERO	priestess
EUTERPE	Muse	HILARY	term
EVE	first lady	HOPE	with Faith and Charity
	first mate	IDA	eider, *say*
	is half cl/eve/r		princess
	leading lady		Fr/ida/y's girl
EVELYN	diarist	INGRID	*goes* [riding]
EVITA	showgirl	IO	cowgirl
FAITH	trust	IRA	*captured by* p/ira/tes
	with Hope and Charity		terrorists
FANNY	by gaslight	IRENE	*in* d/ire ne/ed
	PRICE		*upsets* [ERNIE]
FLEUR	flower girl	IRIS	flag
	growing girl		flower girl
FLORA	flower girl		*is almost* Iris(h)
	growing girl		growing girl
	MACDONALD		part of eye
	ROBSON		rainbow
FLORENCE	army nurse		rainbow goddess
	city girl	ISABELLA	is a beautiful
	NIGHTINGALE		*Italian*
FREDA	[fared] *badly*		Miss Wilfer
GEMMA	bud	ISADORA	dancer
	growing girl		DUNCAN
GEORGE	SAND	IVY	climber
GIGI	Joe's double		growing girl
GINA	*has some*	JANE	EYRE
	ima/gina/tion		Genoese coin
GINA *TURNER*	*makes* [gain]		[JEAN]
GLENDA	*badly* [angled]		Tarzan's mate
GRACE	darling girl		woman
	WG	JEAN	cloth
GRETA	*is a* [great] girl		[JANE]
GRISELDA	patient		GENE, *say*
HAZEL	growing girl		(pl) trousers
	is a nut case	JEANETTE	light twilled cotton
HAZEL's	protector nutshell		MACDONALD
HEATHER	erica	JENNY	country lass
	growing girl		in-off

	LIND	LOIS	*breaks* [soil]
	owl		*found in* [silo]
	she ass=assess		*makes* [oils]
	spinner	LORNA	DOONE
	womanish man	LORRAINE	part of France
	wren	LUCY	Miss Locket
JESSIE	effeminate man	LYDIA	*works* [daily]
JEZEBEL	shameless woman		languish
JILL	flirt	MAB	fairy queen
	Jack's girl	MABEL	*apportions* [blame]
	tumbler		Lucy Attwell
JO	sweetheart		*may* [amble]
JOYCE	HAW-HAW		[MELBA]
JULIET	cap	MADGE	barmaid
	CAPULET		barn-owl
JUDY	frump		leaden hammer
	girl		magpie
	Mrs Punch	MAE	WEST
	odd-looking woman	MAE WEST	life-jacket
JUNE	May's follower	MAGDALEN(E)	asylum
	summer girl		college
	wander around		hospital
KATE	shrew		repentant prostitute
KATIE	girl who did	MAME	took the blame
	KT, *say*	MARGARET	MEG
KAY	after Jay		peg
	K, *say*	MARGUERITE	flower girl
KITTY	cat		growing girl
	jack (bowls)		Queen of Navarre
	(jack)pot	MARIA	West Side girl
	jail	MARIE	LLOYD
	pool (cards)	MARINA	*could be* [airman]
LACHESIS	Fate	MARTINA	*could be* [Martian]
LIL	[ill]-treated	MARY	*in the* [Army]
LILIAN	*makes* [Ian ill]		MOLL(Y)
LILITH	Adam's first wife		[MYRA]
LILY	flower girl		nursery gardener
	growing girl		shepherdess
	lote	MARY's follower	LAMB
	lotus	MATILDA	bushman's swag
	of Laguna		liar
	of the valley		tank
LILY MARLENE	war record		waltzer
LISA	*may be in* [sail]	MAUD	in the garden
	MONA		plaid

MAUD AND RUTH	truth
MAVIS	songbird
	thrush
MAY	[AMY]
	flower girl
	follower of April
	growing girl
MEG	bit of a nut
	MARGARET
MEGAERA	Fury
MEGAN	million to one girl
	Welsh girl
MELBA	[MABEL]
	takes [blame]
MELISSA	*is* [aimless]
MELPOMENE	Muse
MERLE	blackbird
	OBERON
MEROPE	tragic woman
MILDRED	of the soft left
	pinkish girl
MIMI	dual carriageway
	has very cold hand
	seamstress
MINNIE	mine
	moaner
	MOUSE
MIRIAM	right *in* [Miami]
MOIRA	*could be* [Maori]
MOLL	FLANDERS
	gangster's girl
MOLLY	little Mary
	milksop
MONA	island
	LISA
MOPP, Mrs	char
MYRA	*in the* [Army]
	[MARY]
MYRTLE	growing girl
	in the shrubbery
	her husband, Bushman
NADIA	AIDAN<
	[DIANA]
NANCY	city girl
	effeminate male

	French city
	milksop
NAOMI	*brokenly* [I moan]
	is not ruthless
	perhaps [Omani]
	Ruth's friend
NELL	a little woman
	Charlie's girl
	king's mistress
	knell, *say*
	orange-seller
NELLY	petrel
NETTA	*retires* at ten<
NIOBE	daughter of
	Tantalus
	stone maiden
	weeper
NORA	is no painter
NORMA	constellation
	may be [Roman]
	nearly norma(l)
	opera girl
	standard article
OCYPETE	Harpy
OLGA	[gaol]-*break*
	in [gaol]
	in [goal]
OLIVE	colour
	drab
	fruit
	growing girl
	in the drink
	OBE
	Popeye's girl
	sailorman's girl
	stony-hearted
	wood
PAM	card game
	knave of clubs
PANSY	effeminate man
	flower girl
	growing girl
PARTLETT, Mrs	hen
PATIENCE	card game
	kind of dock

	sufferance
PEARL	can handle a gun
	gem
	gets fruit *by* the pound
	grey
	loop of lace
	may be [paler]
	purl, *say*
	type size
	WHITE
	woman of wisdom
PEG	dolly
	takes hat and coat
PEGGY	roofing slate
	warbler
	whitethroat
PHOEBE	ARTEMIS
	moon-goddess
PIGGY, Miss	gilt
PODARGE	Harpy
POLLY	parrot
	pretty girl
	repetitive type
POLYHYMNIA	Muse
PRIMROSE	flower girl
	growing girl
	League
PRUDENCE	caution
PRUNELLA	hedgesparrow
PYTHIA	priestess
RACHEL	du Maurier's
	cousin
REBECCA	Mrs de Winter
	Welsh rioter
REGAN	Lear's daughter
	princess
	wicked sister
RENEE	born again
RITA	*found in* B/rita/in
ROSE	colour
	flower girl
	growing girl
	is from Picardy
	is from Tralee
	sprinkler

	stood up
	wine
ROSEMARY	growing girl
	in the shrubbery
ROSIE	cider-drinker
	[osier]-*weaver*
	tea-girl
RUBY	kind of gem
	kind of type
	sparkling girl
RUTH	babe
	bookmaker
	friend of Naomi
	gleaner
	OT book
	pity
	wife of Boaz
SADIE	*changes* [aides]
	has peculiar
	[ideas]
SELINA	*is* [saline]
SALLY	aunt
	flight
	part of bellrope
	quip
	repartee
	sortie
	willow
	witty girl
SALOME	dancing girl
	stripper
SANDRA	beach artist
SHEILA	Aussie girl
	[ELISHA]
SIBYL/SYBYL	prophetess
	sorceress
SOPHIA	wisdom
SUE	will prosecute
SUSIE	*may take* [issue]
SYLVIA	warbler
TABITHA	*has strange*
	[habitat]
TERESA	[Easter] *break*
TESS	Hardy's girl
	Miss Durbeyfield

	Wessex girl		TILLEY
THATCHER, Mrs	MAGGIE	VICTORIA	carriage
	MEG		city girl
THELMA	*makes* [Hamlet] *mad*		plum
TINA	metal article		queen
TISIPHONE	Muse		station
UNA	*some* l/una/tic		water lily
URANIA	Muse	VIOLA	fiddle
VANESSA	butterfly		flower girl
	Red Admiral		growing girl
VENUS	is (h)armless		pansy
VERA	a/vera/ge girl	VIRGINIA	creeper
	magnetic recorder		growing girl
VERONICA	growing girl		stock
	in shrubbery		tobacco
	pass in the bullring		US state
	patron saint of bullring		VA
	speedwell		water
VESTA	goddess	WENDY	housemaid
	match		
	planet		

APPENDIX 3

A COMPILER'S ALPHABET

A list of words for which the single head-letter may be used.

A
academician
accepted
ace
ack
acre
active
adult
advanced
afternoon
aleph
alpha
alto
amateur
ampere
an
ana
ane
angstrom
annus
answer
ante
are
argon
associate
atomic
atto-
Austria
ay
aye
before (ante)
blood group
bomb
effect
electric current
examination
film

fifty
first character
first-class
first letter
five hundred
five thousand
high-class
it
key
level
mass number
note
nucleon number
one
paper
road
string
top mark
un
vitamin
year (annus)

B
a follower
Bach
bachelor
baron
bass
bay
bedbug
bee
Beethoven
bel
Belgium
beta
beth
billion

binary
bishop
black
blood group
bloody
book
born
boron
bowled
boy
Brahms
breadth
Britain
British
inferior
key
magnetic flux
note
paper
road
second-class
second letter
three hundred
three thousand
vitamin

C
about
approximately
capacitance
cape
caput
carbon
Catholic
caught
cedi
cee

Celsius
cent
centi-
centigrade
centime
century
chapter
Charles
circa
city
clef
club
cold
colony
complex number
computer language
Conservative
contralto
copyright
coulomb
Cuba
cubic
electrical capacitance
hundred
hundred thousand
key
lot
many
note
number
roughly
san
sea
see
speed of light
spring
tap
vitamin

D
damn
date
daughter
day
dead

deci-
Dee
degree
dele
delete
delta
Democrat
deserted
deuterium
Deutsch
diameter
diamond
died
differential operator
doctor
duke
electrical flux
five hundred
four
Germany
key
lot
many
mark
note
notice
number
Schubert's works
string
vitamin

E
Asian
Balearic Islands
boat
bridge player
Canary Islands
east(ern)
Ecstasy
Edward
eight
eight thousand
electron charge
Elizabeth
energy

England
English
epsilon
eta
European
exa-
five
food additive
key
layer
logarithm base
low-grade
note
orient(al)
Spain
string
two hundred and fifty
two hundred and fifty
    thousand
universal set
vitamin

F
clef
Fahrenheit
farad
Faraday's constant
farthing
fathom
fellow
female
feminine
femto-
filly
fine
fluorine
folio
following
foot
force
forte
forty
forty thousand
France
frequency

Friday
Helmholtz   free
    energy
hole
key
loud
noisy
note
vitamin

G
acceleration
agent
clef
conductance
four hundred
four hundred
    thousand
gamma
gamut
Gauss
gee
George
Germany
Gibb's function
giga-
girl
good
gram(me)
grand
gravity
guinea
gulf
key
man
note
shear modulus
string
suit

H
bomb
complex cube root
Dirac's constant
enthalpy

Hamiltonian
hand
hard
heart
heat content
hecto-
height
Helmholtz free
    energy
henry
horse
hospital
hot
hotel
hour
house
Hungary
husband
hydrant
hydrogen
magnetic field
    strength
Planck's constant
tap
total energy
two hundred
two hundred
    thousand
vitamin

I
a
an
ane
ay
aye
che
electrical current
eye
imaginary number
individual
iodine
iota
island
Italy

line
lunch time
moment of inertia
one
single
square root of -1
straight line
un
upright
yours truly

J
curve
heat
Jack
Japan
jay
joule
judge
justice
knave
one
pen
square root of -1

K
Boltzmann's constant
conductivity
constant
dissociation constant
kalium
Kampuchea
kappa
Kay
kay
kelvin
Khmer Republic
kilo
king
Kirkpatrick
knight
Köchel
monarch
Mozart's works
potassium

radius of gyration
Scarlatti's works
thousand
two hundred and fifty
vitamin

L

angle
apprentice
Avogadro number
corner
driver
el, ell
elevated railway
fifty
fifty thousand
half-century
hand
inductance
Labour
lake
la(m)bda
lambert
latent heat
Latin
latitude
league
learner
learning
left
length
Liberal
libra
licentiate
line
lira/lire
litre
live
long
lumen
Luxembourg
many
new driver
novice
number plate
overhead railway

port
pound
pupil
quantum number
railway
side
sovereign
student
tyro
vitamin

M

Bond's boss
em
emma
Frenchman
lot
Mach number
magnetisation
maiden
male
Malta
man
many
mare
mark
married
masculine
mass
master
medium
member
meridian
meso-
meta-
metre
mile
mille
milli-
million
modulus
Monday
monsieur
month
moon

motorway
mu
noon
number
quantum number
roof
small number
small square
spymaster
thousand
vitamin

N

Avogadro number
born (née)
bridge player
en
half an em
indefinite number
knight
name
nano-
natural numbers
natus
neper
neuter
neutral
neutron number
new
newton
ninety
ninety thousand
nitrogen
noon
north(ern)
Norway
note
noun
nu
number
quantum number
unknown number
unlimited number
viscosity

O
allrounder
around
aught
bald patch
ball
band
blob
blood group
cavity
cipher
circle
circular letter
circuit
dial
disc
duck
egg
eleven
eleven thousand
empty
examination
full moon
globe
gulf
hole
hollow
hoop
loop
love
naught
nil
nothing
nought
Ohio
omega
omicron
opening
orb
ortho-
ought
oval
oxygen
pellet
pill

ring
round
spangle
vacancy

P
Angola
Cape Verde Islands
Celt
copper(s)
four hundred
four hundred
    thousand
Kelt
momentum
Mozambique
page
parity
park(ing)
participle
pawn
pea
pedal
pee
peg
penny
peta-
phosphorus
pi
piano
pico-
poise
Portugal
Portuguese Guinea
Portuguese Timor
power
president
pressure
Principe Islands
prince
quiet
rho
Sao Tome
soft
vitamin

Q
boat
Celt
cue
electric charge
farthing
five hundred
five hundred
    thousand
Kelt
koppa
quadrans
quality
quark
Quebec
queen
Queensland
query
question
queue
quintal
rational number

R
are
arithmetic
canine letter
castle
eighty
eighty thousand
gas constant
hand
king
monarch
month
queen
radius
rain
rand
reading
real numbers
Réaumur
received
recipe

Regina
registered trademark
Republican
resistance
Rex
rho
right
road
Roger
Romania
röntgen unit
rook
rotund character
royal
run
rupee
Ryberg's constant
side
writing

S
as
Bach's works
bend
bob
bridge player
dollar
entropy
es
ess
God's
has
his
hiss
is
largesse
Old Bob
paragon
part of collar
Sabbath
saint
Saturday
Schmieder
second
seven

seventy
seventy thousand
shilling
side
siemens
sigma
sister
snow
society
son
soprano
south(ern)
spade
square
stokes
sulphur
sun
Sweden
us

T
bandage
bar
bone
cart
cloth
cross
crossed
half-dry
hundred and sixty
hundred and sixty
    thousand
isotopic spin
junction
kinetic energy
model
perfect letter
period of function
plate
rail
shirt
square
tau
te
tea

tee
temperature
tenor
tera-
tesla
Thailand
the
theta
time
ton(n)e
transmittance
tritium
Tuesday

U
acceptable
aristocratic
bend
boat
bolt
educational
    establishment
ewe
film
high-class
posh
superior
trap
tube
turn
union
Unionist
universal
universe
university
upper-class
upsilon
uranium
Uruguay
Utah

V
against
agent

bomb
chevron
day
electric potential
   difference
five
five thousand
frequency
look
neck
neckline
notch
nu
see
sign
vanadium
Vatican
vee
velocity
verb
verse
versus
very
victory
vide
volt
volume
win

W
bridge player
complex cube root
tungsten
watt
weak
Wednesday
Welsh
west(ern)

whole numbers
wicket
width
wife
William
wolfram
woman

X
across
body
chi
Christ
chromosome
cross
draw
ex
Exe
film
illiterate's sign
kiss
particle
PM's address
ray
reactance
sign of the times
spot marked
takes
ten
ten thousand
thousand
times
unknown
vitamin
vote
wrong sign
xi
Xmas

Y
alloy
chromosome
level
moth
one hundred and fifty
one hundred and fifty
   thousand
track
unknown
why
yard
year
yen
young
youth
yttrium

Z
atomic number
bar
bend
cedilla
impedance
integers
izzard
last character
last letter
omega
proton number
sound of sleep
two thousand
Zambia
zed
zee
zero
zeta

APPENDIX 4

A COMPILER'S VOCABULARY

This list gives just a few of the words, abbreviations, etc., frequently used in crosswords. For a more complete list, see the author's *Crossword Dictionary*, also published by Collins.

A

able seaman	AB.SAILOR	agreement	AY.AYE.YEA
	SALT.TAR	—foreign	DA (Russ.).JA (Ger.)
about (approx.)	C.CA		OUI (Fr.).SI (Span.)
about (concerning)	RE	aircraftsman	AC.LAC
about turn	U	airline	BA.BAC.BEA
academic	MA.PROF	airman	PO
academician	A.ARA.PRA.RA	alcoholic state	DT
academy	RA.RADA	alien	ET
acceptable	OK.U	all right	OK
accepted	A	alpha	A
account	AC	alternative	OR
accountant	AC.ACA.CA	always	AY.AYE
acre	A	amateur	A
acting	ON	amateur's department	DIY
active	A	ambassador	HE
actor	TREE	American	AM.AMER.US
admitting	AM.IAM.IM	—detective	FED.G-MAN
adult	A	—lawyer	DA
advanced	A	—man	BO
advertisement	AD	—policeman	BULL
aeroplane	MIG	—railway	EL
a follower	B	—soldier	GI
after date	AD	ampere	A
afternoon	A.IAM.PM	an/ane	A.I
after the style of	ALA	anaesthetic	NUMBER
again	RE	anarchist	RED
against	CON.V	ancient	
aged	AE.AET	—city	TROY.UR
agent	SPY	—times	BC
		and (Fr.)	ET

angle	L	**B**	
Anglo-Saxon	AS	bachelor	B.BA
angstrom	A	Bach's works	S
annual meeting	AGM	bad French	MAL
answer (one answer)	ANS	bald patch	O
	(IANS)	ball	O
ante	A	banker	RIVER (q.v.)
appeal	SOS	bank rate	BR
apprentice	L	barbarian	HUN
approval	OK	bark	WOOF
approx(imately)	C.CA	batting	IN
	SOME	beady	BD
archbishop	CANTUAR	bee(s)	B (BB.BS)
	EBOR.LAUD	before	A.AN.ERE.OR
archer	TELL	before Christ	AC.BC
are	R	before the day	AD
are (metric)	A	beginning	ALPHA
argy(-bargy)	RG	bend	S.U
arrive/arrival	AR.ARR	bender	KNEE
ars	RR	beta	B
articles:		bible	AV.RV
—English	A.AN.THE	big	OS
—French	LE.LA.LES	—banger	TNT
—German	DER.DIE.DAS	—guns	RA
—Italian	IL.LA	—noise	VIP
—Spanish	EL.LA.LOS	bikini	ATOLL
artillery	RA	bill	AC
artist	ARA.ETTY.LELY	bird	PRISON
	PRA.RA	bishop	B.BP.ODO
art nouveau	RAT.TAR	black	B
arty	RT	blob	O
as above	US	blockbuster	SCULPTOR
Asian	E	bloody	B
associate	A	bloomer	FLOWER (q.v.)
at home	IN	blue	SAD
atomic	A	bluetit	NUN
at one on	-ATION	boasting	AM.IAM.IM
authorisation	OK	bob	S
autobiography	CV	Bond's boss	M
average	AVE.AVER	bone	T
Avogadro's number	N	book	B.BK.LIB.TOME.VOL
award	CH.OBE.OM	bookmaker	AMOS.JOB.etc.
away	OUT	books	BB.NT.OT
ay(s), aye(s)	A(AS).I(IS)	born	B.N.NAT.NE.NEE

239

bound	BD	central heating	CH
bowled	B	century	C
bowler	DRAKE	certain	SURE
boy	B	champion	ACE.CH
branch	BR	chapter	C.CAP.CH
Brazilian	PARA	chemical	NITRE
breadth	B	chemist	MPS
bridge	BR	chief	CH.CID
—opponents	NE.NW.SE.SW	child	BRAT.CH
—partners	EW.NS	childless	SP
—players	N.S.E.W	children	SEED
brief reply	ANS	chimney (Scot.)	LUM
brig	BR	china	MING
Britain/British	B.BR	China area (Far East)	FARE
British company	BL	Chinese dynasty	HAN.MING
British Museum	BM	Christ	X
brother	BR.BRO	Christian era	AD
brown	BR	Christmas period	DEC
business	ADO.BIZ.CO.FIRM	church	CE.CH.RC
buzzer	BEE	cipher	O
by	PER	circle	DISC.O.RING
		circuit	O
		circular letter	O
C		cities	*see* towns
cagey	KG	city	EC.ELY
Cakesville	ECCLES	—(old)	TROY.UR
can	-ABLE.MAY.TIN	civil service	CS
cape	C	class	CL
Capek's play	RUR	classical musician	ORPHEUS
capital (authority)	AI (GLC)	clause	CL
captain	CID.OLD MAN	clear	RID
car	MINI.RR	cleric	BD.DD
carat	CAR.CT	close (old word)	NIE
car test	MOT	club	C
castle	R	Cockney girl	ER
cat	MOG.REX.TOM	cold	C
cattle	KINE.NEAT	collection	ANS
caught	C.CT	college	ETON.POLY
cave (beware)	KV	commander	CINC.CO
cavy	KV		COM.OC
cayenne	KN	commanding officer	CO
cedi	C	commotion	TODO
Celsius/centigrade	C	communist	RED
censor	CATO.EDIT	company	CO.FIRM.TWO
cent/centime	C.CT		

complex number	C
concerning	RE
condition	IF
Conservative	BLUE.C.CON
	TORY.U
conspirator	CADE.OATES
contemporary	AD
continent	ASIA.EUR
copper	CU.D.P
copyright	C
corner	L
Cornwall	SW
correct	OK
coulomb	C
counter	GEIGER.GM
countries:	
Albania	AL
America	AM.US.USA
Australia	AUS
Austria	A
Belgium	B
China	CH
Colombia	CO
Cuba	C
Czechoslovakia	CS
Denmark	DK
Egypt	ET
France	F
Germany	G
Great Britain	GB
Greece	GR
Hungary	H
Iceland	IS
India	IND
Iran	IR
Ireland	IRL
Israel	IL
Italy	I
Jamaica	JA
Japan	J
Khmer Republic	K
Libya	LAR
Luxembourg	L
Malta	M

North America	NA
Northern Ireland	NI
Norway	N
Panama	PA
Peru	PE
Poland	PL
Portugal	P
Puerto Rico	PR
Romania	R
South Africa	SA
—America	SA
Soviet Union	SU.USSR
Spain	E
Sweden	S
Switzerland	CH
Tanzania	EAT
Thailand	T
Turkey	TR
United Kingdom	UK
Uruguay	U.URU
Zaire	ZR
Zambia	Z
	see also territories
county	AVON.CO
	DOWN.SOM
—council	CC
court	CT
cow	LOWER
credit	CR
—notes	-IOUS
cross	TAU.X
crown	CR
cry of delight	OLE
cry of triumph	IO
cue	Q
current	AC.DC
cutie	QT

D

Dad's Army	HG
daily	CHAR.TIMES
dark blue	OXONIAN
date	D
daughter	D

dawn	NUS
day(s)	D(DD)
day's date	DD
dead/died	D.OBIT
dead reckoning	DR
dear (Fr.)	CHER(E)
decentralise	CORE
decimally	INTENS-
Dee	D
deep	MAIN.SEA
degree	BA.D.DEG.MA
delete	D
Democrat	D
deserted	D
deserter	RAT
desert fighter	RAT
designer	DIOR
dessert	FOOL
detective	DET.TEC
detectives	CID.YARD
Deutsch	D
Devon	SW
dial	O
diameter	D
diamond	ICE.ROCK
difficulty	ADO.ER
dime (Amer.)	IOC
diplomat	CD
Dirac's constant	H
directions	N.S.E.W
directors	BOARD
disadvantage (drawback)	WARD
disc	O
District Attorney	DA
ditch	HAHA
divine	DD
doctor	BM.DR.GP
	MD.MO.WHO
doctrine	-ISM
dog	MUTT
dollar	S
donkey	ASS.NED
don't change it	STET
double	BI-.DI-.KA

—act	DODO
doubt	UM
dram	DR
drawer	DR
dressmaker	SATIN.SILK.etc.
dry	SEC.TT
duck	O
duck's eggs	OO
duke	FIST
Durham area	NE
Dutch uncle	OOM

E

early morning	IAM
ease	EE.ES
east/eastern	E
east (Ger.)	OST
economist	MILL.SMITH
ecstatic	SENT
editor	ED
educated man	MA
educational	
—journal	TES
—establishment	ETON.U
EEC	TWELVE
egg	O
el(s)	L (LL.LS)
elected	IN
electoral system	PR
electrical	
—capacity	C
—charge	Q
—current	I
elements:	
aluminium	AL
barium	BA
boron	B
calcium	CA
carbon	C
chlorine	CL
cobalt	CO
copper	CU
deuterium	D
fluorine	F

gold	AU.BULL.OR	existing state	ASIS
helium	HE	exotic	ET
hydrogen	H	expert	ABLE.ACE.DAB.PRO
iodine	I	explosive	HE.TNT
iron	FE	extraterrestrial	ET
krypton	KR	extremity	TOE
lead	PB	eye(s)	I (II.IS)
magnesium	MG	eyesore	STYE
mercury	HG		
neon	NE	**F**	
nickel	NI	fabulous	
oxygen	O	—bird	ROC
palladium	PO	—hare	LOSER
platinum	PT	—tortoise	WINNER
potassium	K	Fahrenheit	F
silicon	SI	fairy queen	MAB
silver	AG	farad	F
sodium	NA	farewell	VALE
sulphur	S	farthing	F.Q
tin	SN	fashion	RAGE.TON
tritium	T	fashionable	IN
uranium	U	fast car	GT.ROD
vanadium	V	Fates	*see* Numbers, Part 2:23
yttrium	Y	father	DAD.FR.PA
ell(s)	L (LL.LS)		POP.TIME
em(s)	M (MM.MS)	fathom	F
empty	O	favoured	IN
—container	-TION	fellow	F.GENT.MAN
energy	E	female	F.HEN.HER.SHE
engineers	CE.RE.REME	feminine	F
England/English	E.ENG	fertiliser	NITRE
en(s)	N (NN.NS)	fifty-fifty	LL
envy	NV	fighter	GI.MAN
ergo	SO	figures	*see* Numbers, Part 2:23
essay	SA	film	A.ET.U.X
Essen	SN	final	
Essex	SX	—letter	OMEGA.Z
estimated time of arrival	ETA	—message	OBIT.RIP
ever	AY.AYE.ER.EER	—word	AMEN.OMEGA
ewe(s)	U (US.UU)	fine	F.OK.SCOT
ex, Exe	X	firm	CO.FAST
examination	ORAL.TEST	first	-IST
excel	XL	—character	A.ADAM.ALPHA
excellency	HE	—class	A.AI

—item in sale	LOTI	—queen	REINE.SM
—lady	EVE	—wine	VIN
—letter	A.ALPHA	frequency	F
—mate	EVE	frequently	FR
—murderer	CAIN	friar	TUCK
—person	ADAM.I.ME	Friday	F.MAN
—victim	ABEL	from	EX
fish	COD.EEL.GAR.ID	from (Fr.)	DE
	IDE.-LING	from the (Fr.)	DELA.DU
fleet	RN	full moon	O
fliers	RAF	Furies *see* Numbers, Part 2:23
flourished	FL	
flower	ROSE.etc.	**G**
flower	RIVER (q.v.)	Gaelic	ERSE.GAEL
flowers	LEI	gallery	TATE
fly-by-night	BAT.MOTH	gangster	AL
folio(s)	F (FF).FO.FOL	garden	EDEN.PLOT
following(s)	F (FF)	gases:	
foot	F.FT	carbon monoxide	CO
football	FA.RU	chlorine	CL
footnote	PS	fluorine	F
for	PRO	helium	HE
force	F	hydrogen	H
forced	FZ	neon	NE
for each	PER	nitrogen	N
for example	EG.VG	oxygen	O
former	EX	gauss	G
forte	F	gee	G
fortissimo	FF	general	GEN.GRANT.LEE
four feet	ELL	—service	GS
fourth man	SETH	—staff	GS
fox	TOD	generation	ERA
fragment	FR	Genesis	GEN
franc	FR	genius	ID
Franco-German		German	HUN
agreement	OUIJA	gift	GAB
free	RID	gin cocktail/sling	IGN.-ING
—of charge	FOC	girl	G
—on board	FOB	globe	O
—on rail	FOR	god	PAN
French	FR	goddess	ATE.ATHENA
—art	ES		HEBE.ISIS
—king	ROI.SM	good	A.AI.PI
—man (men)	M (MM).RENE	—book	NT.OT

—bye	TATA.VALE	head	NESS.PATE.RAS
—man	DEAN.ST	healer	DR
Gort's men	BEF	heart	H
Gotham	NY	Hebrew letters	ALEPH.BETH
government issue	GI		LAMED.RESH.TETH
governor	HE		VAU.etc.
gradually	ERIC	hedge	HAW
grain	GR	height	H
gram(me)	G.GR	Hell	DIS.PIT
grammar	GR	henry	H
grand (Amer.)	G	here in Rome	HIC
graphite	KISH	here is	HS
gravity	G	hesitation	ER.UM.UR
Greek	GR	high-class	A.AI.U
Greek letters	ALPHA.BETA	hill	MT.TOR
	CHI.ETA.IOTA	hole	O
	LA(M)BDA.MU.NU	hollow	O
	OMEGA.PHI.PI. etc.	Holy Writ	NT.OT
greeting	AVE.HI	honour	CH.OBE.OM
group of workers	BEE	hoop	O
grouse	GR	horse	ARAB.BARB.GEE
guinea	G.GU		GG.H.NAG
gulf	G	—race	DERBY.NATIONAL
gun	ARM.BREN.GAT		OAKS
	LEWIS.MAXIM.STEN	hospital	H
gunmen	GRS.RA	hot	H
gypsy	CHAL.ROM	hour	H.HR
—woman	CHAI	house	CO.COT.H.HO.SEMI
		hunter	ORION
H		husband	H.MAN
hail	AVE	hush	SH.ST
hairdresser	COMB	hydrant	H
half	DEMI-.HF.SEMI-	hymns	AM
—century	L		
—day	AM.PM	**I**	
—ditch	HA	I	A.AN.ANE.AY.AYE.EYE
—dozen	VI	—am	AM.IAM.IM
—dry	T	—had/have	ID.IVE
—minute	MIN.MO.UTE	—say	AYE.EYE
hand	AB.H.L.MAN.R	—see	IC
hard (very hard)	H (HH)	—shall/will	ILL
—ground	HEARTH	identification	ID
—water	ICE	if (old word)	AN
Harpies *see* Numbers, Part 2:23		if it (old word)	ANT

245

illegal army	ETA.IRA.PLO	journalist	ED
illiterate's signature	X	joyful cry	IO
illness	FLU	judge	J
image building	PR	junction	T
in		justice	J
—bed	B-ED.BE-D		
—charge	IC	**K**	
—the main	DE-EP	kale	KL
—the same place	IB.IBID	Kay	K
—the style of	ALA	kelvin	K
indeed	DE-ED	kewpie (doll)	QP
indefinite number	N.NO	key	A.B.C.D.E.F.G
individuality	KA	killer	CAIN
inductance	L	kilo	K
infantry	FOOT	king	CR.ER.GR.HM.K
inferior	B		LEAR.R
—horse	TIT	—(Fr.)	ROI.SM
informer	GRASS.NOSE	—emperor	RI
instinct	ID	Kirkpatrick	K
integers	Z	kiss	X
intended	-MENT	knew (old word)	WIST
international	CAP.UN	knight	K.KT.N.SIR
—organisation	UNO	Köchel	K
invariably	EER		
inventor	EDISON	**L**	
Irish house	DAIL	label	TAB.TAG
Irish police	RUC	laboratory	LAB
is (Fr.)	EST	Labour	LAB
island	AIT.EYOT.I.INCH	lady	DAME.EVE.SHE
	IOM.IS.MAN	lake	ERIE.L.LOCH
—our islands	GB	lambert	L
—this island	UK	large letters	OS
issue	SON	largesse	S
it	SA	last	
ivy	IV	—letter	OMEGA.Z
		—month	DEC.ULT
J		—word(s)	AMEN.OBIT.RIP
Jack	*see* sailor	late	EX
jade	YU	Latin	L
jammed cylinder	SWISS ROLL	latitude	L
jay	J	laugh	HA.HAHA.HEHE
jazz fan	CAT	lawgiver	MOSES
jolly (marine)	RM	lawman	BL.DA.EARP
joule	J	lawyer(s)	BL.DA.(BAR)

layer	HEN	main road	AI.MI
leading	NOI	male	HE.HIM.M
league	L	man	IOM.ISLE.M
learner	L	man/Roman	VIR
leaves	TEA	managed	RAN
left	L.PORT	management	ADMIN
left-hand	LH.VO	manuscript(s)	MS (MSS)
leftist	RED	many	C.D.L.M
leg	ON	Marine	JOLLY.RM
legal document	DEED	mark	DM.M
legate	HE	married	M
length	L	Marshal	NEY
Liberal	L.LIB	masculine	M
licentiate	L	mass	M
life symbol	ANKH	master	M
light	VERY	match	TEST
like	AS	maths function	LOG.SINE
line	I.L		TAN
liner	SS	Mayfair	WI
lines/landline	BR.RLY.RY	meal ticket	LV
lira/lire	L	meant	-MENT
litre	L	measure	EL.ELL.EM.EN
little	WEE		FT.Y.YD.M
—horse	GEE.GG.NAG.NED	medal	MC.MM.TD
—way	RD.RY.ST	meeting	AGM
live	BE	member	ARM.LEG.M
lived so long	AV		MP.TOE
local	INN.PH.PUB	Merchant Navy	MN
loch	NESS	Merchant of Venice	POLO
lock keeper	HAIR NET	meter (metre)	M
look	LA.LO.SEE.V.VIDE	midday	A.M.N
loud (very loud)	F (FF)	midnight	G
love	O	mile	M
low	MOO	miller's corn	GRIST
lower	COW	miners	NUM
low grade	E	minor	WEE
lumen	L	misanthrope	TIMON
luminance	L	missiles	AMMO
lunchtime	ONE.I	modern times	AD
		modulus	M
M		mole	PIER.SPY
maiden	IO.M.OVER	monarch	ER.K.R
mailboat	RMS	Monday	M.MON
main	DEEP.SEA	money	BRASS.CENT.L.TIN

monsieur	M	—(Scot.)	NA.NAE
monstrous regiment	WOMEN	—date	ND
month(s)	M.MO(S)	—good	NG.US
morning	AM	—one	NOI
mother	DAM.MA.MAM	—way	ORD
	MUM	non-commissioned	
motoring organisation	AA.RAC	officer	NCO.RSM.SGT.SM
motor race	CARNATION	noon	M.N
motorway	M.MI	north(ern)	N
mountain	ALP.MT.TOR	North Pole	NP
mountaineer	SHERPA	not	
mountain retreat	PLA	—(old word)	NE
mounted	UP	—(Scot.)	NA.NAE
mouthpiece	LIPS	—at home	OUT
Mozart's works	K	—clear	NL
murderer	CAIN	—far	NL
murder victim	ABEL	—out	IN.NO
Muses *see* Numbers, Part 2:23		—permitted	NL
music school	RAM	—specific	NS
Muslim leader	AGA	notch	V
		note	A.B.C.D.E.F.G
			DO.DOH.UT.RE
N			ME.MI.FA.FAH
name	N		SO.SOH.SOL.LA
named	DIT		LAH.SI.TE.TI
namely	SC	nothing	NIL.O
name unknown	NU	nothing to America	-OUS
nationalists	SDP	notice	AD
native	ABO	noun	N
naught	O	novice	L
naval commander	CORN	now	AD.ANON
Navy	RN	nowadays	AD
near (old word)	NIE	number	N.NO
neat	CATTLE.COW	number one	ADAM.I
	KINE.OX		ME.NOI
—sound	LOWING.MOO	—(Fr.)	UN.UNE
neckline	V	—(Ger.)	EIN
neper	N	—(Ital.)	UNA.UNO
neuter	N	—returning	-ION
new	N	numbers:	
newton	N	one	A.ACE.AN.ANE.I
New York opera	MET	two	II.PR
no	O	two (double)	BI-.DI-
—(Fr.)	NON	two (twice)	BIS

three (triple)	TER-.TRI-	—injury	TEEN.TENE
four, five, six	IV.V.VI	—Irish Magistrate	RM
nine	IX	—king	COLE.LUD.OFFA
ten, eleven	X.XI	—man	DAD.PA.POP
12½ cents (US)	DIME	—paint	LIMN
twenty-five pounds	PONY	—penny	D
thirty seconds	MIN	—people	ICENI
fifty, fifty-one	L.LI	—Prime Minister	EDEN.PITT
ninety	XC	—railway	LNER.SR.etc.
ninety-nine	IC	—scholar	ERASMUS
hundred	IC.C	—shilling	BOB.S
hundred and fifty	CL	—ship	ARGO
hundreds	CS.D	—style	OS
two hundred	CC	—thing	RES
thousand	G.K.M	—way	VIA
hundred thousand	LAC	—wedding	BRIDAL
	LAKH	—woman	MA
many	C.D.L.M	omega	Z
nurse	SRN.VAD	on	LEG
		one	A.AN.ANE.I.UN
O		—(dialect)	UN
objector	CO	—fifteen	ASIDE
occupational therapy	OT	—member	AMP.IMP
odds	SP	—pound	*see* pound
of (Fr.)	DE	—time	EX
of the (Fr.)	DELA	one's	AS.IS
	DES.DU	on purpose	-MENT
of the (Ital.)	DEL	opener	KEY
officer	LT.CO	opening	O
—commanding	OC	Open University	OU
—in-charge	OIC	operating	ON
ogee	OG	operation	OP
oh(s)	O (OO.OS)	opposite	OP
oh, why	OY	orb	O
old		orchestra	LSO
—age	ELD	order	CH.OBE.OM
—Bob	S	orient	E
—boy	OB	oriental	E.INE
—city	TROY.UR	otorhinolaryngology	ENT
—English	OE	ought	O
—Etonian	OE	our man	HE
—fiddle	GU.GUE	our time/era	AD
—fighter	GLADIATOR	out of print	OP
—goat	GATE	outsize	OS

over	RE.SUPRA
owe(s)	O (OO.OS)
own	
—(Scot.)	AIN
—goal	OG
ox	KINE.NEAT
Oxford dreamer	SPIRE

P

page(s)	P (PP)
painter	ARA.PRA.RA
paper(s)	MS (MSS)
paradise	EDEN
paragon	S.SAINT.ST
park(ing)	P
part	PT
participle	P
partnership	EW.NS.SN.WE
party	CON.DO.LAB.LIB TORY
pawn	P
paying guest	PG
pea(s)	P (PP.PS)
peacekeepers	UN
peacemakers	ACAS
peavy	PV
pedal	P
pee(s)	P (PP.PS)
peg	P.T.TEE
penny	P
people	MEN.NATION.RACE
perfect letter	T
performing	ON
period	AD.BC
philosopher	BACON.PLATO
piano	P
pianissimo	PP
piece (chess)	MAN.PAWN
pilot	GEORGE
pint	P.PT
Planck's constant	H
play (Jap.)	NO(H)
playing	IN.ON
Pluto	DIS

PM's address	TEN.X
poet	AE
point	N.S.E.W HEAD.NESS.PT.TOR
poise	P
pole	N.NP.PO.ROD.S.SP
police	CID.FORCE.MET
policeman	MP.PC
politician	CON.LIB.LAB MP.TORY
poor horse	ROSINANTE.TIT
port	ADEN.L.RIO
—authority	PLA
posh	U
post town	PT
pound	EZRA.L.LB
—one pound	AL.ALB.IL.ILB L.LB
—twenty-five pounds	PONY
—fifty pounds	LL
power	P
present day	AD
preservationists	NT
president	CHAIR.P.PR.PRES
pretty girl	CUTIE.DISH
priest	ELI.REV
—(Fr.)	ABBE.CURE
primitive	UR
prince	P.PR.RAS
princess	ANNE.DI.IDA INA.REGAN
printer's measure	EL.EM.EN
prison	BIRD.CAN.COOLER HOCK.JUG.NICK QUAD.STIR
private	GI
prominence	TOR
promises to pay	-IOUS
prophet	ELI
provided/providing	IF
psychotic state	DT
public relations (officer)	PR(O)
puff	AD
pupil	L

250

Q	
QE	ER
quality	Q
quart	QT.QU
quarter	N.S.E.W
	NE.NW.SE.SW
queen	BESS.ER.HM.MAB
	Q.QU.R
question	Q
quiet	P.QT
fairly quiet	MP
very quiet	PP
quintal	Q
queue	CUE.Q
R	
rabbit	BRER
race	—NATION.TT
radius	R
railway	BR.RLY.RY
American railway	EL
rain	R
rand	R
rate	MPH
rating	AB
rational numbers	Q
real numbers	R
Réaumur	R
recipe	R.REC
record	DISC.ENTRY.EP
	LOG.LP
Regina	R
relation	SIB
remains	ASH
reported	DIT
representative	MP
reserves	TA
resident magistrate	RM
resistance	R
revolutionary	CHE.RED
rev up	VER
riding	UP
right	R.RT
right-hand	RH.RO

ring	DISC.O
—road	ORD
river	AIRE.ALPH.CAM
	DEE.EXE.FAL
	ISIS.OUSE.PO.TAY
	TEES.URE
road	AVE.R.RD.ST
Romans/Roman people	PR
röntgen unit	R
rook	R
roughly	C.CA
row	ADO.TIER
rowing boat	EIGHT.FOUR
royal	R
—badge	ER
rubber	ULE
rugby	RU
run	R
runner	RIVER (q.v.)
running	ADMIN
—water	EA
S	
Sabbath	S
said (Fr.)	DIT
sailor/salt/seaman	AB.JACK
	TAR
sailors	RN
saint(s)	S(SS).ST(STS)
salesman	REP
Sandhurst	RMA
same	DO.ID.IDEM
same place	IB
sapper	RE
Saturday	S.SAT
say (Fr.)	DIT
Scarlatti's works	K
Schmieder	S
scholar	BA.MA
school	ETON
Schubert's works	D
science centre	LAB
scope, plenty of	A-Z
scorer	COMPOSER

Scot/Scotsman	IAN.JOCK
	MAC.MON
screecher	SWIFT
scriptures	NT.OT
scruple	SCR
sea	C.DEEP.MAIN
—(Fr.)	MER
Seabee (Amer.)	CB
seas	CC.CS
second	B.MO.S.SEC
—child	ABEL
—class	B
secretary	TEMP
secret service	CIA
see	ELY.C
	V.VID.VIDE
seedy	CD
seer	EYE.OPTIC
see why	CY
see you	CU
self-confessed	AM.IAM.IM
self-contained	SC
senior	SR
sergeant	NCO.SGT
service	ACE.LET.MASS
	RAF.RN
serving man	GI
sex appeal	IT.SA
shark	NURSE
shilling	S
ship	SS
shipping company	LINE
shirt	T
short	
—answer	ANS
—break	HOL
—time	MO.SEC.T
show-ring	MANIFESTO
side	L.R.XI.XV
siemens	S
sign	V
sign of the times	X
signs of the Zodiac	
see Numbers, Part 2:23	

silence/silent	MUM.SH
	ST.TACE
single	I
sister	S.SIS
six-footer	ANT.BEE.INSECT
sixth sense	ESP
skipping	OMITTING
sloth	AI
small	TINY.WEE
—capitals	SC
—change	P
—illustration	FIG
—measure	CC.EL.EM.EN
—quantity	CC
—square	EM.M
—weight	CT.GR.OZ.WT
smuggle(d)	RUN (RAN)
snake	ASP.BOA
so	ERGO
soccer blunder	OG
socialist	RED
socially acceptable	U
social worker	ANT.BEE
society	S
soft (very soft)	P (PP)
soldier	ANT.MAN
airborne soldier	PARA
American soldier	GI.JOE
German soldier	SS
soldiers	IMPI.MEN.RA.RE
	SAS.TA
son	S
song	AIR.ARIA.LAY
soprano	SOP
source	PARENT
south(ern)	S
South Pole	SP
spade	S
Spanish hero	CID
speakers	LIPS
species	SP
specifically	AS.SC
spectacles	OO
speculator	BEAR.STAG

speed	MPH.RATE	submariner	NEMO
—of light	C	summer time	BST
spies	CIA	sun	S
sports car	GT.ROD	sun-god	RA.SOL
spot marked	X	superior	U.UP
spymaster	M	support	BRA.LEG
square	S.T	surgeon	VET
square root of −1	I	sweetheart	JO
starting price	SP	swimmer	COD.EEL
states (Amer.):			LING.etc.
Alabama	AL.ALA	swindle	CON
Alaska	ALAS		
California	CAL	**T**	
Connecticut	CT	take	REC
Florida	FLA	tales	ANA
Georgia	GA	tanner/sixpence	VID.VIP
Illinois	ILL	Tantulus's prisoner	DECANTER
Iowa	IA	tar	AB
Kentucky	KY	tax	SCOT.VAT
Louisiana	LA	te	T
Massachusetts	MASS	tea(s)	T (TS.TT)
Mississippi	MISS	teachers	NUT
Missouri	MO	team	SIDE.XI.XV
New York	NY	tea-time	IV
North Dakota	ND	tee(s)	PEG.T (TS.TT)
Ohio	O	teepee	TP
Rhode Island	RI	telepathy	ESP
South Dakota	SD	territorials	TA
Utah	U	territories:	
Virginia	VA	Channel Islands	CI
steamship	SS	East Africa	EA
stokes	S	Home Counties	SE
stone	ST	Humberside	NE
stop	COLON.PT	Isle of Man	IOM
street	ST	London area	SE
—(Fr.)	RUE	Merseyside	NW
strikebreaker	RAT	Northern Territories	NT
strings (violin)	A.D.E.G	Quebec	Q
strong (very strong)	F (FF)	Queensland	Q
student	L	South Island	SI
students' (union)	NUS	Tyneside	NE
study	CON.DEN	Washington	DC
stumped	ST	terrorists	ETA.IRA.PLO
stunner	KO		PROVOS

tesla	T
test	ORAL.MOT
text	MS
thanks	TA
that is	IE.SC
that (old word)	YT
—(Lat.)	ID
the (old word)	YE
—(Fr.)	LA.LE
—(Ger.)	DAS.DER.DIE
—(Ital.)	IL.LA
—(Span.)	EL.LA
them	EM
theologian	BD.DD
third man	ABEL
this	
—(Fr.)	CE.CET
—(Lat.)	HIC
—country	UK
—era	AD
—year	HA
thousand	G.K.M
thrice	TER-.TRI-
through	PER
thus	SIC.SO
time	AGE.EON.MO.SEC.T
times	X
tinker	SLY
today	AD
ton(ne)	T
torpedo boat	MTB.TB
Tosti's song	TATA
to the (Fr.)	ALA.AU.AUX
towns:	
(city)	EC.ELY
Los Angeles	LA
New Jersey	NJ
New Orleans	NO
New York	GOTHAM.NY
Washington	DC
Westminster	WI
tradesmen	TU
traffic signal	GO.STOP
trainee	L

training	PE.PT
trains	BR
tramp	HOBO
transaction	TR
transatlantic	US
translation	TR
transport	BR.BUS.CAB.CAR CART.RLY.RY.TRAM
tree	ACTOR.ASH.FIR YEW.etc.
—ring	MAYO
trendy	IN
tribe	DAN.GAD
triumphant cry	IO
trivial sum	IP
trouble	ADO.AIL
Tuesday	T
turn	U
tyro	L

U

U-boat	SUB
un	A.AN.I
uncle	SAM.PAWNBROKER
undersecretary	US
understood	-MENT
underworld	DIS
undivided	ONE
unfashionable	OUT.SQUARE
unfavourable aspect	N
unidentified	NU
union/Unionist	U
unit	A.I
universal	U
—set	E
university	U
at university	UP
unknown	X.Y
—number	N
upper class	U
upright	I.PI
use	US.UU
useless	US

V

various years	VY
Vatican	V
vee	V
velocity	V
verb	V.VB
verse	V
versus	V
very	V
—(Fr.)	TRES
—(Scot.)	UNCO
—black	BB
—large	OS
—loud	FF
—quiet/soft	PP
—strong	FF
victory	V.VE.VJ
vide	V
violin string	A.D.E.G
viscount	VIS
viz	SC
volt	V
volume	V.VOL
vote	X

W

wall (Fr.)	MUR
warning	CAVE.FORE
warship	SUB
water	AQ.EA
waterfall	RAIN
watt	W
way	AVE.RD.RLY.RY.ST
way of working	MO
weak	W
Wednesday	W
weight	CT.G.GR.OZ.ST TON(NE).WT
Welsh	W
Welsh riots	REBECCA
west(ern)	W
what (Fr.)	QUE
who (Fr.)	QUI
whole numbers	W

why	Y
wicked sister	REGAN
wicket	W
wife	DUTCH.RIB.UX
wine	ASTI.PORT.TENT
wings	ALA
winner	ACE
wise	YS.YY
with a tenant	LET
without	SIN.SINE
—a day fixed	SD
—children	SP
—date	SA
woman	EVE.F.HER.SHE.W
work	OP.OPUS
worker	ANT.BEE.HAND MAN
writer	ELIA.NIB.PEN
writing	MS

Y

yard	Y
year	Y.YR
—of reign	AR
yearly meeting	AGM
yes	AY.AYE
—(Fr.)	OUI
—(Ger.)	JA
—(Ital.)	SI
—(Russ.)	DA
—(Span.)	SI
yew(s)	U (US.UU)
you	U
—are	UR
—queue	UQ
—see	UC
—will, say	YULE
young feller	WASHINGTON
yours truly	I
youth leaders	WISE.YS

Z

Zodiac	*see* Numbers, Part 2:23